Québec City

SACHA JACKSON

Contents

Maps

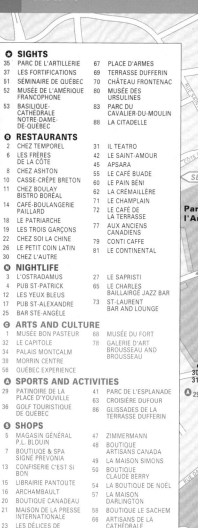

SIGHTS

35	PARC DE L'ARTILLERIE	67	PLACE D'ARMES
37	LES FORTIFICATIONS	69	TERRASSE DUFFERIN
51	SÉMINAIRE DE QUÉBEC	70	CHÂTEAU FRONTENAC
52	MUSÉE DE L'AMÉRIQUE FRANCOPHONE	80	MUSÉE DES URSULINES
53	BASILIQUE-CATHÉDRALE NOTRE-DAME-DE-QUÉBEC	83	PARC DU CAVALIER-DU-MOULIN
		88	LA CITADELLE

RESTAURANTS

2	CHEZ TEMPOREL	31	IL TEATRO
6	LES FRÈRES DE LA CÔTE	42	LE SAINT-AMOUR
8	CHEZ ASHTON	45	APSARA
10	CASSE-CRÊPE BRETON	55	LE CAFÉ BUADE
11	CHEZ BOULAY BISTRO BORÉAL	60	LE PAIN BÉNI
14	CAFÉ-BOULANGERIE PAILLARD	62	LA CRÉMAILLÈRE
18	LE PATRIARCHE	71	LE CHAMPLAIN
19	LES TROIS GARÇONS	72	LE CAFÉ DE LA TERRASSE
22	CHEZ SOI LA CHINE	77	AUX ANCIENS CANADIENS
26	LE PETIT COIN LATIN	79	CONTI CAFFE
30	CHEZ L'AUTRE	81	LE CONTINENTAL

NIGHTLIFE

3	L'OSTRADAMUS	27	LE SAPRISTI
4	PUB ST-PATRICK	65	LE CHARLES BAILLAIRGÉ JAZZ BAR
12	LES YEUX BLEUS	73	ST-LAURENT BAR AND LOUNGE
17	PUB ST-ALEXANDRE		
25	BAR STE-ANGÈLE		

ARTS AND CULTURE

1	MUSÉE BON PASTEUR	68	MUSÉE DU FORT
32	LE CAPITOLE	78	GALERIE D'ART BROUSSEAU AND BROUSSEAU
34	PALAIS MONTCALM		
39	MORRIN CENTRE		
56	QUÉBEC EXPERIENCE		

SPORTS AND ACTIVITIES

29	PATINOIRE DE LA PLACE D'YOUVILLE	41	PARC DE L'ESPLANADE
36	GOLF TOURISTIQUE DE QUEBEC	63	CROISIÈRE DUFOUR
		86	GLISSADES DE LA TERRASSE DUFFERIN

SHOPS

5	MAGASIN GÉNÉRAL P.L. BLOUIN	47	ZIMMERMANN
7	BOUTIUQE & SPA SIGNÉ PREVONIA	48	BOUTIQUE ARTISANS CANADA
13	CONFISERIE C'EST SI BON	49	LA MAISON SIMONS
15	LIBRAIRIE PANTOUTE	50	BOUTIQUE CLAUDE BERRY
16	ARCHAMBAULT	54	LA BOUTIQUE DE NOËL
20	BOUTIQUE CANADEAU	57	LA MAISON DARLINGTON
21	MAISON DE LA PRESSE INTERNATIONALE	58	BOUTIQUE LE SACHEM
23	LES DÉLICES DE L'ÉRABLE	66	ARTISANS DE LA CATHÉDRALE
24	BOUTIQUE L'ÉCHELLE	74	PAYOT INSTITUTE
28	PREMIÈRE ISSUE	76	LAMBERT & CO.
46	BIBI ET COMPAGNIE	82	GALERIE D'ART LES TROIS COLOMBES

HOTELS

9	HÔTEL MANOIR VICTORIA	59	HÔTEL STE-ANNE
33	LE CAPITOLE DE QUEBEC	61	AUBERGE PLACE D'ARMES
38	AUBERGE INTERNATIONALE DE QUÉBEC	64	HÔTEL CLARENDON
		75	FAIRMONT LE CHÂTEAU FRONTENAC
40	HÔTEL LE CHAMPLAIN	84	LA MARQUISE DE BASSANO
43	CHEZ HUBERT	85	HÔTEL CHÂTEAU BELLEVUE
44	HÔTEL LE CLOS SAINT-LOUIS	87	HÔTEL CAP DIAMANT

SEE MAP 2

QUAI SAINT AANDRÉ

RUE RIOUX

RUE SAINT PIERRE

RUE SAINT PAUL

CÔTE DE LA CANOTERIE

RUE DU SAULT AU MATELOT

REMPARTS

RUE DES REMPARTS

Hôtel-Dieu
de Québec

RUE DE LAVAL

RUE HÉBERT

RUE DE LA VIEILLE UNIVERSITÉ

RUE COUILLARD

1 🄲

51 ✪

Séminaire de
Québec

HARLEVOIX

RUE COUILLARD

RUE CHRISTIE

RUE SAINTE-FAMILLE

RUE FERLAND

RUE SAINT FLAVIEN

3 Ⓝ
2

5 Ⓢ
4 Ⓝ
46 Ⓢ

RUE GARNEAU

6 Ⓡ

RUE DE L'HÔTEL-DIEU

CÔTE DE LA FABRIQUE

47 Ⓢ 48

RUE DES REMPARTS

49
50 Ⓢ

Musée de l'Amérique
Francophone

Parc
Montmorency

AVE PIERRE OLIVER CHAUVEAU

🄲 52

Basilique-
Cathédrale Notre-
Dame-de-Québec

✪ 53

RUE DE BUADE

CÔTE DE LA MONTAGNE

54 55
58 Ⓢ 56

57 Ⓢ

RUE SAINTE ANNE

59 60 61
Ⓗ Ⓡ

RUE DU TRÉSOR

RUE DU FORT

68

RUE COOK

Ⓡ
62

Ⓐ Ⓗ Ⓝ
63 64 65

Cathedral of
the Holy
Trinity

67

Place
d'Armes

funicular

69 ✪

Terrasse
Dufferin

VIEUX-QUÉBEC

Ⓢ 66

RUE DES JARDINS

RUE DU TRÉSOR

RUE DU PETIT CHAMPLAIN

BLVD CHAMPLAIN

Musée des
Ursulines

✪ 80

RUE DONNACONA

77

79

81 Ⓡ Ⓡ

RUE SAINT LOUIS

Ⓢ 76

71,72 73
Ⓡ Ⓝ Ⓢ Ⓗ
70   74 75

RUE SAINT LOUIS

RUE HALDIMAND

78

Château
Frontenac

82 Ⓢ

86
Ⓐ

RUE DES CARRIÈRES

RUELLE DES URSULINES

RUE CORPS DE GARD

Jardin des
Gouverneurs

PLACE TERRASSE DUFFERIN

43

Ⓗ 44

83 ✪

RUE MONT CARMEL

RUE DES GRISONS

RUE DE LA PORTE

Parc du Cavalier-
du-Moulin

84

85

AVE SAINTE GENEVIÈVE

RUE SAINT LOUIS

Ⓡ 45

RUE DE BRÉBEUF

87

AVE SAINT DENIS

| 0 | | 100 yds |
| 0 | | 100 m |

🌙

DISTANCE ACROSS MAP
Approximate: 1.1 mi or 1.7 km

Parc de
l'Esplanade

BLVD CHAMPLAIN

La Citadelle

88 ✪

SEE MAP 3

© AVALON TRAVEL

Vieux-Port de Québec

Musée de la Civilisation

VIEUX-QUÉBEC

Rue Sous-le-Cap

Parc Montmorency

La Fresque des Québécois

Place Royale

Église Notre-Dame-des-Victoires

Cathedral of the Holy Trinity

Funiculaire du Vieux-Québec

Le Château Frontenac

St. Lawrence River

Quartier du Petit-Champlain

Jardin des Gouverneurs

0   100 yds
0   100 m
DISTANCE ACROSS MAP
Approximate: 4.2 mi or 6.9 km

SEE MAP 1

© AVALON TRAVEL

SIGHTS

- 1 FONTAINE DE TOURNY
- 2 HÔTEL DU PARLEMENT
- 3 OBSERVATOIRE DE LA CAPITALE
- 4 PARC DES PLAINES D'ABRAHAM
- 6 MANÈGE MILITAIRE
- 8 LA GRANDE-ALLÉE
- 18 TOUR MARTELLO 1
- 19 TOUR MARTELLO 2
- 46 MUSÉE NATIONAL DES BEAUX-ARTS DU QUÉBEC

RESTAURANTS

- 11 CASA CALZONE
- 13 LE COSMOS
- 14 VOO DOO GRILL
- 21 SEBZ THÉS AND LOUNGE
- 25 BÜGEL FABRIQUE DES BAGELS
- 26 MILANO PIZZA
- 30 MORENA
- 32 CAFÉ KRIEGHOFF
- 35 BISTRO B
- 36 GLACIER ABERDEEN
- 38 MÉTROPOLITAN EDDIE SUSHI BAR
- 39 GRAFFITI
- 40 LE FASTOCHE
- 47 RESTAURANT DU MUSÉE DES BEAUX-ARTS

NIGHTLIFE

- 9 LES VOÛTES NAPOLÉON
- 10 L'INOX
- 12 LE DAGOBERT
- 15 LE MAURICE
- 16 SOCIÉTÉ CIGARE
- 17 LE CHARLOTTE ULTRA LOUNGE
- 31 LE JULES ET JIM
- 33 PUB GALWAY
- 34 RIDEAU ROUGE
- 42 BLAXTON PUB AND GRILL

ARTS AND CULTURE

- 20 GRAND THÉATRE DE QUÉBEC
- 29 CINÉMA
- 43 MAISON HENRY-STUART

SPORTS AND ACTIVITIES

- 5 PARC DES PLAINES D'ABRAHAM
- 23 ASHTANGA YOGA QUÉBEC
- 44 PARC DU MUSÉE
- 45 PISCINE PARC DU MUSÉE

SHOPS

- 22 IZBA SPA
- 24 KETTO
- 27 URBAIN PRÊT-A-PORTER
- 28 ZONE
- 37 SILLONS LE DISQUAIRE
- 41 LES HALLES DU PETIT QUARTIER

HOTELS

- 7 HÔTEL CHÂTEAU LAURIER

SEE MAP 4

Parc de l'Amérique Française

Parc des Champs-de-Bataille

Musée National des Beaux-Arts du Québec

© AVALON TRAVEL

SEE MAP 1

Fontaine de Tourny

1

Parc de l'Esplanade

Hôtel du Parlement

2

Parlement du Québec

Observatoire de la Capitale

3

Parc de la

Francophonie

Parc des Plaines d'Abraham

4 5

La Grande-Allée

9

8

10

7

6

12

11

Manège Militaire

13,14

15-17

PARLIAMENT HILL

Tour Martello 2

19

AVE VACHE   AVE GEORGE VI

Parc des Champs-de-Bataille

Tour Martello 1

18

RUE GARNEAU   AVE ONTARIO   RUE PETIT CHAMPLAIN   BLVD CHAMPLAIN

0   100 yds

0   100 m

DISTANCE ACROSS MAP
Approximate: 1.2 mi or 1.9 km

SIGHTS
- 33 RUE SAINT-JOSEPH
- 53 JARDIN SAINT-ROCH
- 61 ST-MATTHEW CHURCH AND CEMETERY
- 76 RUE SAINT-JEAN
- 80 ÉGLISE SAINT-JEAN-BAPTISTE

RESTAURANTS
- 1 LA PETITE BOÎTE VIETNAMIENNE
- 12 TAVERNE STEAKHOUSE LE TONNEAU
- 16 CAMELLIA SINENSIS
- 18 LES BOSSUS
- 27 VERSA
- 28 YUZU SUSHI BAR
- 37 BRÛLERIE SAINT-ROCH
- 39 LA BOÎTE À PAIN
- 41 NEKTAR
- 42 LE CERCLE
- 44 LE CLOCHER PENCHÉ
- 47 PAIN ET PASSION
- 48 CAFÉ BABYLONE
- 56 LE COMPTOIR
- 57 SNACK BAR ST-JEAN
- 63 TUTTO GELATO
- 70 LE MOINE ÉCHANSON
- 72 LIBRAIRIE ST-JEAN-BAPTISTE
- 73 CRÊPERIE LE BILLIG
- 78 LE SULTAN
- 82 LE CARTHAGE
- 84 LE PAIN GRÜEL
- 85 AU BONNET D'ÂNE
- 88 CHEZ VICTOR

NIGHTLIFE
- 4 LA BARBERIE
- 7 MO
- 17 LE LARGO
- 26 LE BOUDOIR
- 46 TAVERNE JOS DION
- 49 LA CUISINE
- 50 LES SALONS D'EDGAR
- 51 SCANNER
- 58 LA NINKASI
- 64 PUB NELLIGAN'S
- 65 LE DRAGUE
- 66 BAR LE ST-MATTHEW
- 68 LE TEMPS PARTIEL
- 74 FOU-BAR
- 79 LE SACRILÈGE

ARTS AND CULTURE
- 2 LE LIEU
- 3 MORGAN BRIDGE
- 11 GALERIE D'ART FACTORY
- 35 CENTRE MATERIA
- 38 THÉATRE LA BORDÉE
- 40 IMPÉRIAL DE QUÉBEC
- 43 LE CERCLE
- 54 MÉDUSE

HOTELS
- 31 HÔTEL PUR
- 36 AUBERGE L'AUTRE JARDIN
- 52 AUBERGE LE VINCENT
- 67 AUBERGE J.A. MOISAN
- 81 LE CHÂTEAU DU FAUBOURG
- 87 CHÂTEAU DES TOURELLES

SHOPS
- 5 LE KNOCK-OUT
- 6 DÉJÀ VU
- 9 CHAMPAGNE LE MAÎTRE CONFISEUR
- 9 TOHU BOHU
- 10 SWELL & GINGER
- 13 FANAMANGA
- 14 LIBRAIRIE PHYLACTÈRE
- 15 LA QUINTESSENS
- 19 LALIBERTÉ
- 20 BENJO
- 21 SIGNATURES QUÉBEÇOISES
- 22 MADEMOISELLE B
- 23 PHILIPPE DUBUC
- 24 FLIRT
- 25 COSMÉTIQUES BLOOMI
- 29 BALTHAZAR
- 30 KITSCH
- 32 MOUNTAIN EQUIPMENT CO-OP
- 34 RUE SAINT-JOSEPH
- 45 BOUTIQUE LUCIA F.
- 55 ESTHER P
- 59 JUPON PRESSÉ
- 60 POINT D'EXCLAMATION
- 62 SCHÜZ
- 69 CHOCO-MUSÉE ERICO
- 71 EPICERIE EUROPÉENNE
- 75 LOBO LAVIDA
- 77 RUE SAINT-JEAN
- 83 ROSE BOUTON
- 86 CD MÉLOMANE

SEE MAP 3

⊛ SIGHTS
28 AQUARIUM DU QUÉBEC

Ⓝ NIGHTLIFE
18 LE PUB DE
L'UNIVERSITÉ LAVAL
24 L'OZONE LAURIER

Ⓖ ARTS AND CULTURE
15 LE CLAP

Ⓐ SPORTS AND ACTIVITIES
1 MEGA PARC
DES GALERIES
DE LA CAPITALE
4 REMPARTS DE QUÉBEC
5 ROC GYMS
6 BAIE DE BEAUPORT
7 DOMAINE MAIZERETS
8 PARC
CARTIER-BRÉBEUF
9 PARC LINÉAIRE DE LA
RIVIÈRE ST-CHARLES
10 POINTE-AUX-LIÈVRES

11 PARC VICTORIA
12 LES CAPITALES
DE QUÉBEC
13 CORRIDOR
DES CHEMINOTS
16 PARC DU
BOIS-DE-COULONGE
17 LE ROUGE ET OR
27 PARC DE LA PLAGE
JACQUES-CARTIER
29 LE CHAMPLAIN AND
LE PYLÔNE
30 LA TEMPÊTE

Ⓢ SHOPS
2 GALERIES
DE LA CAPITALE
3 UNIVERS TOUTOU
14 LATULIPPE
19 LAURIER QUÉBEC

20 PLACE DE LA CITÉ
21 LA MAISON ANGLAISE
22 HOLT RENFREW
23 PLACE STE-FOY

Ⓗ HOTELS
25 HÔTEL SÉPIA
26 CHÂTEAU BONNE
ENTENTE

L'ANCIENNE-LORETTE

Québec City
Jean Lesage
International Airport

LA SUÈTE

Lac
Laberge

Le Grand-Village

Le Faubourg - L'Erpiniére

SAINT AUGUSTIN

Lac
St-Augustin

Club de Golf
de Cap Rouge

St. Lawrence River

Saint-Nicolas

CHEMIN SAINT JOSEPH

CHEMIN AUBIN

© AVALON TRAVEL

LEBOURGNEUF

LAIRET

VIEUX-LIMOILOU

VANIER

SAINT-ROCH

Québec City

SAINT-JEAN-BAPTISTE

VIEUX-QUÉBEC

Lévis

PARLIAMENT HILL

Battlefields Park

St. Lawrence River

SILLERY

SAINTE-FOY

PLACE-DU-VIEUX-MOULIN

ST LOUIS

Aquarium du Québec

SAINT-ROMUALD

Place-Normandie

SAINT-JEAN-CHRYSOSTOME

Moulin-Gosselin

0   1.5 mi

0   1.5 km

DISTANCE ACROSS MAP
Approximate: 18.7 mi or 30 km

DISCOVER
Québec City

The province of Québec is a place all its own: It's a country within a country with its own traditions, architecture, and language. Perched on a cliff above the St-Lawrence River, Québec City is the soul of the province: the first city to be founded in Canada, the seat of the Québec government, and the self-proclaimed "Capitale Nationale."

The historic landmarks and 17th-century architecture are captivating. But what will impress you the most is the infectious energy that people exude here. Temperatures drop below freezing in winter but bars and restaurants are still packed, with windows steaming with that unmistakable joie de vivre.

You can still walk the narrow, cobblestone streets of Vieux-Port or pose next to one of the many cannons that line the city's walls. But a youthful revolution in the old working-class neighborhoods is bringing a daring new quality of art and culture to this historic city.

Clockwise from top left: Fountaine-de-Tourny; St-Jean-Baptiste Basilica; Parvis Church in St-Roch; Québec City as seen from the Vieux-Port.

Planning Your Trip

Where to Go

Vieux-Québec's Upper Town

Les Fortifications surround Vieux-Québec's Upper Town, a 400-year-old neighborhood where the history of the winding streets and original architecture remains safe from the ravages of time. Protected by these walls is the **Château Frontenac,** Québec City's most famous sight, and the **Séminaire de Québec,** one of the city's oldest sights.

Vieux-Québec's Lower Town

The stone Norman-style buildings and cobblestone streets of **Place Royale** mark the country's birthplace. History is unavoidable here, from the narrow lanes of **Quartier du Petit-Champlain** to the historic **Vieux-Port,** with its converted warehouses, antiques shops, and trendy hotels.

Parliament Hill and the Plains

Outside of the walls are the **Plains of Abraham and Battlefield Park,** the site of France's historic defeat by the British. The seat of the provincial government is to its north, housed in **Hôtel du Parlement.** Running alongside the government building are the nightclubs and bars of **La Grande-Allée,** the city's nightlife destination. Also in the Plains is **Musée National des Beaux-Arts du Québec,** which holds the largest existing collection of Québec art.

Saint-Jean-Baptiste and Saint-Roch

Once working-class neighborhoods, Saint-Jean-Baptiste and Saint-Roch are now **trendy, bohemian neighborhoods,** home to the city's coolest kids,

the entrance into Vieux-Québec's Upper Town

Les Fortifications, a popular place to take a break in the summer

and the area where you'll find the best bars, browse independent boutiques, and catch the latest bands. It's also a major **arts hub,** and the contemporary arts complex **Méduse** is located here.

Greater Québec City

In the areas surrounding the center of the city, find kid-friendly destinations like the **Aquarium du Québec** and the beautiful, sprawling gardens of **Parc du Bois-de-Coulonge.** The slopes of **Mont-Sainte-Anne** are fun for the whole family.

Excursions from Québec City

Just a half-hour drive from the city are the picturesque towns of **Île d'Orléans** and **Côte-de-Beaupré,** while an hour north, the **Charlevoix** region has some of the most spectacular scenery in the region.

When to Go

Though **summer** is the busiest time to visit, it's also the best time to explore the cities' neighborhoods, and you'll get to experience fun summer events like the Festival d'Été.

It's no surprise that prices drop considerably **October-April,** so if you can handle a bit of cold, your pocketbook will thank you. Plus, the cold isn't so bad when it's hockey season and 98 percent of the people—and you—are crowded into bars watching the game. Quebéc City **winters** can be particularly freezing, but **December-March** is an ideal time to visit if you love skiing or other winter recreational activities. October is particularly pretty thanks to the changing fall foliage, and even February has a couple of bright spots with the Carnaval de Québec's unadulterated celebration of snow.

Before You Go

Passports and Visas

All visitors must have a **valid passport** or other accepted secure documents to enter the country; even those entering from the United States by road or train must have these documents.

Citizens of the United States, Australia, New Zealand, Israel, Japan, and most Western European countries don't need visas to enter Canada for stays up to 180 days. U.S. permanent residents are also exempt.

Nationals from South Africa, China, and about 150 other countries must apply for a **temporary resident visa** (TRV) in their home country. Full details can be found at **Citizen and Immigration Canada. Single-entry visitor visas** are valid for six months and cost $75, while **multiple-entry visas** cost $150 and last for two years, as long as a single stay doesn't last for longer than six months. A separate visa is required if you intend to work in Canada.

Transportation

Most visitors arriving by **air** will land at Montréal's **Pierre Trudeau International Airport,** the main hub for both national and international air travel to the province. Direct flights are also available to Quebéc City's **Aéroport International Jean-Lesage de Québec.** It's about 15 kilometers from downtown, but there are no shuttles to downtown from this airport.

If you're arriving by **train** you'll arrive at Québec City's **Gare du Palais** near the Vieux-Port. Those arriving by **bus** in Québec City will also arrive at the Gare du Palais.

Québec City's **transit system** is limited to buses, but they are fast and efficient in getting you up those steep hills. **Taxis** are useful when the winter hits, though they can be hard to flag down, depending on the area. Although **driving** the city streets is straightforward enough, if you're not used to ice and snow, it's better to leave it to the pros.

The Best of Québec City

Four days is the perfect length of time to visit Québec City, allowing you to dedicate enough time to experience the city's historic center with a few side trips.

Day 1

Drop off your luggage at your hotel in Vieux-Québec's Upper Town then head directly to **Café-Boulangerie Paillard** for some fresh croissants. Browse the shops and historic buildings on **Côte de la Fabrique** until it brings you to **Terrasse Dufferin** in the shadow of **Château Frontenac**. Snack on a beaver tail pastry as you stroll the promenade and look out over the St-Lawrence, then head into the chateau for a guided tour.

Tour the historic **Citadelle** and then wander through the winding streets and alleys of **Upper Town**.

For dinner, take your pick of the restaurants along **rue St-Louis** or splurge at **Le Patriarche**. After dinner, walk along **Les Fortifications** and finish the night at a *boîte à chansons,* such as **Le Pape-Georges,** or with a nightcap at the cozy **Bar Ste-Angèle**.

Day 2

After breakfast at **Crêperie le Billig** take the **Escalier du Casse-Cou** or ride the **Funiculaire du Vieux-Québec** down to one of the oldest streets in North America, **rue du Petit-Champlain**. Browse the independent boutiques and follow the cobblestone lanes that will eventually lead you to **Place Royale**. Take a peek at **La Fresque des Québécois** and see if you can point out the famous characters. Whether you fail the test or not, head to the **Musée de la Civilisation** and brush up on your history.

La Citadelle

Musée de la Civilisation

The Escalier du Casse-Cou connects Upper and Lower Town.

After visiting the museum, head west along **rue St-Paul** to browse antique stores. Or skip the stores and take the well-hidden **rue Sous-le-Cap** until it brings you to **Galerie Madeleine Lacerte.** Check out the latest exhibit and then cross the street for a drink at **Taverne Belley** and watch the locals playing petanque.

On your way to **Saint-Roch,** stop to admire the graffiti murals on the highway overpass, then head for a bistro dinner at **Les Bossus.** Cap the night off with a show at **Le Cercle** and a bit of dancing at **La Cuisine.**

Day 3

Have a hearty breakfast at **Le Petit Coin Latin,** then head to the **Fontaine de Tourny** and take a trip around the statues at the **Hôtel du Parlement.** Stroll the rolling hills of the **Parc des Plaines d'Abraham** and make a stop at **Tours Martellos.** Continue through the park all the way to the **Musée National des Beaux-Arts du Québec.** After seeing the latest exhibit, grab launch at **Morena** on **avenue Cartier.**

Follow Cartier south, down the sloping hill, and take a right on **rue St-Jean,** where you can spend the rest of the afternoon popping in and out of stores and drinking coffee at the many cafés. Don't miss **Auberge J.A. Moisan,** the oldest grocery store in North America, or the quiet shade of **St-Matthew Church and Cemetery.**

While you've got the European vibe going why not continue with a French wine and regional cuisine at **Le Moine Échanson.** After your meal, head over to **La Grande-Allée** for a taste of sophisticated nightlife at **Le Charlotte Ultra Lounge.**

Day 4

Head down to **Cyclo Services** and rent bikes for the day. Pack your bags with sandwiches and goodies from the **Marché du Vieux-Port** and then take the **Corridor du Littoral** heading west. Ride about three kilometers and make a stop at the historic park **Domaine Maizerets.** After a wander

Get Outside

No matter where you are in the province or how low the temperature drops, you're never far from serious outdoor fun.

· **Baie de Beauport,** just outside of the city, is a great place to canoe, kayak, sail, or play beach volleyball.

· **Parc des Plaines d'Abraham** is the place in the city to run, walk, bike or even swim. Come winter you can cross-country ski, ice skate, or snowshoe.

· A 20-minute drive out of the city will bring you to the bird-watching and hiking heaven that is **Cap-Tourmente.**

· **Corridor du Littoral** follows the coast of the river and is ideal for experienced (or determined) cyclists.

· **Domaine Maizerets** is great for biking, skating, cross-country skiing, snowshoeing, and tobogganing.

· Some of the best skiing in the country is just an hour's drive away at **Le Massif.**

· Ski station **Mont-Sainte-Anne** is busiest throughout winter, but in summer, the area offers camping and mountain biking trails.

· **Parc de la Plage Jacques-Cartier,** just outside of the city, offers boating, mountain climbing, and 2.5 kilometers of hiking trails.

· **Parc du Bois-de-Coulonge,** which is easily accessible from downtown, offers cycling, a number of walking trails, and lawn bowling in summer.

· **Parc Linéaire de la Rivière St-Charles,** with 32 kilometers of trails to choose from, offers opportunities for biking, rollerblading, snowshoeing, cross-country skiing, and even ice-skating.

among the ancient trees and lily-pad ponds, get back on your bike and ride another nine kilometers to the impressive park Chute Montmorency.

Leave your bike and follow the path closest to the falls and cool off in the mist. If you have any energy left, climb the stairs to the top for a view of the falls and mythic Île d'Orléans.

After you've taken in the view, go for a well-earned dinner at L'Aventure, then get back on your bikes and return to the city. Once there, leave the bikes at the rental place and head for a late-night stroll around the Vieux-Port, grabbing a treat at Le Marché du Vieux Port along the way.

Head back to your hotel for a good night's rest before heading home the next morning.

Romantic Weekend Getaway

For a short, romantic getaway, Québec City is considered one of the most romantic cities in North America. The winding cobblestone streets, classic New France architecture, and overall charming ambience have a tendency to bring out the amorous side in visitors. But nothing seems forced about it—instead, the city carries its romantic status quite naturally.

Day 1

Check into your suite at the plush **Auberge Saint-Antoine** and then go exploring along the cobblestone streets of **Quartier du Petit-Champlain.** Stop for a coffee or a cool drink on the corner terrace of **Lapin Sauté** and be charmed by the traditional music of street performers. Head to **Place Royale** and check out the small but beautiful chapel in **Église Notre-Dame-des-Victoires.**

Browse antiques and galleries on **rue St-Pierre** and **rue St-Paul.** Stroll among the boats and quays of the **Vieux-Port,** then head to Quai Chouinard and board the *Louis Jolliet.*

Enjoy views of **Chute Montmorency, Île d'Orléans,** and the illuminated city on this four-hour boat cruise as you dine on a five-course meal.

Day 2

Breakfast at **Panache** and then take the **Funiculaire du Vieux-Québec** to **Terrasse Dufferin.** Snap the requisite shots of **Château Frontenac** before taking the stairs at the far end to the **Parc des Plaines d'Abraham.** Stroll through the park to the **Musée National des Beaux-Arts du Québec.** After browsing the largest existing collection of Québec art, pick up some gourmet treats at **Les Halles du Petit Quartier** on Cartier, then grab a cab to

Église Notre-Dame-des-Victoires, on Place Royale

a quaint staircase in the historic Quartier du Petit-Champlain

Château Frontenac sits majestically over the St. Lawrence.

Life in Québec City completely changes once winter hits. And though it might seem like the perfect season to hibernate, the mounting snow is no excuse to stay indoors. Whether you're in the city or the country, there's a variety of things to do when the mercury drops.

- Drive an hour north to **Le Massif,** the highest ski mountain in the province. The ski runs offer 49 different trails and have the most breathtaking views of the St-Lawrence River.

- Bundle up and head to **Château Frontenac** for some serious winter sledding down the **Glissades de la Terrasse Dufferin.**

- The sweet treat known as ***tire sur la neige*** (maple syrup frozen on snow) can be found at just about every corner come winter.

- A typical après-ski meal of **raclette** is the perfect end-of-the-day fare. It can be procured in the cozy confines of restaurant **Le Petit Coin Latin.**

- **Carnaval de Québec,** which takes place between the end of January and early February, is two weeks of mostly free outdoor fun, from dog-sled races and ice-canoeing to outdoor dance parties and snow sculpture competitions.

Parc du Bois-de-Coulonge. Picnic overlooking the St-Lawrence River, then wander the grounds, and don't miss the arboretum close to the shore.

Hail a cab back to Upper Town and shop the independent boutiques along **rue St-Jean.** Freshen up back at the hotel and cab it to your reservation in the glass dining room at **Le Saint-Amour.** After dinner, take a moonlight tour through the streets in a **caléche** (horse-drawn carriage), stopping to admire the view at the **Parc du Cavalier-du-Moulin.** Then grab a cozy nook at **Pub St-Alexandre** for a nightcap.

Québec City skyline at dusk

Day 3

Rise early and drive to the base of the **Chute Montmorency,** about 20 minutes outside of Québec City, where you'll board the train **Le Massif** for a leisurely trip up-river. Take in the stunning views of the **Charlevoix** region and the St-Lawrence from this luxury locomotive. Disembark at **Baie-Saint-Paul,** check out the modern and ecofriendly hotel **La Ferme** before exploring the town's cultural heritage at the many galleries and artisanal shops. If all that walking makes you thirsty, grab a local micro-brew at **Le Saint-Pub.**

Hop back on the train heading a farther 40 minutes north to the majestic **Fairmont le Manoir Richelieu** in **La Malbaie** for an overnight stay. Located on the banks of the river, it's one of the prettiest spots in the region and a perfect place to kick back for the night. When you're settled in your room, relax next to the outdoor pool and get a massage at the in-house spa.

In the evening have dinner at **Vices Versa,** and get a taste of the local cuisine.

Sights

Highlights

★ **Most Iconic Sight:** The most photographed hotel in the world, **Château Frontenac** has become an indelible image of Québec City (page 30).

★ **Best Views:** Stroll along the top of **Les Fortifications** for the most stunning views of the city from both within and outside of the historic walls (page 32).

★ **Best Museum:** Dedicated to the history of Québec, **Musée de la Civilisation** offers an in depth look at Québécois culture (page 39).

★ **Most Historic Sight:** The site of the first settlement in Québec, **Place Royale** is the birthplace of both the French-Canadian nation and Canada itself (page 40).

★ **Most Picturesque Neighborhood:** Once home to Irish immigrants and dock workers, **Quartier du Petit-Champlain** has been revived and rejuvenated by a co-op of artists (page 41).

★ **Most Unusual City Street: Rue Sous-le-Cap** is a charming three-meter-wide street that runs along the cliff-face, lined with tiny old cottages (page 42).

★ **Best Collection of Québécois Art:** With a 19th-century prison incorporated into its design, the **Musée National des Beaux-Arts du Québec** beautifully mixes history and art (page 45).

★ **Most Patriotic Site:** The **Parc des Plaines d'Abraham** is the site of the historic 1759 battle between the French and British, an event that changed the course of North American history (page 47).

★ **Most Historical City Street:** Learn about the city's history in the older buildings that line **rue Saint-Jean** as you wander down what is now one of the busiest commercial streets in the city (page 51).

The only fortified city left in North America, Québec City is like no other place on the continent. Constructed on the top of Cap Diamant, a cliff that looks out over the St-Lawrence River, the city is defined by its natural hills and cliffs, though from afar it's not always easy to notice. Québec City

is the cradle of Canadian society, where in 1608 the first settlers arrived. Led by Samuel de Champlain, they built the first habitation on the site that's now called Place Royale. It was under French rule until 1759, when it fell to the British at the Battle of the Plains of Abraham, but this political feat did not alter the existing French-Canadian culture and way of life. Despite 100 years of British rule and the eventual founding of the Canadian Dominion, the city's ties to the early settlers remain remarkably intact. It's this lineage and incredible architectural heritage that give it its own unique (albeit European) feel.

Quebéc City is divided into two main areas, Haute-Ville (Upper Town) and Basse-Ville (Lower Town). They are easy to differentiate thanks to their geography. Upper Town constitutes the area on the top of the cliff, while Lower Town constitutes everything below it. It's in Upper Town that you'll find Les Fortifications, the walled defenses that encircle Old Québec's Upper Town and many of the biggest sights, including Château Frontenac and La Citadelle.

Directly below, between the cliff and the river, is Vieux-Québec's Basse-Ville (Old Québec's Lower Town). This is where the first European settlement was established, near Place Royale, and where historic areas like the Vieux-Port (Old Port) and the Quartier du Petit-Champlain are situated.

Previous: Place Royale, Vieux-Québec's Lower Town; Les Fortifications, Upper Town; Église Notre-Dame-des-Victoires, Lower Town.

Getting from the lower to the upper part of the city isn't complicated, provided the winding, hilly streets aren't sheets of ice. Taking the Escalier Frontenac (Frontenac Stairs) is the easiest way, but the funicular and the brand-new Ecobuses offer some good alternatives.

Though separated by a cliff, Vieux-Québec is quite small and dense, so it's easy to cover by foot. In fact the best way to get around the city, in winter or summer, is by walking. Expect to get quite a workout, though, thanks to the hilly geography. No matter where you are in the city, if you want to get down or up, there are likely stairs involved, or at the very least, a city bus. Due to the density of the city, even peripheral areas like the Plains (just outside of the walls in Upper Town) and Saint-Roch (the city's coolest post code, located in Lower Town) are only a 15-minute walk from Vieux-Québec.

Of course, Québec is a vastly different city with a completely different landscape in winter than in summer. Many sites close during the winter or have truncated hours. What constitutes the different seasons, however, is a complicated matter. A good general rule of thumb is the following: Summer hours usually run from June 24, Saint-Jean-Baptiste day and the province's national holiday, to Labor Day, the first Monday in September. Winter hours, meanwhile, could start as early as Labor Day or Canadian Thanksgiving (the second Monday of October) and run until May or June. Many of these dates fluctuate according to the weather, so make sure to double-check hours if there's a particular sight you want to visit.

With so many interesting historical sites just about everywhere you turn in Québec City—even a stroll down Faubourg Saint-Jean Baptiste is a lesson in the city's evolution—there's no time for a dull moment.

Vieux-Québec's Upper Town

Map 1

Basilique-Cathédrale Notre-Dame-de-Québec

It was on this site, high above the St-Lawrence River, that explorer Samuel de Champlain built Québec's first church in 1647. Later, in 1664, the Basilique-Cathédrale Notre-Dame-de-Québec became the first parish church in North America. It was given the title of cathedral 10 years later, when the diocese of Québec was established with the arrival of Monsignor de Laval, the first bishop of New France.

Destroyed by fire during the English conquest in 1759, it was entirely reconstructed a few years later, only to be remodeled again in 1843, by Thomas Baillairgé. Inspired by Sainte-Geneviève in Paris, Baillairgé, whose father François designed the church's interior, gave it a neoclassical facade. That, too, had to be reconstructed when the church was once again ravaged by fire—arsonists used the fire to steal priceless paintings—in 1922. During this rebuilding period, however, the builders tried to stay as true as possible to the original building, working off of François Baillairgé's original 18th-century drawings for the interior. Despite the fact that it has

Confession: Québec City's Love Affair with Churches

If you weren't convinced about the Catholic Church's involvement in the development of New France, you will be after a trip to Québec City. There are so many churches in the city that a single trip alone couldn't cover them all. Most are free and open to the public for both prayer and sightseeing.

- **Chalmers-Wesley United Church:** A neo-Gothic Protestant church, this one was completed in 1853 and was designed by architect John Wells. Its steeple is the tallest inside the walls of Old Québec at 164 feet above the sidewalk (78 rue Ste-Ursule).

- **Chapelle Historique Bon Pasteur:** Designed by Charles Baillairgé in 1868, the slanting roof hides an ornate baroque-style interior (1080 rue de la Chevrotière).

- **Église Saint-Dominique:** Run by Dominican monks, this church

and former monastery boasts a stunning wood-beamed ceiling reminiscent of medieval architecture (175 Grande-Allée).

- **Holy Trinity Anglican Cathedral:** Inspired by St-Martin's in the Fields in London, this was the first Anglican cathedral to be built outside of the British Isles (31 rue des Jardins).

- **Sanctuaire Notre-Dame-du-Sacré-Coeur:** Tucked back from the road, this slender, neo-Gothic church was built in 1901 by François-Xavier Berlinguet and is renowned for its stained-glass windows and marble plaques that line the walls (71 rue Ste-Ursule).

- **St. Andrew's Presbyterian Church:** This congregation had its start among the Scottish Fraser Highlanders that were part of Wolfe's Army in 1759 (106 rue Ste-Anne).

SIGHTS VIEUX-QUÉBEC'S UPPER TOWN

been rebuilt a number of times, the bell tower and portions of the walls are from the original structure.

Long and narrow, the interior is a soft buttery yellow with a high arched ceiling, lined with windows and intricate moldings. A stunning gold-plated baldaquin stands at the altar, and other items include paintings of the Virgin Mary that date back to the French regime, the bishop's original throne, and a chancel lamp that was a gift of Louis XIV.

Between 1654 and 1898 over 900 people were buried in the crypt below the church, including 20 bishops and four governors. It's also rumored that Samuel de Champlain himself is buried nearby; archaeologists have been searching for the grave for over 50 years. Hour-long guided tours of the crypt and basilica are available but must be reserved in advance, so call ahead.

MAP 1: 16 rue de Buade, 418/692-2533, www.notredamedequebec.org; Nov.-Apr. Mon.-Fri. 7:30am-4pm, Sat. 7:30am-6pm, Sun. 8:30am-6pm; May-Oct. Mon.-Fri. 7:30am-5pm, Sat. 7:30am-6pm, Sun. 8:30am-6pm; free

Proudly holding the title of "most photographed hotel in the world," Château Frontenac is one of the most stunning buildings in Québec. The fortress-like architecture and its location on the top of the Cap Diamant, a bluff overlooking the St-Lawrence, give it an especially majestic feel.

Built in 1893, it is part of a chain of "château style" hotels that were constructed across the country by the Canadian Pacific Railway. Since Québec was one of the North American ports before the long trip across the Atlantic, the hotel was designed to rival any European counterpart and grab the attention of travelers. The building's architect, Bruce Price, drew from both the Middle Ages and Renaissance and used elements like the turrets found on Scottish castles and the bastion towers of French châteaus.

Named after Louis de Buade de Frontenac, who was governor of New France twice between 1672 and 1698, the hotel sits on the site of what was once Château St-Louis, the official residence of the governor of New France and later home of the British governors. The ruins of the many incarnations of the residence lie just in front of the hotel.

It has been the temporary residence of everyone from Queen Elizabeth II to Charles Lindburgh, as well as the site of Alfred Hitchcock's *I Confess,* but the hotel's proudest moment took place in 1943. It was the site of the Québec Conference of World War II, where U.S. president Franklin D. Roosevelt, British prime minister Winston Churchill, and Canadian prime minister William Lyon Mackenzie King discussed the eventual invasion of France. **MAP 1:** 1 rue des Carrières, 866/840-8402, www.fairmont.com/frontenac; daily 24 hours; free

La Citadelle

The largest British fortress in North America, La Citadelle is also the largest defense on the continent to have never seen battle. Covering 2.3 square kilometers and perched on the edge of the cape at the highest point in the city, overlooking the St-Lawrence, this strategically placed defense is an imposing figure, standing out along the rolling plains and the copper roofs of Vieux-Québec.

Built under the direction of British officer Lieutenant-Colonel Elias Walker Durnford, the design is entirely French. Modeled in the style of military engineer Vauban, it is shaped like a four-pointed star and as such has no blind spots. Construction on the Citadelle started in 1820, took 30 years to complete, and incorporated two existing buildings from the French regime, the oldest of which is a battery dating back to 1750. The winding gate that is used as entrance into the Citadelle is also the only real gate remaining from the French regime, and is reminiscent of what all gates into the city were once like.

Though it never saw any action, the Citadelle continues to be the official residence of the Royal 22e Régiment, the only Francophone infantry regiment in the Canadian Forces Regular Force. The low stone barracks are a mix of English and French influences with symmetric casement windows and doors and pitched tin roofs. A brand new museum, completed in 2014, commemorates the regiment's 100th anniversary. Housed in a

A Tour of One's Own: Québec City's Best Walking Tours

There's more than one way to see the city, but the best way to see it is on foot. Here are a few fun, kookier ways to get to know the town.

If you like to be spooked, **Ghost Tours of Québec** (418/692-9770, www.ghosttoursofquebec.com) is for you. Reservations are recommended for these nighttime tours that whisk participants down darkened streets while talking about the city's 400-year-old history and all the ghosts and hauntings that go with it. Guides will even take visitors into one of the most haunted buildings in the city, though taking a pass and staying outside is totally okay. Learn about the previous job experience needed to qualify for the job of executioner in the 1600s, or how the murder of an American in Québec could be the source of an unexplained haunting.

Equally exciting but slightly less grim, **La Compagnie des Six Associés** (418/692-3033, www.sixassocies.com) offers a handful of walking tours, all with a different theme. They always involve a stop at a bar. Lust and Drunkenness is one such tour; it will take you past and into some of the forgotten brothels and taverns of the 19th century and give you an idea of how both the rich and the poor spent their free time and money. Things get a little darker with their Crime and Punishments tour, which lets visitors follow the wife of a French torturer through the streets by lantern-light as they learn about various crimes, the criminals, and inevitably their punishment.

If you love the history but hate the gore (well, some of it anyway), **Les Tours Voir Québec** (866/694-2001, www.toursvoirquebec.com) hits up all the important sights on their Grand Tour. The architecture, the events, the history—it's all here, along with a few lesser-known sights. If you're not quite full yet, take a second helping and try their Food Tour, which looks at the influence of British, French, and Amerindian cooking in the kitchen. Of course, a taste of local wine, beer, chocolate, cheeses, pastries, and crêpes will only give you a better idea of exactly how this whole mix has come together.

Fed up with walking? **Tours Ludovica** (418/655-5836, www.toursludovica.com) does the work while you sit back and relax. Guides ride around on bikes while visitors sit and enjoy the scenery, in a sort of mash-up between a rickshaw and a horse-drawn carriage. Going off map, Tours Ludovica offers tours of lesser-known areas like Saint-Roch, Saint-Sauveur, and Limoilou. A ride out to Saint-Sauveur lets visitors take in the historical architecture of a neighborhood that—had Samuel de Champlain's plans gone through—would have become a large city called Ludovica. It's here that you'll find many old seminaries and other church buildings as well as the Hôpital Général de Québec, the city's original hospital and the oldest building in the city. Up-and-coming Limoilou can also be explored by pedicab; let the guide lead you through the history of this emerging neighborhood before hopping out to grab a coffee at one of the sidewalk cafés.

historic building on the site, the museum is dedicated to the regiment's distinguished military history. Starting with the early days and Québec's most important battles, the exhibits continue up to the modern day with the regiment's tour in Bosnia and other United Nations missions. One exhibit is dedicated to the war heroes of the 22e Régiment who fought in World Wars I and II, summarizing their duties, showing personal artifacts, and in one case showing a spy's various identity cards.

As early as the 1860s there was talk of tearing down the Citadelle, but then Governor General Lord Dufferin refused, instead pointing to the fortifications' historical importance. Since that time, his residence became the official residence of the governor general of Canada. It is here too that Georges Vanier, the first French-Canadian governor general and a war hero, was laid to rest in a battery turned chapel.

Since it is still an active military residence, the only way to get inside the Citadelle is to take a tour. Both the regiment and city get equal tour time, and though there's a lot to see, the most interesting aspects, such as the barracks and doors that lead inside the walls, are off-limits.

MAP 1: 1 Côte de la Citadelle, 418/694-2815, www.lacitadelle.qc.ca; bilingual tours Apr. daily 10am-4pm, May-Sept. daily 9am-5pm, Oct. daily 10am-3pm, Nov.-Mar. daily at 1:30pm; $10 adults, $9 seniors and students, $5.50 children, children 7 and under free

★ Les Fortifications

Québec is the only fortified city in North America, and its walls encircle the entirety of Upper Town, covering 4.6 kilometers, which you can walk for free. The Fortifications offer some of the most stunning views of the city and environs and are a great place to hang out in the summer and have a picnic or take a break from sightseeing. One of the best places to start is at the St-Louis Gate on rue St-Louis. As it's here that you're mostly likely to recognize the ramparts. As you walk along the walls, every angle of the city can be explored, from the defenses of the Citadelle to the lookouts over the river. Lined with cannons and grass-covered in spots, the stone walls of the Fortifications frame the city in a way that transports visitors back to the days when they were a practical defense against attacks. It's along this part, surrounding the Citadelle, where you'll find the best views.

Built in a classic urban style, the Fortifications are characterized by the geometry of flanking and the adaptation of the walls to the city's topography, which sees the walls grow in height and depth at different parts. Though Québec was a bustling city by 1700, its defense system was inadequate, and the city was a maze of temporary and permanent structures. It wasn't until the fall of Louisbourg, a fort in Cape Breton off the coast of Nova Scotia, in 1745, that serious consideration was given to the state of the Fortifications. It was Governor Beauharnois who, following Chaussegros de Léry's designs, authorized a new enceinte that permanently closed the city to the open countryside.

In the late 19th century, citizens complained about the impracticality of the gates, complaining that they stopped circulation and were a nuisance—the gates would close at curfew, and, up until the British troops left, the ramparts were for military and pedestrian use only. Though Lord Dufferin, then governor general of Canada, understood their complaints, he also saw the historical importance of the fortifications—during the summer-long siege of Québec, it was these walls that kept the citizens from British invasion—and instead suggested the gates be dismantled and then rebuilt to make them wider.

The Interpretation Centre of the Fortifications of Québec is located by the St-Louis Gate, beneath the city's ramparts. It offers information about the history of the city's defenses as well as exhibits and guided tours, which depart from Terrasse Dufferin.

MAP 1: 2 rue d'Auteuil, 418/648-7016; Interpretation Centre May-Sept. daily 10am-6pm; tours June 1-24 daily 2pm, June 25-Sept. 6 daily 10am and 2pm, Sept. 7-Oct. 11 2pm; Interpretation Centre $4 adults, $3.50 seniors, $2 children; tours $9.80 adults, $7.30 seniors, $4.90 children

Musée de l'Amérique Francophone

Entering the modernized foyer of the museum you're almost not prepared for the historic chapel that you enter shortly after. Full of green marble pillars, beautiful stained-glasses windows, golden busts of important members of Québec's history, and a 1753 organ, the most alluring part of this exhibit is the baroque music that is played throughout the day.

After a bit of maze-like wandering—through the chapel, into an elevator, and across an outdoor walkway—you arrive at the building that houses the Musée de l'Amérique Francophone, an old building that once belonged to the Séminaire de Québec. The first exhibit on the ground floor looks at the history of the seminary itself, with artifacts like old keys, chalices, and furniture that once belonged to the seminary.

Moving on to the museum's permanent collection, visitors get a well-rounded view of the history and trajectory of the Francophone population, not just in Canada but within the whole of the continent. It retraces the roots of Francophone explorers and guides who helped explore the United States and found American cities like Detroit, Pittsburgh, Buffalo, and St. Louis.

The design of the exhibit is modern and easy to navigate, even in high season when there are more crowds. For the most part, however, it's rarely overcrowded and visitors can wander the exhibits at their leisure.

MAP 1: 2 Côte de la Fabrique, 418/692-2843, www.mcq.org; early Sept.-mid-June Tues.-Sun. 10am-5pm, mid-June-early Sept. daily 9:30am-5pm; $8 adults, $7 seniors, $5.50 students, $2 children, children under 12 free

Musée des Ursulines

Founded in 1639 by Marie de l'Incarnation, an Ursuline nun, and Madame Marie-Madeline de Chauvigny de la Peltrie, a rich widow, the Couvent des Ursulines is the oldest school in North America dedicated to the teaching of women. Girls still study at this institution, which now boasts a museum and a chapel alongside the schoolrooms and courtyard playgrounds.

The first Ursuline nuns landed in Québec on August 1, 1639, and soon started teaching, though at the time the French-Canadian population was so small, the majority of their students were First Nations girls. Just outside of the convent's walls is the Musée des Ursulines de Québec, which tells the story of these pioneer women who were both teachers and students. Newly reopened and renovated, the new permanent collection, The Young Ladies' Academy, allows visitors into the heart of the boarding school and the daily lives of the nuns and pupils that passed through the convent's halls. Artifacts from the time of the French regime are also on view, including teaching materials, personal objects, and sacred artwork.

When French governor Montcalm died after the Battle of the Plains of Abraham, he was buried in the convent chapel by night so as not to arouse suspicion. For a long time his skull was part of the museum's permanent collection, to the delight of visiting schoolchildren.

Despite the simple, austere pews found in the small Ursuline chapel, it has some of the most beautiful sculpted wood in Québec. The carvings were created by master craftsman Pierre-Noël Levasseur between 1723 and 1739, and it was the Ursulines themselves who gilded the carvings, which now adorn the nave of the chapel. The tomb of founder Marie de l'Incarnation can also be found here. The chapel is open to the public from May to October, and entry is free.

MAP 1: 12 rue Donnacona, 418/694-0694, www.museedesursulines.com; May-Sept. Tues.-Sat. 10am-noon and 1pm-5pm, Sun. 1pm-5pm, Oct.-Nov. and Feb.-Apr. Tues.-Sun. 1pm-5pm; $8 adults, $6 seniors and students, $4 children

Parc de l'Artillerie

The position of the Parc de l'Artillerie, looking out over the west of the city and across the St-Charles River, has made it a strategic military site since the late 17th century. Four vastly different buildings trace the city's history from the French regime right up to the 1940s. Of the four buildings that make up the site, the Dauphine Redoubt is the most striking, with massive white supports that plunge down the side of a hill. Built in 1712 and completed in 1748, it was army barracks both before and after the British conquest and eventually became the home of the superintendent. During the summer, characters in period costume bring the barracks to life with demonstrations and tours through the rooms, which have been decorated to reflect various periods in the building's evolution.

Kitty-corner to the Redoubt is the interpretation center, a former foundry used to make an arsenal for the Canadian military, from the Boer War up to World War I and II, and even the Korean War. The site now holds a 200-year-old scale model of Québec. Constructed in 1806-1808, by draftsman Jean-Baptiste Duberger and John By, a military engineer, it was sent to England in 1810 to convince the British government that the city needed new fortifications. Alongside uncovered ruins, there are artifacts that were found on and around the site, including toothbrushes, children's toys, and belt buckles.

MAP 1: 2 rue d'Auteuil, 418/648-7016, www.pc.gc.ca; early May-early Sept. daily 10am-6pm, early Sept.-Oct. daily 10am-5pm; $4 adults, $3.50 seniors, $2 children

Clockwise from top left: the Fontaine de Tourny, Parliament Hill; the Funiculaire du Vieux-Québec, Vieux-Québec's Lower Town; the Séminaire de Québec, Vieux-Québec's Upper Town.

Parc du Cavalier-du-Moulin

This tiny little park tucked away at the end of a quiet residential street is one of the city's best-kept secrets. Passing through the park's wrought-iron gates, visitors enter onto Mont-Carmel, the spot of an old windmill (*moulin* in French). Originally a military outpost, the small 1,500-square-meter park was one of the few defenses constructed by the French military in the 17th century. This small defensive outpost was then named "cavalier," a nod to its solitary position. In 1663, the windmill was erected here and included in the military fortification. By 1700, with the building of the first surrounding walls, *le cavalier du moulin* was no longer needed.

Nowadays the park acts as a window onto history, allowing visitors to imagine a city that once had nothing but fields beyond this hillock. It's adorned with a cannon to remind people of its past life as a military defense; the cannon juts out over the hill, directed at the houses and winding streets beyond.

MAP 1: rue Mont-Carmel; daily 24 hours; free

Place d'Armes

The history of Place d'Armes is the history of Québec. Once situated behind Château St-Louis, which was at the time also a fort, it was in this public square, safely behind the defenses, that the military would perform their various parades and military inspections. When construction of the Citadelle was undertaken in 1820, however, the military moved and the regular parades went with it, moving instead to the Parc de l'Esplanade in front of the fortress and running alongside the city walls.

Though it lost its military importance, the square continued to be a popular meeting place, and in 1915 a monument was erected to the notion of faith. Dedicated to the Récollets, the first religious community to live in New France, the monument today stands in the shadow of the Château Frontenac at the center of a bustling square surrounding by busy restaurants and cafés.

MAP 1: between rue du Trésor and rue du Fort

Séminaire de Québec

Established in 1663 by Monsignor François de Laval, the first bishop of New France, to train young men for the priesthood, this seminary was expanded five years later to include the Petit Séminaire, which, in a push to Gallicize the indigenous population, accepted both Indian and French students to study at the Collège des Jésuites. It continued to be the training ground of future priests right up until the conquest, when its connection to the priesthood was somewhat lost. The studies instead began to focus on the liberal arts, and the school began accepting students who didn't want to become priests. By 1852 the college part of the Séminaire de Québec became the University of Laval.

Laid out according to 17th-century principles, the *séminare* has various wings, all of which center around interior courtyards (you can enter one through the Musée l'Amérique Francophone). Though the time periods vary there is continuity in the architecture, with stone masonry covered with stucco, casement windows, steep roofs with dormers, and raised fire-walls evident in all of the buildings. The bursar's wing in particular is interesting. Designed from 1678 to 1681 and restored in 1866 after a fire, its vaulted kitchen is still intact, along with the chapel of Monsignor Briand, who was bishop of Québec in 1766-1784.

Today, it remains both a school and seminary, with Laval's school of architecture located on the site and priests who continue to live here and dedicate their lives to the church.

MAP 1: 1 rue des Remparts, 418/692-3981, www.seminairedequebec.org

Terrasse Dufferin

Along the front of Château Frontenac, looking out over the St-Lawrence River and across to Lévis, is the wide boardwalk of Terrasse Dufferin. Created in 1879 by the governor general of Canada, Lord Dufferin, the 671-meter-long promenade was designed by Charles Baillairgé, the same designer behind the kiosks and street lamps that line the boardwalk.

It was during his summer stay at the Citadelle, now at the opposite end of the promenade, that Lord Dufferin conceived of the idea to build the boardwalk, a place for residents and visitors to take their daily stroll. The use of wooden planks gives the whole thing an air of summer, even in the middle of winter. Though he left his post in 1879, Dufferin himself inaugurated the project and put down the first stone.

Beneath the *terrasse* lie the ruins of the former St-Louis Fort and Château, which was destroyed by fire in 1834. Visitors are able to visit the excavation site thanks to a new interpretation center, cleverly hidden by the boardwalk. Only a few steps down and you're face-to-face with the foundations of the original building and some of the artifacts they uncovered here.

During the winter, a huge slide is built at the Citadelle end of the *terrasse* and children of all ages line up to take a super-fast ride down *les glissades* overlooking the frozen river.

MAP 1: Intersection of rue des Carrières and Place d'Armes

Vieux-Québec's Lower Town

Map 2

Église Notre-Dame-des-Victoires

The oldest stone church in Québec, Église Notre-Dame-des-Victoires was built on Place Royale in 1688, on the site of l'Abitation, Québec's first building. In the basement of the church you can still see one of the building's walls, and archaeological digs have uncovered one of the building's original turrets in the church's facade. The king's storehouse also stood on this site, and it was this particular location that attracted François de Laval, the bishop of New France. For years Laval requested a chapel be built on the site of the king's storehouse, an extension of Upper Town's Notre-Dame-de-Québec church, but it was his successor, Monsignor de Saint Vallier, who would see the work completed in 1723.

Sky High: Édifice Price

Completed in 1931, Édifice Price is the only skyscraper in Vieux-Québec. Built as the headquarters for Price Brothers Limited, one of the biggest printing companies in Québec at the time, it was designed by Montréal firm Ross and Macdonald. Despite heavy criticism from the public, the government ignored accusations that it wasn't protecting Québec's historic area—two historic houses were demolished to make way for the new building—and gave the company a building permit anyhow.

Completed within a year, the art deco building is reminiscent of the Empire State Building in New York, though much smaller. The design uses setbacks to gradually taper the build-ing's width. Unlike the Empire State Building, however, the roof is classical in design, with a château-style steepled copper roof that blends well with its surroundings. The interior includes bas-reliefs that depict the origins of the Price company, which was forced into bankruptcy during the Depression.

Since 2001, the 16th and 17th floors have become the official residence of the premier of Québec, and the two-floor apartment includes a 14-guest dining room, two bedrooms, and offices. Decorated to reflect the province's history, it boasts maple hardwood floors, traditional Québec style furnishings, and paintings by local artists.

Designed by Claude Baillif, the church was originally named l'Enfant Jesus, but it's name was changed twice. In 1690 the British admiral Phipps was defeated by Governor Frontenac, and the church was renamed Notre-Dame-de-la-Victoire. In 1711, the city was again saved when the fleet of Admiral Walker, on its way to attack Québec, was shipwrecked in the St. Lawrence. This time the name change was easy; they made it plural. Despite two failed attempts, the British would eventually destroy the church in 1759 during the siege of Québec. The subsequent reconstructions were meticulous and took place in 1762-1766 under the eye of Jean Baillairgé.

The interior itself is rather austere, with a few pews and a tiny, circular staircase leading up to the organ. Designed by students of Thomas Baillairgé, it was constructed in 1854-1857 and features several paintings from the 17th, 18th, and 19th centuries. The oldest part of the church is the tabernacle; originally found in the Sainte-Geneviève Chapel, it dates from 1724. Unique to Québec, the frescos on either side of the main altar retrace the history of the church and city, and were done by local painter and decorator Jean-M. Tardivel. The most striking church accent, however, is the single ex-voto, a model of a vessel that arrived in 1664, transporting the Carignan Regiment and the Marquis de Tracy, which hangs suspended over the pews.

MAP 2: Place Royale, 32 rue Sous-le-Fort, 418/692-1650, www.notredamedequebec.org; daily 9am-5pm; tours May-Oct., reservations required mid-Oct.-Apr.; free

Reaching nearly three stories tall and covering 420 square meters, La Fresque des Québécois is the largest and most historical trompe l'oeil in the city. Unveiled in 1999, it took 12 artists to complete the immense mural that cleverly shows the city's history and its important figures. Sixteen important Québécois are featured in the painting, including historical figures like Jacques Cartier, Samuel de Champlain, and Lord Dufferin, as well as cultural icons like singer/songwriter Félix Leclerc and politician Louis-Joseph Papineau. Also shown in the mural are typical Québécois buildings through whose windows the important figures peek. One of the gates figures prominently, as do the famous L'Escalier du Casse-Cou and the province's four seasons.

A popular tourist sight (it's fun to try and slip yourself in among the historical figures), it kicked off a trompe l'oeil craze around the city, and many buildings are now covered in historically clever murals.

MAP 2: Place Royale

Funiculaire du Vieux-Québec

The only funicular of its kind in North America, the Funiculaire du Vieux-Québec was built in 1879 and designed by William Griffith. Wood-covered and steam-powered, it operated six months a year as an alternative to horse and buggy, transporting passengers and merchandise from Lower Town to Upper Town. The arrival of electrical power in 1907 meant it could work year-round, which it did until 1945, when the wooden structure caught fire and was subsequently rebuilt with metal shelters. It lets passengers off and on at Terrasse Dufferin.

Transportation is still its main function, though today it transports more tourists than merchandise since it allows incomparable views of Lower Town, the port, and Lévis, across the water.

The entrance of the funicular is situated in a historical house, built in 1683 by Québec architect Baillif, that once belonged to one of the country's first European explorers, Louis Jolliet. Jolliet, along with Father Jacques Marquette, was the first European to explore and map the Mississippi River. Jolliet lived here until his death in 1700.

MAP 2: 16 rue du Petit-Champlain, 418/692-1132, www.funiculaire-quebec. com; early Sept.-June 19 daily 7:30am-11pm, June 20-early Sept. daily 7:30am-midnight; $2.25

★ Musée de la Civilisation

In the heart of the port district, not far from the shores of the St-Lawrence and surrounded by historical buildings, the modern facade of the Museum of Civilization strikes out against its surroundings. Designed by Moshe Safdie, the architect behind Montréal's Habitat 67, the front of the museum is built into an incline, tucking the museum away and adding a touch of nature, with a glass roof and greenery sprouting from along the sides. Inaugurated in 1988, the museum is dedicated to the history, present, and future of Québec civilization, as well as that of cultures from around the world.

Crossing the St-Lawrence: Québec-Lévis Ferry

SIGHTS
VIEUX-QUÉBEC'S LOWER TOWN

One of the best views of the city is from across the river in the city of Lévis. Get there by hopping on the **Québec-Lévis Ferry** located right on the port (10 rue des Traversiers, 877/787-7483, www.traversiers.gouv.qc.ca, $3.25 adult, $2.25 child, $7.75 car). The views of the city are stunning, especially at night, and the 10-minute trip on the commuter ferry will give you a new appreciation for the city's geography. The ferry runs all year long, several times an hour 6am-6pm and hourly 6pm-2:30am. In July-August, a bus tour to Lévis is also available and includes such sights as Fort No. 1, which was built by the British as a defense between 1865 and 1872.

Inside, the harmony with the surroundings continues with a large open lobby, full of glass and light. The three-story building accommodates 10 exhibits simultaneously, 3 of which are permanent exhibits rooted in the region's history. Le Temps des Québécois is an overview of the history of this nation within a nation, from the first explorers to Expo 67. It's a fun exhibition with bits of pop culture—like videos of iconic TV presenters and shows from the 1980s and 1990s—placed within context next to religious iconography, old tramway signs, sabers, and World War II ration boxes. Presented in conjunction with the National Film Board of Canada (the NFB), historic films, political speeches, and important cultural events are shown on film here.

With a focus on the province as a whole, Territoires looks at the various regions of the province and the problems the areas, and their inhabitants, face. Not an overly optimistic exhibit, it examines issues like suburban sprawl and the Amerindians' lost connection to the land, and tries to provide solutions. The breathtaking photos and videos of the regions give visitors a good overview of the expansive province.

Those wanting to learn more about Québec's First Nations will enjoy Encounter with the First Nations, which looks at the 11 different tribes that inhabit the province and includes videos, artifacts—a birch canoe, a tepee, Inuit sculpture—as well as a look at the history and migration patterns of the particular tribes. Admission is free on Tuesdays November-May.

MAP 2: 85 rue Dalhousie, 418/643-2158, www.mcq.org; mid-June-early Sept. daily 9:30am-6:30pm, early Sept.-mid-June Tues.-Sun. 10am-5pm; $15 adults, $14 seniors, $10 students, $5 children, children 11 and under free

★ Place Royale

For all intents and purposes this is the birthplace of Canada—or more specifically the birthplace of the French-Canadian civilization. It was here that Samuel de Champlain, founder of Québec, built l'Abitation, the first establishment in Québec, and though the structure itself is long gone, slate stones mark where the building once stood. As early as 1623, the square started to take on a life of its own alongside the settlement's second habitation. A military parade ground, marketplace, and the surrounding houses burned to the ground during a fire that destroyed Lower Town in 1682. Place Royale got its name in 1686 when Intendant Jean Bochart de Champigny erected a bust of King Louis XIV in its center. As in all towns in France, it was the custom to have a square dedicated to royalty, but unlike in France, there was nothing ceremonious about the square or its surroundings; in fact, the merchants complained that the bust took up valuable space, and so it was removed and placed at the intendant's house.

Damaged during the Seven Years' War, the square was gradually rebuilt, and by the 19th century the square was part of an urban complex that included warehouses, two markets, and a number of businesses. Up until the early 20th century many of the buildings went through major transformations; floors were added, roofs were flattened, storefront windows were built on the ground floor. It wasn't until an economic downturn in the 1960s forced the city to reconsider its purpose that the area was restored.

After restoring a few buildings (the Chevalier hotel, the Maison Fornel, and the Notre-Dame-des-Victoires church), the government decided it wanted to recreate the ambience of the early 17th century and went about completely renovating the buildings to closely resemble how they would have looked during the French regime. Following the detailed plans of the original structures, the buildings were rebuilt using Norman construction with firewalls, stone, spirits to hold up the walls, and ladders on the roofs.

Set on the same square is the Place Royale Interpretation Center. Opened in 1999, it's in the former home of merchant François Hazeur as well as part of the Smith home next door. Exhibits here include a scale model of the original settlement, which would've been situated just outside the modern glass doors. Built against Côte-de-la-Montagne—the steep road established by Samuel de Champlain in 1623—it also houses a public staircase that links the Lower Town with the street above. Admission is free on Tuesdays November-May.

MAP 2: 27 rue Notre-Dame, 418/646-3167, www.mcq.org; mid-June-early Sept. daily 9:30am-5pm, early Sept.-mid-June Tues.-Sun. 10am-5pm; $7 adults, $6 seniors, $5 students, $2 children, children 12 and under free

★ Quartier du Petit-Champlain

The charming restaurants, quaint boutiques, and tourist-packed cobblestone streets of this picturesque neighborhood often belie its rich and interesting history. The oldest street in the city, rue du Petit-Champlain in the 17th century was little more than a dirt path down which residents would walk to get their water. Over the next 200 years, the street would grow to become a bustling area full of houses and businesses of many working-class families and men who worked in the port.

In the mid-1800s, the area saw an influx of immigrants. The Irish Potato Famine saw the Irish fleeing the country in boatloads and consequently arriving in Québec, one of the first ports of call. Many of these immigrants stayed, settling on la rue du Cul-de-Sac and la Petit rue Champlain, calling it instead Little Champlain Street. In time, the Francophones adopted the name as well, turning it into rue Petit-Champlain. This was a poor, working-class neighborhood, and the reconstruction of the nearby Place Royale in the 1970s forced a change in Petit-Champlain as well. The low rent meant that many artists had moved into the area, and it was the artists who rejuvenated it, financing renovations themselves and doing much of their own work. Since none of the buildings were entirely destroyed, a walk through this quarter gives visitors a view of the city's architecture through the ages, with buildings from different eras lovingly preserved.

At one end of rue Petit-Champlain you'll find L'Escalier du Casse-Cou, or the Breakneck Stairs, a narrow and steep set of steps that are one way to get from Upper Town to Lower Town. First built in 1660, the steps are squished between two buildings and can get icy in winter. The unusual name is rumored to come from American soldiers during their attempted invasion. At the other end of the street, you'll find La Fresque de Petit Champlain, which represents the life and history of the area, including the 1759 siege and the fires that came with it.

MAP 2: Between rue du Petit-Champlain and Place Royale

★ Rue Sous-le-Cap

La rue Sous-le-Cap, which means "street beneath the cape," is unlike any other street in the city and totally enchanting. Wedged between the cliff face and the backs of the houses that face rue St-Paul, it was the only road that pedestrians could use at the beginning of the 19th century to get from their homes in this section of Lower Town to the Côte du Palais, a winding street that would take them to Upper Town. What today are the backs of houses fronting on rue St-Paul used to be front entrances of homes along the waterfront, and during high tide, the roadway would be submerged under water.

The narrow street, which measures three meters across, was also at one time the city's red-light district, with a number of brothels operating on the street. Characterized by the stairs and walkways that cover almost all of the street, it's here that you'll find tiny, slightly crooked houses and some of the prettiest private patios in the city.

MAP 2: Behind rue du Sault-au-Matelot; between rue de la Barricade and rue St-Paul

Vieux-Port de Québec

At the base of Cap Diamant, where the waters of the St-Lawrence and St-Charles Rivers converge, the Vieux-Port de Québec (Old Port) is steeped in history. Lined with buildings that are both old and new, it maintains a connection to the past while looking to the future. The basins that once accommodated large cargo and passenger ships are now marinas docked with pleasure cruisers and sailboats, though the old locks of Louise Basin are still in use.

During its heyday in the 19th century, it was one of the world's five biggest ports, a hub of activity with commerce and transatlantic voyages. It was and still is a major contributor to the economic development of the region. Ships from here deal in commercial trade with over 60 countries, and the city is a popular cruise destination. On the very outskirts of

Bunge du Canada

Bunge Silo

A number of imposing silos occupy the far end of Québec City's port. Known as the **Bunge of Canada** (300 rue Dalhousie), these grain silos have been in operation for more than 40 years, enabling Canadian and American shippers to store a massive amount of grain before sending it overseas. They are some of the only silos in the eastern region of the country and a reminder of the city's history as a bustling and crucial port. The Bunge du Canada remains an important part of the city's landscape and its economic strength.

Petit-Champlain, one of the areas that border the Vieux-Port, are some of the city's oldest defenses. Low walls, cannons, and a moat are the only remnants of what was once part of the Lower Town's fortifications. To celebrate the city's 400th anniversary in 2008, the waterfront was rejuvenated with a number of bike paths that follow the water's edge and takes cyclists right in to the Old Port. It's here along the quays and among the docked boats that people stop for an ice cream or a cold drink in the summer and look back at the city that stands, perfectly lit, on the hill. The newly built Vieux-Port Interpretation Centre presents exhibitions related to the timber trade and shipbuilding, and characters in period costumes evoke a sense of history as they tell old-time tales. Guided walking tours of the port are also available. **MAP 2:** 100 Quai St-André, 418/648-3300; May-Aug. daily 10am-5pm, Sept.-Oct. daily noon-4pm; free

Parliament Hill and the Plains

Map 3

Fontaine de Tourny

Fontaine de Tourny was a gift from La Maison Simons (one of the oldest department stores in the province) to Québec City for its 400th anniversary in 2008. It came to its place in front of the Parliament by a circuitous route. Created in France in 1854, it won an award at the Universal Exposition in Paris the following year before being installed, in 1857, in the heart of Bordeaux in the Allées de Tourny. By 1960, however, the city no longer wanted the fountain, which was in a state of near disrepair. It was dismantled and stored in the Château Larivière near Bordeaux before being sold to a Parisian antiques dealer at the beginning of the 21st century.

During a trip to Paris in 2003, Peter Simons, president of the department store, discovered it in a flea market and had it shipped to Québec for restoration. Measuring seven meters high and four meters wide, it's adorned with 43 jets and decorated with statues, by sculptor Mathurin Moreau, of one man and three women symbolizing water, which matches well with the history of the port city. Five other statues were made from the same mold and can be found in cities across Europe, including Geneva in Switzerland and Porto in Portugal.

MAP 3: Ave. Honoré Mercier between La Grande-Allée and blvd. René-Lévesque

La Grande-Allée

Dubbed the "Champs d'Elysées of Québec," La Grande-Allée is one of the larger boulevards in the city and is the city's nightlife hot spot. It's lined with grand Victorian mansions, and the homes have been converted into cafés, restaurants, and nightclubs. Once lined with terraced houses, it was the chichi neighborhood of Québec, but many of those homes were torn down to make way for the Hôtel du Parlement, found on the south end of the *allée,* just in front of the St-Louis Gate.

It is the Grande-Allée that separates the rest of the city from the Plains of Abraham, which run along its back. The architecture of the strip's buildings is still stunning, with much of the stonework dating from the late 19th century.

MAP 3: Between Fontaine de Tourny and rue de l'Amérique Française

Hôtel du Parlement

The Parliament Building, house of the National Assembly of Québec, is one of the most impressive buildings in the province's capital city. Located on one of the highest spots of Upper Town, just outside the city walls, the quadrilateral building was constructed between 1877 and 1886 by the French architect Eugène-Étienne Taché. Inspired by the Louvre in Paris, the style of building, Second Empire neo-French Renaissance, is unique in North America. The front of the building also features a pantheon representing the province's rich history.

Incensed by the Durham Report, in which the British Lord said that the French-Canadians could not be civilized because they had no history, Taché included 15 statues depicting important figures in the province's history, to show that they did indeed have a strong past. Figures include Samuel de Champlain, Louis de Buade de Frontenac, James Wolfe, the Marquis de Montcalm, and, at the very top, an indigenous family. As the province's political life continues to grow, so does the number of statues; there are now 22 in front of the Parliament Building.

Since it is still a functioning government office, the only way to see the interior of the building is to take a free guided tour. At 30 minutes long, the tour provides a great opportunity to appreciate the unique architecture of the building, as well as gain insight into Québec's history and political scene. Make sure to have a photo I.D. with you, however, otherwise you won't pass the security check. In the summer, outdoor tours are also given to discover the surrounding gardens, which highlight the many trees and flowers of Québec and also give an overview of the many sculptures. All tours leave from the visitors center.

MAP 3: 1045 rue des Parliamentaires, 866/337-8837, www.assnat.qc.ca; first Tues. of Sept.-June 23 Mon.-Fri. 9am-4:30pm; June 24-first Mon. of Sept. Mon.-Fri. 9am-4:30pm, Sat.-Sun. 10am-4:30pm; free

Manège Militaire

This iconic piece of Canadiana was destroyed by fire in 2008, and though 90 percent of the museum's artifacts were saved, only the shell of the historic drill hall remains. Built in 1887, between the Plains of Abraham and the Grande-Allée, the Manège Militaire is home to the Voltigeurs de Québec, a primary reserve regiment founded in 1862. It was designed by Eugène-Étienne Taché, who also designed the Parliament Building, and the architectural style is inspired by the French chateaus of the 14th and 15th centuries, with circular turrets, pointy roofs, and high dormer windows. This particular style, extremely unique in North America, is recreated in countless other important structures in the country. It is one of the most recognized Canadian military buildings in the world.

MAP 3: 805 ave. Wilfrid-Laurier

★ Musée National des Beaux-Arts du Québec

Located in the middle of the Plains of Abraham, Musée National des Beaux-Arts du Québec holds the largest existing collection of Québec art, with works dating from the 17th century onward. The major focus here is on fine art, and the exhibits rarely revolve around the work of contemporary artists, though plans for a new addition will hopefully change that.

The musueum consists of three distinct structures: the Gérard-Morisset Building, the Charles-Baillairgé building, and the Grand Hall. Each has its own atmosphere and the work exhibited therein reflects that. Inaugurated in 1933, Gérard-Morisset is classical in style. It was designed by architect Wilfrid Lacroix and built in a neo-Italian Renaissance style. The first of the buildings to hold the museum's collection, it's full of white marble, wide Victorian steps, sculpted ceilings, and columns, and it's here that

Clockwise from top left: Basilique-Cathédrale Notre-Dame-de-Québec, Lower Town; the hidden rue Sous-le-Cap, Lower Town; the Musée National des Beaux Arts, Parliament Hill and the Plains.

you'll find permanent collections dedicated to Québécois artists like Emile Bourdos and others.

Much less conventional is the Charles-Baillairgé building, a former prison. It was incorporated into the museum in 1991 but retains a number of cells, which visitors are invited to explore. Opened in 1867, the prison was modeled after the Auburn Penitentiary in New York state and was all about rehabilitation through isolation. Overpopulated from the beginning, it sheltered not only criminals but the poor and needy. Despite its old-fashioned design, it housed inmates until 1970.

The Grand Hall joins these two structures with its pyramid-like glass facade, which adds light and airiness to the entire structure. A monument directly out front of the museum commemorates the place where General James Wolfe was shot and killed.

MAP 3: Parc des Champs-de-Bataille, 418/644-6460, www.mnba.qc.ca; June-Aug. Thurs.-Tues. 10am-6pm, Wed. 10am-9pm, Sept.-May. Tues. and Thurs.-Sun. 10am-5pm, Wed. 10am-9pm; $18 adults, $16 seniors, $10 youth (13-30), children 12 and under free

Observatoire de la Capitale

It might not look like much on the outside, but on the 31st floor of the building is one of the best views of the city. Perfect for a general overview of Québec, at 221 meters high the *observatoire* is the highest spot in Québec and offers 360-degree views of the city and its environs.

As you look out over the city at various vantage points, you will see important buildings and monuments, pointed out and explained on the easy-to-read plaques that adorn the windows. Sights like the far-off Québec bridge are easily seen, along with the Laurentian mountains and the St-Lawrence River. Alongside points of interest, the Observatoire de la Capitale also gives you information on the province and its history, such as the destruction of Chinatown, which took place to make way for highways to the suburbs. Temporary exhibits, including photographs of local sights, are also on view.

MAP 3: 1037 rue de la Chevrotière, 418/644-9841, www.observatoirecapitale.org; Feb.-Canadian Thanksgiving daily 10am-5pm; $10 adults, $8 seniors and students, children 12 and under free

★ Parc des Plaines d'Abraham

It was here on the Plains of Abraham on September 13, 1759, that the French fell to the British, forever changing the course of North American history. After Champlain's arrival in 1608, there were skirmishes on and off with the British, who at the time were fighting for control of the North American colonies against the French, but it wasn't until 1759 that the real battle took place.

Led by General James Wolfe, the British army advanced up the St-Lawrence in the spring of 1759, setting up camp north of Québec. During that summer, they laid a near constant siege on the city, destroying houses and monuments but not breaking French general Montcalm's reserve. For all intents and purposes, life continued within the walls of the city amid

Bridge over Troubled Water: Le Pont de Québec

The longest cantilever bridge in the world, the Pont de Québec is also the easternmost bridge to cross the St-Lawrence River. Measuring 987 meters long, 29 meters wide, and 104 meters high, it has three highway lanes, one rail line, and one pedestrian walkway, and connects Québec City in the north with Lévis in the south.

Before the bridge was completed, after two disasters, the only way to get from one side of the St-Lawrence to the other was by ferry. Politicians and government officials were looking into building a bridge as early as 1852, but it wasn't until the turn of the century that construction got underway, headed by the Phoenix Bridge Company out of Pennsylvania.

In the summer of 1907, with three years of work nearing completion, the bridge collapsed, killing 75 workers, the majority of which were Mohawk steelworkers from the Kahnawake reserve near Montréal. Though engineer Norman McClure had noticed abnormalities in the foundation structure, his eventual call to halt production never made it to Québec. That same afternoon the southern arm and central section collapsed into the river in 15 seconds.

After a Royal Commission of In-quiry, construction started on a second bridge. This time construction was headed by three engineers: Canadian H. E. Vautelet, Maurice Fitzmaurice from Britain (who worked on the construction of the Forth Bridge in Scotland), and Chicago's Ralph Modjeski. With the bridge nearing completion, the central span was raised into position on September 11, 1916, only to crash into the river, killing 13 workers. Because it was in the midst of World War I, rumors quickly spread that it was German sabotage. It soon became clear, however, that it was another unfortunate accident.

Reconstruction started almost immediately after the collapse and the project was granted special permission to use steel, which was in high demand because of the war effort. After nearly 20 years of construction, the bridge opened for rail traffic on December 3, 1919. Today it is still one of the most impressive engineering feats in North America. Though it's not visible from downtown Québec City, those traveling to and from Québec City by Autoroute Duplessis or heading for a stroll beside the river in Parc de la Plage Jacques-Cartier will get a stunning view of the bridge in all its glory.

the bombardments and fires. The siege lasted three long months. With winter approaching, Wolfe discovered the Canadians were awaiting a shipment of supplies from France to arrive on September 13. The supplies never arrived, but Wolfe continued with his plan regardless, maneuvering his men through the hard-to-navigate narrows in rowboats and mounting the cliff by way of a dried-up creek. By the time the Canadians arrived on the battlefield, the British army was already in formation. It was all over in 15 minutes. Wolfe was shot and killed on the spot, but Montcalm was only wounded; he was rushed back inside the city walls, where he was taken to a friend's house and died the following day. Five days later, Québec capitulated.

The peculiar name Plains of Abraham can be traced as far back as 1635, when Abraham Martin, a pilot of the St-Lawrence and a friend of Samuel de

Champlain, was given 12 acres of land in the area and an additional 20 acres 10 years after. Today there is little trace of the battle on the rolling green hills of the plains that border the cliff above the river. The grandiose stone building set back from the Plains houses the interpretation center, which offers a multimedia exhibit of its history, from the battle to its popularity with prostitutes in the 19th century and as a choice spot for duels, hangings, and the Stanley Cup playoffs. The park itself was part of the 300th anniversary celebrations and was designed by Frederick Todd. Many of the cannons that line the park were gifts from other nations to remind people that this was once a battlefield.

If you're interested in doing more than just strolling and picnicking in the park, you can head to the **Discovery Pavillon** on the Plains where you can visit the Odyssey exhibit about the battle ($10 adults, $8 seniors and students, 12 and under free).

MAP 3: 835 ave. Wilfrid-Laurier, 418/649-6157, www.theplainsofabraham.ca; daily 10am-5pm; free

Tours Martellos

In 1807 the United States Congress closed U.S. ports to all exports and restricted imports from Britain because of British and French interference with U.S. merchant ships during the Napoleonic Wars. Dubbed the American-Anglo crisis, it prompted Sir James Craig, then governor in chief of Canada, to increase the city's fortifications. Built between 1808 and 1812, four Martello towers were constructed around Québec as defenses and were positioned at various points outside of the city walls, mostly along the Plains of Abraham.

Round in shape, with limited openings, the west sides of the towers were built stronger than the east sides, based on the idea that if an attack were to happen, it would likely come from the west. In the event that the Martellos were under siege from the east, the eastern wall could easily be battered down and the men would be able to escape and continue fighting.

The smooth sandstone was cut in such a way that the constructions are perfectly rounded. Each Martello has a single door, placed at 4.5 meters above ground, 2.5 times the height of men at that time. It was originally reached by a ladder.

They became obsolete in the 1860s but continue to stand as monuments of and windows onto the city's past. Tour Martello 1, located on the Plains of Abraham, hosts an exhibition in summer (mid-June-early Sept.) inviting visitors to discover the military history and examine the lives of the soldiers who occupied the towers. Tour Martello 2, located not far from the Plains on the corner of Taché and Wilfrid-Laurier, invites you to drink beer in 19th-century style while you discuss the appropriate punishment for a British solider with the locals. These are hosted daily July-August and on weekends from late August to early September. An adult must accompany those under 18.

MAP 3: Parc des Champs-de-Bataille, 418/648-5371, www.ccbn-nbc.gc.ca; mid-June-early Sept. daily 10am-5pm; $14 adults, $10 seniors and students, $4 children (included with entrance into Plains of Abraham's Odyssey tour)

Saint-Jean-Baptiste and Saint-Roch

Map 4

Église Saint-Jean-Baptiste

Built in 1882, this parish church is one of the most stunning in Québec City. Situated outside of the walls in Saint-Jean-Baptiste, a neighborhood that at the time was home to blue-collar workers of both French-Canadian and Irish origin, it's now surrounded by shops, restaurants, and residential homes.

A fire destroyed the previous church and much of the neighborhood in 1881, and the job of rebuilding the church was passed on to Joseph-Ferdinand Peachy. Of mixed Québécois (his mother) and Irish (his father) descent, Peachy was an ideal choice for an architect in this region. First learning the craft under Thomas Baillairgé, he started his own architecture firm in 1866. Inspired by both a church built in the 12th century and Église-de-la-Sainte-Trinité in Paris (which was built a mere 10 years earlier), Église Saint-Jean-Baptiste is a combination of very distinct styles: neo-Renaissance, neo-Roman, and Second Empire.

Though the facade is unmistakably Second Empire, and almost a direct copy of the Sainte-Trinité, the interior styles are subtler. The gallery features semicircles under the windows as well as triptychs in the arcade, both neo-Roman elements. Neo-Renaissance, meanwhile, can be seen in the use of blue pastel for the roof and in the placement of the window.

The church opened to the public in 1884, but it wasn't until 1896 that the church would be completely finished. Staying close to its parish roots, much of the financing for the church came from the public, and many of the church's embellishments, from the pews to the baldaquin, were made in Québec City, by members of the parish. Only three elements came from outside of the province: the Italian ceramic floor tiles, the paintings of the stations of the cross, and the three types of white marble that are used throughout, on the pillars and for the statues. Even the organ was built by local Napoléon Déry in 1885, though it was reconstructed by the Casavant brothers in 1921.

MAP 4: 400 rue St-Jean, 418/525-7188, www.jeandominique.org; Mon.-Sat. noon-4pm, Sun. 11am-4pm; tours daily; free

Jardin Saint-Roch

Once an empty dirt lot, the Jardin Saint-Roch has become a symbol for the ongoing revitalization of the Saint-Roch (pronounced ROCK) area in the city's Lower Town. Inaugurated in 1992, it was one of the first places to get a much-needed facelift. With the opening of the park, the centerpiece of which is a waterfall featuring local stone, other businesses came to the area, taking up residence in old warehouses and factories and transforming them into workable, creative environments.

Displayed in the park are busts of René Richard, Alfred Pellan, and Horatio Walker, three important Québécois painters. Though their styles differed wildly, they represent the diversity and the richness of art and culture in Québec. The park is now surrounded by gaming companies, art studios, galleries, and theaters.

MAP 4: Between Côte d'Abraham and blvd. Charest at rue du Parvis and rue de la Couronne; daily 24 hours; free

★ Rue Saint-Jean

This section of rue St-Jean, part of the area known as Faubourg Saint-Jean-Baptiste, is a continuation of the St-Jean found within the city's historic walls. And though these two sides of the street—within and without the walls—are linked by a shared past, their appearance and history are markedly different. The word *faubourg* refers to "outskirts" in English, and during the early days of the city, when its gates were opened in the morning and closed in the evening, that's exactly what Faubourg Saint-Jean Baptiste was, an outskirt with no services or protection available from the city center once the gates were locked.

In the beginning of the 18th century, craftsmen built their workshops and homes along the inside walls of the fortifications. In 1745, however, the defenses were expanded, forcing many to move. This construction pushed them outside of the walls and they quickly established themselves and took their trades to the *faubourg,* bringing commerce to the area for the first time. In 1845, however, the first of two fires would decimate the area. Two churches, three schools, and 1,300 homes were burned to the ground during the 1845 fire, which subsequently led to the widening of the street. This and other fire prevention measures, such as restrictions on the layout of foyers in homes, were soon put into practice. In 1881 the area was hit with a second fire, and in just seven hours the church went up in flames and 5,000 were left without homes. This time the architectural restrictions were more drastic and wood was banned in construction.

These two disasters and the resulting architectural restrictions, coupled with a meshing of cultures that came later (the working-class Protestants and Catholics), have created the vibrant street today. The *faubourg* remains a vital part of day-to-day life as one of the busiest commercial streets in a busy residential neighborhood. As you wander along the street, the city's history is mapped out before you in the various architectural styles and businesses telling the story of each important epoch.

MAP 4: Between Autoroute Dufferin and ave. Salaberry

Rue Saint-Joseph

From the end of the 19th-century until the 1960s, this was one of the most important commercial streets in the city. Akin to Fifth Avenue in New York, it was the chichi shopping district, the home of upscale shops and historic department stores. The construction of large shopping centers on the outskirts of town in the 1950s and '60s, however, drew consumers out of the downtown core. Soon the stores left too, moving to new digs in the suburban malls, leaving the stores boarded up and the street run-down.

With hopes of luring business and shoppers back to the street, the city decided to turn it into the closest thing they could to a mall. In 1974, they

New Québec:
Up-and-Coming Limoilou

Like its neighbor Saint-Roch, Limoilou is fast becoming one of the coolest neighborhoods in the city. Full of cozy bars and cafés, artist boutiques, kid-friendly restaurants, and some of the best food shops in Québec City, it's an ideal place to spend the day wandering and scouring for antiques.

Situated across the St-Charles River, it is one of the oldest boroughs in the city. The first thoroughfare, now called 1e avenue (1st Avenue) was built in 1665. The area was entirely rural up until the end of the 19th century. Its proximity to downtown and placement alongside the river allows for an exceptional view of the city. It's a predominantly residential neighborhood, and the majority of shops and cafés are found in Vieux-Limoilou, easily reached by crossing the rue du Pont in Saint-Roch. Inspired by the grid system used in New York, the streets and avenues are numbered. The majority of cafés and shops are concentrated on 3e avenue, a continuation of rue du Pont on the other side of the St-Charles River. Cafés and neighborhood shops are on 1e avenue, while 2e avenue is perfect for taking in the old Victorian architecture and apartment blocks with spiral staircases.

Open and bright with a modern, minimalist decor, **Le Fun en Bouche** (1073 3e ave., 418/524-7272, www.lefunenbouche.com,

Tues. 9am-2pm, Wed.-Sun. 8am-2pm, $10) is a neighborhood bistro in the heart of Vieux-Limoilou. Head here for the daily brunch and try the eggs Benedicts or French toast. The lunch selections include bagel with smoked trout and blueberry port spread, and smoked chicken, leek, and parmesan quiche. If you're in the mood for something to warm you up, **Soupe et Cie** (522 3e ave., 418/948-8996, www.soupecie.com, daily 11am-9pm, $15) has hearty soups and open-faced sandwiches on the menu. Closer to the bridge but still in the center of the community, this long restaurant with brick walls, old chandeliers, and tons of bright cushions is a cozy place to grab a bite. Despite its chic decor, it's kid-friendly—in fact, kids rule here and their exuberance and chitchat make up most of the ambience.

Just down the block is **Hosaka-Ya** (491 3e ave., 418/529-9993, Tues.-Fri. 11:30am-2pm and 4:30pm-9pm, Sat.-Sun. 4:30pm-9pm, $10), a relaxed Japanese restaurant inspired by the traditional *izakaya*. The menu is more well-rounded than most, offering classic dishes like *gyoza* and udon noodles as well as seasonal sushi dishes. They've also opened a **Ramen** (75 St-Joseph E.) in St-Roch. If you're looking for a drink, stop into **Le Bal du Lézard** (1049 3e ave., 418/529-3829, www.lebaldulezard.

covered the majority of the street with a Plexiglas arcade. Instead of drawing business, however, the new scheme attracted the marginalized and disenfranchised—the arcade was ideal shelter against the elements. Except for department store Laliberté and the Brunet pharmacy next door, who resisted the original exodus, most businesses consisted of cheap cafés and diners and five-and-dime stores.

It was Mayor Jean-Paul L'Allier, who governed for four terms, who would eventually bring business back to the area and the street. His first gamble was convincing Université Laval to move its art school from its campus on the fringes of the city to an old, unoccupied corset factory. The gamble paid com, daily 2pm-3am), a friendly little neighborhood bar that's been a staple here since 1985. It has a laid-back feel and features a foosball table and nice sidewalk *terrasse* come summer. For a cozy, rustic bar, you can't do much better than **La Souche** (801 Chemin de la Canardière, 418/742-1144, www.lasouche.ca, Mon.-Wed. 11am-1am, Thurs.-Fri. 11am-3am, Sat. 3pm-3am, Sun. 3pm-1am, $7), or "The Stump" in English. This local bar offers a number of local brews in a relaxed, stump-strewn setup. They also have a patio come summer.

Decked out in red and green tablecloths and multicolored streamers adorning the walls, **Restaurant la Salsa** (1063 3e ave., 418/522-0032, Tues.-Sat. 11:30am-10pm, $15) is one of the most authentic Mexican restaurants in the city. The interior might border on kitsch, but their *pupusas,* enchiladas, and tamales are nothing but classic. Cheese lovers should make a stop at **Yannick Fromagerie** (901 3e ave., 418/614-2002, www.yannickfromagerie.ca), which specializes in specialty cheese from Québec, while a fresh baguette from **La Fournée Bio** (1296 ave. 3e, 418/522-4441, Mon.-Wed. 7am-6:30pm, Thurs.-Fri. 7am-7pm, Sat.-Sun. 7am-5:30pm, $10) acts as the perfect accompaniment. Open for over 14 years, La Fournée Bio is an artisanal organic bakery that makes

everything from croissants to sourdough and even serves a good cup of coffee.

New on the scene is **La Planque** (1027 ave. 3e, 418/914-8780, www.laplanquerestaurant.com, Tues.-Fri. 11:30am-2pm and 5:30pm-close, Sat. 5:30pm-close, $25), a casual fine-dining restaurant with a young, superstar chef whose creations, like scallop "ratatouille" and roasted pig's foot, garnered the establishment a nomination for best new Canadian restaurant in 2013, as well as clients from across the St-Charles River.

For a bit of antiquing, head into **Le Retour du Passé** (500 1e ave., 418/524-8885, www.leretourdupasse.net, Mon.-Sat. 9am-5pm, Sun. 9am-4pm), an antiques store that deals in old electronics like radios, clocks, and record players, as well as the usual mishmash of stuff. **Aarticle 721** (721 3e ave., 418/742-4333, Tues.-Sun. 11am-6pm) specializes in locally made products for the home and for the child, man, or woman in your life. They've got everything from pineapple printed pillows to googly-eyed baby onesies. **La Boutique du Skate** (412 3e ave., 418/781-2030, Tues.-Fri. and Sun. noon-5pm, Sat. 10am-4pm) has a selection of skateboarding shoes as well as a huge selection of boards—perfect if you're traveling with your teen.

off, and slowly but surely other businesses, drawn by incentives, returned to the strip. Sections of the Plexiglas eyesore, however, remained. It was fully removed for the city's 400th anniversary in 2008, but there are still sections along this diverse and interesting street where you can see where the arcade roof once sat.

MAP 4: Between rue St-Dominique and rue Caron

St-Matthew Church and Cemetery

Distinctly English with its slender steeple and neo-Gothic stonework, reminiscent of medieval English parish churches, St-Matthew Church and

Cemetery stands out in an otherwise French-influenced Faubourg St-Jean Baptiste. The first cemetery in the city to exclusively bury Protestants, it encircled the church and was in use from 1772 to 1860. It is the burial place of many of the earliest English settlers in Canada and is the oldest cemetery in Québec City.

The church was originally the city gravedigger's house. It was only in 1822 with the arrival of French-speaking Protestant immigrants from the Channel Isles that services started to be held in French. By 1827, the services had become so popular, with a French service in the morning and an English one in the evening that the house was modified into a chapel. Destroyed by the great fire of 1845, it was rebuilt into today's incarnation by John Cliff. The interior, which now houses a public library, maintains its late-19th-century architecture with its exposed beams, rounded moldings at the top of the arcades, and delicate embellishments in the stonework.

Today it is a public library, and visitors can stroll among the bookshelves and admire the preserved interior, which has remained virtually untouched.

MAP 4: 755 rue St-Jean, 418/641-6798, www.bibliothequesdequebec.qc.ca; Mon.-Tues. and Thurs. noon-5:30pm, Wed. noon-8pm, Fri. 10am-5:30pm, Sat.-Sun. 1pm-5pm; free

Greater Québec City   Map 5

Aquarium du Québec

Staying true to its roots, this aquarium specializes in boreal and arctic wildlife, though over 10,000 animals call this place their home. It's divided into eight areas, both indoor and outdoor, and the main attraction is the Awesome Ocean, a glass tunnel through a massive seawater tank that allows visitors to get up close and personal with the marine life. Species from Québec wetlands and the St-Lawrence River are also here, along with polar bears, harp seals, and walruses from both coasts in the Arctic display. The newest addition is a tropical exhibition space showcasing jellyfish, stingrays, seahorses, and other southern species.

First opened in 1956 as a marine biology laboratory and research center, it soon attracted visitors eager to see the species that occupied the two aquariums. Continuing its slow growth over the next 40 years, the sight was given a major renovation in 2002 that saw it expand with outdoor gardens and seal and polar bear viewing pools. Located just outside of the city in Sainte-Foy, this is a great attraction for families and has drawn over eight million visitors.

In summertime kids can cool off in the adjoining water park or clamber their way through the Abre-en-Abre pathway adventure.

MAP 5: 1675 ave. des Hôtels, Sainte-Foy, 866/659-5264, www.sepaq.com/aquarium; June-early Sept. daily 10am-5pm, early Sept.-May daily 10am-4pm; $17 adults, $15.50 seniors, $8.50 children 3-17

Restaurants

Highlights

★ **Best Views: Le Café de la Terrasse** in Château Frontenac is in a picturesque setting looking out over the St-Lawrence (page 62).

★ **Best Place to Get a Taste of the North:** The menu at **Chez Boulay Bistro Boréal** is full of game and fish, with a focus on meats that are sustainable and come from the northern part of the province (page 62).

★ **Best Late-Night Eats:** Credited with popularizing poutine, **Chez Ashton** is Québec's preeminent fast-food joint and the ideal spot to refuel after a night on the town (page 65).

★ **Best Tasting Menu:** One of the best haute cuisine restaurants in the city, **Restaurant L'Initiale** features tasting menus with local food in a down-to-earth, modern interior (page 68).

★ **Most Authentic Québécois Grub:** Established in 1975, **Buffet de l'Antiquaire** serves heaping portions of traditional cuisine and some great breakfasts in a tiny 1950s-style diner (page 70).

★ **Best Upscale Bistro:** Situated on a tiny street in the Vieux-Port, **L'Échaudé** has both an elegant and relaxed atmosphere with classic bistro dishes (page 70).

★ **Best Café: Brûlerie Saint-Roch** is packed for a reason: The lattes here are the best and the ambience is effortlessly cool (page 78).

★ **Most Authentic Crêpes:** Run by an expat from Brittany, **Crêperie Le Billig** serves up the best crêpes in the city, which are even more delicious when you down them with cider (page 79).

★ **Most Bang for Your Buck:** Eat among savvy locals at **Le Clocher Penché,** where the bistro fare is made with fresh, regional ingredients and the bill is always a pleasant surprise (page 81).

★ **Most Likely to Surprise:** Both the wine and food menu change regularly at **Le Moine Échanson,** an unassuming restaurant that's all about getting you to discover new flavors from various corners of the globe (page 81).

With the most restaurants per capita in the country, Québec City has no shortage of choice when it comes to dining. The challenge here isn't finding a decent place to eat, it's deciding which ones you have time for. The number of noteworthy, award-winning chefs and restaurants in Québec,

well respected for its gastronomy, can be both tiring and exhilarating. Whether serving up a simple breakfast or an intricate haute-cuisine meal, chefs tend toward *terroir*, cooking that uses local produce and ingredients. In this region of the province those ingredients include wild game, such as elk, red deer, and bison, and seafood like scallops and cod.

Whereas the big trend at Montréal restaurants is market-fresh cuisine cooked by up-and-coming chefs in a boisterous atmosphere, the trend in Québec is more traditional, with a focus on details and inventive preparation, though a few young, breakout stars can be found, mostly in the Saint-Roch section of town. Even the decor of some of the city's best restaurants can feel a little staid and reserved—few, if any, of the city's restaurants turn into nightclubs once the tables have been cleared. The ones that do, however, can be found on the Grande-Allée, just outside the old walls.

Since so many of the restaurants offer top-quality ingredients and service, the price tag can also be high, though it's often worth it. One way to circumvent the cost without sacrificing the experience is to order the table d'hôte, which gives you the option of a three-course meal, usually appetizer, main, and dessert, for a set price. Another option is to go to one of the more expensive restaurants for lunch. Following the French tradition, restaurants here serve lunch well into the afternoon (service ends around 2pm),

Previous: Le Cochon Dingue, Lower Town; Chez Boulay Bistro Boréal, Upper Town; pastry chefs in the kitchen of Le Cochon Dingue.

often with a specific lunchtime menu. Also in the French tradition is the city's love affair with cafés and bakeries; they are abundant and delicious.

Barely a street goes by that doesn't feature a cute, independent café or two, most of which serve delectable pastries, light lunches, and choice coffee. Though you can always get your coffee to go, it's rare to see resident Québeckers striding along with their lattes; in fact, there are only two Starbucks in the city, and other chain coffee shops are just as rare. Bakeries, too, can be found in every neighborhood, each offering its own take on freshly-baked bread and pastries.

There are a couple things, however, that the Québec culinary scene is lacking: vegetarian and ethnic restaurants. Though some restaurants offer a vegetarian option, many do not, and doing research ahead of time is sure to save some frustration. Vegetarians who eat fish have abundant choices, but vegans will be sorely disappointed. When it comes to ethnic eats in Québec, Asian cuisines are the most popular; there are good Chinese and Vietnamese restaurants available. Japanese is a little harder to find, but the restaurants that do exist have excellent sushi, thanks to the abundance of fresh fish.

The city is no stranger to tourists, and menus in Québec are often written in English. Even when they're not, there's no reason to be shy; servers are happy to translate for you. A lot of fuss can be made about the dangers of falling into a "tourist trap" when you're visiting a city like Québec, but the reality is, most restaurants, regardless of the number of tourists at their tables, are adept at making some seriously good meals. Whether you're enjoying a tasting menu by one of the top chefs or eating meat pie by candlelight in a laid-back bistro, you'll always find a lively and welcoming atmosphere—the city's most charming and infectious trait.

Vieux-Québec's Upper Town
Map 1

ASIAN
Apsara ®®
If you're fed up with bistro fare and all this "Europe in North America" business, head over to Apsara for some traditional Asian cooking. The decor here doesn't stray far from typical dining rooms, with its white tablecloths and wicker chairs, but a sense of the Far East is evoked in the golden statues, Thai artwork, and traditional masks featured throughout the restaurant. The ambience is quiet and calm with traditional music playing in the background and impeccable service. Apsara specializes in Cambodian, Thai, and Vietnamese cuisine, and with five or six mains available from each region, deciding on a single dish can be tough. Those facing a bout of indecision should go for the Apsara Plate, featuring dishes from each country, including Khemara beef from Cambodia and Vietnamese shrimp d'Anam.

MAP 1: 71 rue d'Auteuil, 418/694-0232, www.restaurantapsara.com; Mon.-Fri. 11:30am-2pm and 5:30pm-10:30pm, Sat.-Sun. 5:30pm-10:30pm

59

Chez Soi La Chine $

The sign at the entrance reads Authentic Chinese Food, a simple but bold statement in a city that isn't overflowing with ethnic food choices. It's located on the down slope of a hilly street, and the sidewalk cuts in front of the door at nearly a 45-degree angle. Inside, the yellow paper lanterns and traditional Chinese music are just about the only Asian touches in this otherwise sparse restaurant. Despite its austerity, it's one of the best Asian restaurants in the city, serving up traditional Chinese fare that is both filling and tasty. It's popular with young locals and the city's Asian community, and specialties like duck with Chinese mushrooms, crispy chicken, and perfectly steamed pork dumplings keep customers coming back. There is, however, one ingredient this place is missing: alcohol. It's a BYOB venue, so don't forget to bring a bottle of wine or beer with you to dinner.

MAP 1: 27 rue Ste-Angèle, 418/523-8858; Tues.-Fri. noon-2pm and 5:30pm-10pm, Sat.-Sun. 5:30pm-10pm

CAFÉS AND CHEAP EATS

Café-Boulangerie Paillard $

Modern and open, the long communal tables of this pastry shop, bakery, and *sandwicherie* are cafeteria-like in style, but the tall ceilings and lots of light make it feel effortlessly spacious. In traditional New York style, you must line up to order, be it a fresh Paillard salad with walnuts, blue cheese, and pears or a frothy cappuccino and almond croissant. They're known for their macaroons, those sweet, one-bite-and-you're-done cookies; they come in a rainbow of colors and flavors and rival any that you'd find in the tiny back lanes of Paris.

MAP 1: 1097 rue St-Jean, 418/692-1221, www.paillard.ca; daily 7am-9pm

Chez Temporel $

Established in 1974, this two-story café on rue Couillard, a quaint and winding side street, has become an institution. A favorite with students and artists, it is frequented by locals who come here to grab a quiet coffee or light lunch, offering a nice alternative in the otherwise touristy and busy part of Old Québec. It's simply decorated, with wood tables, brick walls, and work by local artists on the wall, and the food follows suit with homemade croissants, muffins, soups, salads, and quiches.

MAP 1: 25 rue Couillard, 418/694-1813; daily 7am-1am

Le Petit Coin Latin $

Just inside the city walls on a steep side street you'll find Le Petit Coin Latin, one of the oldest cafés in Québec. Stone walls, a fireplace, and burgundy banquettes give it an intimate, homey atmosphere. Like its surroundings, the food here is unpretentious and includes Québécois classics like *tourtière au caribou* (caribou pie) and *tarte au sucre* (sugar pie). It's a popular place for breakfast and brunch, especially in the summer when the garden

RESTAURANTS

VIEUX-QUÉBEC'S UPPER TOWN

terrace is open out back; their plentiful omelets and *pain doré* will leave you stuffed. In winter, order the hearty and warming raclette.

MAP 1: 8½ rue Ste-Ursule, 418/692-2022; Mon.-Fri. 8am-11pm, Sat.-Sun. 7:30am-11pm

Les Trois Garçons 💲💲

Started by three friends (hence the name, which means "Three Guys" in English) who wanted to create an eatery that towed the line between Parisian bistro and New York diner, Les Trois Garçons serves gourmet burgers and the like. Located on a bustling strip of rue St-Jean, the restaurant has a pleasant sidewalk patio in the summer that's almost always packed; its casual dining style is a nice change compared to some of the city's stuffier (and pricier) dining rooms. Outfitted in red, white, and black, it has a slight 1950s diner feel thanks to the art deco metal railing on the second floor that lets you oversee the diners below. The crowd here are in the know when it comes to food trends, and you'll often see diners chowing down on a Trio of Mini Burgers—the best way to taste them all.

MAP 1: 1084 rue St-Jean, 418/692-3900, www.bistro3garcons.com; Mon.-Wed. 7am-10pm, Thurs.-Fri. 7am-11pm, Sat. 8am-11pm, Sun. 8am-10pm

CRÊPERIES
Casse-Crêpe Breton 💲

No matter the time of day, the line at this bustling crêperie on St-Jean is usually out the door. Luckily, it moves pretty fast and customers are soon seated in the banquettes that line the restaurant's walls or at the bar with a full view of the action. Open since 1983, it can sometimes feel like an upper-class fast-food joint, in the swiftness of service and the way they churn out the crêpes. Choose from a list of suggestions—egg, bacon, mozzarella—or build your own with fillings like berries, chocolate, asparagus, and swiss cheese. While it's not the best crêperie in the city, it's a good choice for a quick and inexpensive meal.

MAP 1: 1136 rue St-Jean, 418/692-0438, www.cassecrepebreton.com; daily 7am-10pm

FRENCH
Le Café Buade 💲

Established in 1919, Café Buade is the oldest restaurant in the city. Not far from Château Frontenac and facing the Notre-Dame-de-Québec Cathedral, it's a popular place with both tourists and long-time regulars. Serving basic family restaurant fare like pasta, pizza, and prime rib, it may not be the best meal you'll eat in the city but it won't break the bank either. If you do find yourself intrigued by the homey and warm atmosphere, opt for a classic club sandwich or one of their generous breakfasts, available daily until noon.

MAP 1: 31 rue de Buade, 418/692-3909, www.cafebuade.ca; May-Sept. daily 7am-11pm, Oct.-Apr. daily 7am-9pm

Clockwise from top left: sidewalk terrasse at Lapin Sauté, Vieux-Québec's Lower Town; Brûlerie Saint-Roch; beef dish at L'Échaudé, Vieux-Québec's Lower Town.

★ **Le Café de la Terrasse** $$$

Situated in Château Frontenac with stunning views of the St-Lawrence, Le Café de la Terrasse is luxury without the price tag. Overseen by Baptiste Peupion, the newly appointed executive chef at Le Champlain, the café's haute-cuisine sibling, the menu varies according to season and tends toward regional gastronomy. The wine list too stays close to home and features many Canadian selections. The restaurant runs along the facade of the hotel, with picture windows onto the river. The soft green decor, reminiscent of a summerhouse, is welcoming and sumptuous. Mains include classics like beef Wellington and lamb with marinated herbs, and buffets are often theme-based, like the lavish brunch buffet. Backpackers and mature travelers alike come here to grab a pre-dinner or post-skiing cocktail, especially in winter when the city of Lévis is lit up across the water.

MAP 1: 1 rue des Carrières, 418/691-3763, www.fairmont.com/frontenac; daily 7am-2pm and 5:30pm-10pm

Le Champlain $$$

Chef Baptiste Peupion, originally from Paris, was appointed executive chef in early 2013 and has revamped the menu by adding touches of local *terroir* cooking to the traditional French cuisine. The storied restaurant (and hotel) went through a major overhaul in 2013-2014, and Peupion's dishes follow suit with a mix of contemporary and classic flavors. Located in the historic Château Frontenac, it has gorgeous views of the river and boasts a glass-roofed sun lounge. With patterned carpets, luxurious chandeliers, and rich wood paneling, the decor is traditionally elegant. Though new flavors have been added to the menu, it retains much of its original charm, including the century-old tradition of afternoon tea, which is served June-October Thursday-Saturday. Reservations and smart casual attire are a must.

MAP 1: 1 rue des Carrières, 418/266-3905, www.fairmont.com/frontenac; daily 6pm-10pm

★ Chez Boulay Bistro Boréal $$$

This new addition to rue St-Jean is unlike any other dinning experience in the city. Jean-Luc Boulay, chef and owner of Saint-Amour, has teamed up with up-and-comer Arnaud Marchand to create a restaurant that's centered on cooking and delicacies from the northern, or boreal, region of the province. The menu is chock-full of game and fish, with a focus on meats that are sustainable. Standout dishes include confit bison cheeks, confit goose legs, and seared black cod with shellfish mousse. The decor is sleek and black with lots of banquette seating and chic white walls in the open concept dining room. Weather permitting, there's also an outdoor patio. Stop in for a three-course lunch if you fancy experiencing the boreal flavors with a smaller price tag.

MAP 1: 1110 rue St-Jean, 418/380-8166, www.chezboulay.com; Mon.-Fri. 11:30am-10:30pm, Sat.-Sun. 10am-10:30pm

Chez L'Autre 🟢🟢

Opened in 2012, this low-key brasserie is the perfect antidote to fussy tasting menus. Located in Le Capitole, a theater/hotel that's also home to Italian restaurant Il Teatro, L'Autre has a prime location just outside the old walls on the Place d'Youville. In the summertime, the flower baskets overflow with color and the *terrasse* is bustling. It's the interior, however, that defines the restaurant. The black and white decor—white walls, white bar, black bistro chairs—is simply elegant and sets the tone for the menu, which features classic French bistro fare. Foie gras torchon, salmon tartar, and beef tenderloin with béarnaise sauce all make an appearance on the menu.
MAP 1: 964 rue St-Jean, 418/694-1199, www.lecapitole.com; daily 11am-10:30pm

La Crémaillère 🟢🟢🟢

Just in front of City Hall, you'll find award-winning restaurant La Crémaillère. Situated in a historic Victorian townhouse, the rooms of the restaurant have been diligently restored to show the intricate moldings and woodwork of a bygone era. The rich, patterned upholstery contrasts nicely with the white walls, giving the setting a bit of a modern kick. Taking inspiration from both French and Italian traditions, dishes are classic in presentation and flavor. House specialties include roasted rack of lamb, milk-fed veal, and lobster in champagne sauce. The atmosphere is elegant and romantic, making it perfect for a date night.
MAP 1: 73 rue Ste-Anne, 418/692-2216, www.cremaillere.qc.ca; Mon.-Fri. 11:30am-2:30pm and 5pm-10pm, Sat.-Sun. 5pm-10pm

Les Frères de la Côte 🟢🟢

A cheerful and festive ambience oozes from this restaurant full of bon vivants. Located on one of the busiest corners in Old Québec, the casual dining room, decorated with checkered tablecloths and banquette seating, can be a bit cramped at times, with neighboring diners squished in beside each other. This is all part of the lively atmosphere, which in summer extends to a tiny sidewalk *terrasse*.

Cuisine here runs the gamut from *bavette de cheval* (horse flank) and osso bucco to thin-crust pizzas and mussels with fries.
MAP 1: 1190 rue St-Jean, 418/592-5445; Mon.-Fri. 11:30am-10pm, Sat.-Sun. 10am-10pm

Le Pain Béni 🟢🟢🟢

Le Pain Béni is all about mixing influences. Located in the 200-year-old Auberge Place d'Armes, the dining room's stone walls are juxtaposed against the ultramodern design of bright orange chairs and simple table settings, creating a fresh and modern take on fine dining. On the menu you'll find dishes inspired by both French and Italian traditions, including lamb ravioli, beef tartare, goose leg confit, and parsnip gnocchi. With popular music on the sound system creating a laid-back ambience, there are few places that mix fine cuisine and contemporary atmosphere so well.

MAP 1: 24 rue Ste-Anne, 418/694-9485, www.aubergeplacedarmes.com; May.-Sept. daily 11:30am-10:30pm; Oct.-Apr. Mon. 11:30am-2pm, Tues.-Fri. 11:30am-2pm and 5:30pm-10pm, Sat. 5:30pm-10pm

Le Patriarche ❸❸❸

Situated in a converted heritage home that was built in 1827, Le Patriarche retains the feeling of an old house, giving it an especially warm and romantic atmosphere and making it a choice spot for couples. It specializes in *gastronomie du terroir,* and the service here is unique: Each course is served as a trio of dishes, sort of like a choose-your-own tasting menu. An order of Québec lamb, for example, comes as mini-servings of roasted lamb rack, pan-fried lamb loin, and braised lamb tongue. Since Patriarche emphasizes *terroir* cooking, wild game features on the menu, but they also have one of the better vegetarian selections, offering three mini-dishes that change daily.

MAP 1: 17 rue St-Stanislas, 418/629-5488, www.lepatriarche.com; July-Aug. daily 5:30pm-10pm, Sept.-June Wed. and Sat.-Sun. 5:30pm-10pm, Thurs.-Fri. 11:30am-2pm and 5:30pm-10pm

Le Saint-Amour ❸❸❸

Le Saint-Amour is one of the most renowned restaurants in Québec. Chef Jean-Luc Boulay has won all the honors, the most recent of which was a visit by Sir Paul McCartney. After his historic concert for the city's 400th anniversary in 2008, the former Beatle and noted vegetarian came here with his band. The French-inspired dishes are creative, though, sadly, not vegetarian-friendly. Try the homemade terrine cooked "sous-vide," stuffed and roasted Scallops from the Iles of Madelaeine, or the red deer seared and served with wild mustard seeds. Art nouveau touches can be found throughout the restaurant, framing the mirrors and illuminating the bar with a beautiful stained-glass mosaic. Watch the kitchen magic happen through the open kitchen design and sip a glass of red from their exquisite wine list, reputed to be one of the best in the country.

MAP 1: 48 rue Ste-Ursule, 418/694-0667, www.saint-amour.com; Mon.-Fri. 11:30am-2pm and 6pm-10pm, Sat. 5pm-10pm, Sun. 6pm-10pm

ITALIAN
Conti Caffe ❸❸❸

The resolutely modern decor of this Italian-style restaurant is a breath of fresh air compared to many restaurants in Old Québec that stick to a staid, traditional look. The little brother of Le Continental, from which it took its name, Conti Caffe has an atmosphere that is younger, more relaxed, and more fun than that of its older counterpart. It serves Italian dishes like veal parmigiana and spaghetti carbonara, and specialties include lamb chops, filet mignon, and pan-fried sea scallops. Of course, the classic brick and stone walls still add an air of charm and romance, but the rich blue walls and contemporary furnishing are a vibrant touch.

MAP 1: 32 rue St-Louis, 418/692-4191, www.conticaffe.com; daily 11:30am-11pm

Le Continental ❸❸❸

Waiters in white dinner jackets prepare mains tableside, making Le Continental the pinnacle of fine dining. Set in an elegant Victorian house, Le Continental is a traditional, rather formal restaurant known for impeccable service and unmatched cuisine. Blending Italian and French traditions, the restaurant is known for its flambé dishes, which include shrimp with whiskey, orange duckling, and flambé sirloin. Other classic dishes include braised veal sweetbreads and steamed snow crabs. Though there is no formal dress code, this is the time to break out your dinner jacket and dress shoes.

MAP 1: 26 rue St-Louis, 418/694-9995, www.restaurantlecontinental.com; Mon.-Fri. noon-3pm and 6pm-11pm, Sat.-Sun. 6pm-9pm

Il Teatro ❸❸

With one of the most eye-catching terraces in the city—with overflowing flower pots and a view of St-Jean Gate—Il Teatro is a no-brainer when it comes to dining alfresco and is popular with theater-goers and tourists alike. It's located in the magnificent Capitole de Québec theater (hence the name), and the interior is modern and welcoming with brick walls, simple decoration, and huge windows that look on to Place d'Youville. Chef Serge Gagné, despite his not-too-Italian name, has been cooking some of the best Italian food in the city for the past 18 years. The risotto al mascarpone and scaloppini del capo are some of the best dishes, and the tuna steak with pepper is perfect for fish lovers. Cap the night off with a cappuccino, a slice of *panforte,* and a stroll around the city's walls.

MAP 1: 972 rue St-Jean, 418/694-9996, www.lecapitole.com/en/restaurant.php; daily 7am-2am

LATE-NIGHT EATS

★ Chez Ashton ❸

Founded in 1969 by Ashton Leblond, Chez Ashton is fast food *à la québécoise.* Sure you can get your burgers and fries here, but what Ashton prides itself on is its poutine. It's the single culinary achievement of the region (origins remain obscure and hotly debated), and Mr. Leblond helped popularize the combination of French fries, cheese curds, and brown gravy that has since gone on to conquer the rest of the province. Add shredded turkey and green peas onto the rest and you have a *galvaude,* a popular selection here. The decor is typical of fast-food chains—neon lights, vinyl banquettes, and a crowd of starving late-night revelers. You can find many Chez Ashton locations in the city, including one in Saint-Roch (830 blvd. Charest, 418/648-0891) and one near the Parliament (640 Grande-Allée, 418/522-3449).

MAP 1: 54 Côte du Palais, 418/692-3055, www.chez-ashton.com; Sun.-Wed. 11am-2am, Thurs. 11am-4am, Fri.-Sat. 11am-4:30am

QUÉBÉCOIS

Aux Anciens Canadiens 🪙🪙

Located in the oldest house in the city (built in 1675), Les Anciens Canadiens is firmly planted in Québécois tradition. It's not hard to fall for its charm, with its white-washed walls, red roof, and miniature stature. It's a huge tourist destination. Servers are dressed in slightly unconvincing old-timey costumes, and the food on the menu is traditional Québécois—that is to say, plentiful and heavy. Despite the kitschy costumes and themed dining rooms, the food is excellent. If you want to discover everything about traditional regional cooking, try the Trapper's Treat (meat pie with a pheasant and bison casserole) or the Québec Tasting Platter (meat pie with meatball and pig's knuckle ragout and baked beans). As for dessert—well, you'd better like maple syrup.

MAP 1: 34 rue St-Louis, 418/692-1627, www.auxancienscanadiens.qc.ca; daily noon-9:30pm

Vieux-Québec's Lower Town

Map 2

CAFÉS AND CHEAP EATS

Les Cafés du Soleil 🪙

Over 40 kinds of coffee, some from as far as India and Japan, line the walls of this Vieux-Port café. Dedicated to the art of coffee and coffee making, this popular neighborhood café, full of locals and browsing tourists, was originally a store selling espresso makers and other coffee accessories and making some *allongée* (long espresso) on the side. It only became a full-fledged café when they decided to make sandwiches and snacks for the customers who were spending more and more time hanging out and sampling their coffee. A small but lively place, it's usually packed with regulars. Besides coffee, they also offer sandwiches, salads, soups, and pastries, as well as a selection of teas.

MAP 2: 143 rue St-Paul, 418/692-1147; winter Mon.-Fri. 7am-5:30pm, Sat. 8:30am-5:30pm, Sun. 10am-5:30pm; summer Mon.-Wed. 7am-7pm, Thurs.-Fri. 7am-10pm, Sat.-Sun. 8:30am-10pm

CRÊPERIES

Café Bistro du Cap 🪙🪙

On a narrow cobblestone street backing onto the sheer cliff face, Café Bistro du Cap is in a gem of a spot. With a small *terrasse* out front and a modest, no-frills interior, the entire atmosphere is unpretentious and intimate. This is a small operation run by a couple; he runs the kitchen while she runs the front of the house, so selection here isn't huge and is often determined by the availability. Praised by both locals and tourists, their menu includes items like pan-fried salmon, lamb shank, and chowder. They are especially known for their crêpes. Savory or sweet, the crêpes are some of the best in the city, and perfect for a mid-afternoon snack.

FRENCH
Café du Monde ⑤⑤

Café du Monde is in the Vieux-Port on a quay that juts out into the river. Aiming to bring a little Rive-Gauche (Left Bank) to Québec, the interior is precisely decorated with black and white checkered tiles, walls of wine, and even black-apron-clad servers (who have tempered their accents in some cases) to really give diners that Parisian feel. Though the atmosphere isn't entirely convincing—since when is the Rive-Gauche surrounded by grain silos and shipping relics?—the food is, with mains like mussels, salmon tartare, and rabbit hindquarter transporting you across the Atlantic in no time.

MAP 2: 84 rue Dalhousie, 418/692-4448, www.lecafedumonde.com; Mon.-Fri. 11:30am-11pm, Sat. 9am-11pm

Le Cochon Dingue ⑤⑤

Started in 1979, French bistro Le Cochon Dingue (The Crazy Pig) has become one of the most popular restaurants in the city. Famous for mussels, steak frites, and pork filet mignon, they also serve breakfast and lunch, with daily specials. Though they've since opened other outlets, including one near rue Cartier (46 blvd. René-Lévesque, 418/523-2013), the original establishment is still the most charming, with brick walls, sharp white tablecloths, and bistro chairs. It's both elegant and relaxed. In summer, their sidewalk *terrasse* takes up almost the entire street, with Le Petit Cochon Dingue at number 24, serving coffees and sweets.

MAP 2: 46 blvd. Champlain, 418/694-0303, www.cochondingue.com; Mon.-Fri. 7am-11pm, Sat.-Sun. 8am-11pm

Lapin Sauté ⑤⑤⑤

Run by the same people who own Le Cochon Dingue, Lapin Sauté (Jumping Rabbit) is more laid-back and romantic than its bustling neighbor. Located in a turn-of-the-20th-century home, the small dining room—it seats 32—has a rustic feel with a low, wood ceiling and a stone fireplace. The food here is rustic as well, specializing in country-style cuisine. Their specialty is rabbit, served in a pie, a cassoulet, or roasted with maple and raspberry sauce. They also have a refined kids' menu that includes grilled salmon and Caesar salad.

MAP 2: 52 rue du Petit-Champlain, 418/692-5325, www.lapinsaute.com; Mon.-Fri. 11am-10pm, Sat.-Sun. 9am-10pm

Le Quai 19 ⑤⑤

Located in an old stone warehouse in the heart of the Vieux-Port, Le Quai 19 (formerly Le 48 St-Paul) couldn't be in a better location. In summer, the large *terrasse* with chic black umbrellas and overflowing flowerpots is one of the most enviable places in the city. Forgoing typical French cuisine to focus on local produce and flavors, the new menu puts an emphasis on

A Quick Guide to Québécois Food

Over the past 400 years or so Québec has developed its own cuisine; some foods are variations on old French recipes and some are creations that are uniquely their own. In the early days of the colony much of Québec society relied on hunting and fishing for sustenance, and wild game is still a big part of cooking in the region. Here's a quick guide to some of the more common but obscure foods you may come across.

· **Caribou:** This is one of the more popular meats, and you'll find it on menus across the city. It's an especially popular ingredient in meat pies.

· **Caribou (the drink):** During the city's world-famous annual Winter Carnival this stuff is available in all the SAQs (liquor stores). This mixture of port, vodka, black-currant liqueur, and maple syrup might be tough to get down but it will keep you warm and give you enough courage to tackle *les glissades*—the enormous toboggan run on Terrasse Dufferin.

· **Cheese Curds:** This is the special cheese they put on top of poutine, but it is also eaten on its own as a snack and can be found at most corner stores. Made from fresh cheddar, it has a rubbery texture and squeaks when it's chewed.

· **Cheval:** Though it's not as common a meat here as in Belgium, horse can still be found on menus across the city, mostly likely listed as *bavette de cheval,* horse steak. Similar to beef in consistency, it is both sweeter and more tender.

· **Cretons:** If you order a traditional Québécois breakfast, there's a good chance you'll find a serving of this on your plate. A salty pork product, it's made by boiling the pork in milk with onions and spices until its consistency is halfway between a spread and a pâté. It's best eaten on toast.

· **Foie Gras:** Made from duck and goose liver (the name literally means "fatty liver"), this typical French dish has turned into an industry in Québec. Locally produced foie gras is now a staple in most bistros and restaurants serving haute cuisine.

freshness, with the majority of the dishes featuring such treats as fish from New Brunswick, veal from Charlevoix, and chanterelle mushrooms from Québec. The interior is cozy but chic with the old gray stone walls providing an austere backdrop to the simple white banquette seating and black tables. **MAP 2:** 48 rue St-Paul, 418/694-4448, www.lequai19.com; daily 7am-11am, 11:30am-2pm, and 5:30pm-11pm

★ Restaurant L'Initiale $$$
One of the most renowned restaurants in the city, this is a must for those who enjoy haute cuisine and is frequented by foodies from the world over. There is no set menu but various tasting menus that change with the seasons and the local products available. Known for his innovative dishes, head chef Yvan Lebrun marries unlikely flavors, such as suckling pig with squash, and crispy sweetbreads with mustard kidneys. Housed in a

- **Galvaude:** A variation on poutine, this dish adds chicken and peas to the fries, gravy, and cheese for a more "rounded" meal.

- **Grand-père dans le Sirop:** A popular dessert during the Great Depression, this is essentially a sweet dumpling made by boiling batter in sugar water, then serving it doused with maple syrup. Translated it means "Grandpa in the syrup."

- **Guedille:** Found mostly in *casse-croûtes* (snack shacks), *guedilles* are hot dog buns stuffed with lettuce, mayonnaise, and just about anything else, including egg, chicken, and fries. Commonly found outside of the cities, it's one version of Québec's take on fast food.

- **Oreilles de Crisse:** Translated this means "Christ's ears." Made from fried salted pork, they've been a snack since the time of Nouvelle France. Variations on this can be found in upscale restaurants across the province, especially those that specialize in *terroir* cooking.

- **Poutine:** Fries, gravy, cheese curds—this is the unofficial national dish of Québec. Though poutine has recently been embraced by food lovers everywhere, it was invented in this region and remains close to locals' hearts.

- **Ragoût de Pattes de Cochon:** This stew made with pig's feet is part of the *réveillon,* or Christmas meal. A variation on this includes *ragoût de boulettes,* which means meatballs, though likely made with pork and not beef.

- **Tourtière:** Otherwise known as meat pie, this is likely the most common of all the dishes as well as the oldest. Records show that it was first being made in Québec as early as 1611. It's usually made with beef or pork, but different regions in the province have different versions. In Montréal, it's a shallow pie filled with ground pork, while in the Lac-Saint-Jean region, north of Québec City, the pie is deeper and made with wild game like moose, caribou, elk, and hare. It's called *cipaille* in most restaurants.

century-old building, the interior of l'Initiale is distinctly modern with a sleek comfortable design. The entire restaurant follows a beige and cream color scheme and this subtly works in achieving a rich atmosphere.
MAP 2: 54 rue St-Pierre, 418/694-1818, www.restaurantinitiale.com; Tues.-Fri. 11:30am-2pm and 6pm-9pm, Sat. 6pm-9pm

ITALIAN
La Pizz $$

The delicious thin and crispy crust may be the trademark of this pizza joint, but the secret of their success is their ingredients. Fresh vegetables from the Marché du Vieux-Port and imported French cheese are mixed to produce unique flavor combinations, like tomato, bacon, egg, and Emmenthal or tomato, crème fraîche, leeks, scallops, and Emmenthal. The restaurant on St-Paul, which has a homey feel with bistro chairs and warm red walls, has been so successful that they recently opened another place right on Place Royale (3A Place Royale, 418/692-3003), making it a default tourist destination. So you can now eat your Frenchified 'za on the oldest spot in Canada.

MAP 2: 299 rue St-Paul, 418/692-5005, www.la-pizz.com; mid-Oct.-late May Mon.-Wed. 11:30am-2pm, Thurs.-Fri. 11:30am-10:30pm, late May-mid-Oct. daily noon-10:30pm

QUÉBÉCOIS

Brynd Smoked Meat ❸❸

Located on the former spot of the famous Thomas Dunn Pub, Brynd specializes in smoked meat sandwiches. This Québec variation, a smoked meat sandwich on rye served with "class" (the "class" seems to apply solely to the fact that you can choose between fries or salad and you don't have to wait in line for an hour to order), is one of the best in the city. The decor is minimally chic with mirrors lining the walls and the wooden banquettes filled with local office workers and hungry tourists. The waiters in all black duds are especially cool and congenial.

MAP 2: 369 rue St-Paul, 418/692-4693, www.brynd.com; Sun.-Tues. 11am-9pm, Wed.-Thurs. 11am-10pm, Fri.-Sat. 11am-11pm

★ Buffet de l'Antiquaire ❸

Set among the chichi bistros and idyllic antiques stores of rue St-Paul, the Buffet de l'Antiquaire is a no-frills diner. Established in 1975, it serves up breakfasts and traditional Québécois grub like *ragoût de boulettes* (meatballs, potatoes, and gravy), *pâté à la viande* (meat pie), and *cipaille* (game meat pie). Usually the busiest place on the block, it's adored by locals and tourists alike for its old-time charm—diner stools, vinyl banquettes, and line cooks in full-view. The all-day-long breakfast is served in heaping amounts and with their unforgettable homemade jam. In summer, tables and chairs are set up on the sidewalk outside for a makeshift patio.

MAP 2: 95 rue St-Paul, 418/692-2661; daily 6am-11pm

★ L'Échaudé ❸❸

With a stainless-steel bar and tables covered with butcher paper, the vibe at this Vieux-Qubébec bistro strikes the perfect balance of relaxed elegance. A new team behind this established name means almost everything (save for the decor) has undergone a makeover. A revamped menu—lobster tempura with risotto, mackerel with mustard sauce—puts the focus on organic and locally sourced food, while the wine list is selected from a sustainable vineyard. Touches of classic bistro fare remain, however. As does the restaurant's dedication to excellent value. They recently introduced a specially priced after-9pm menu, perfect for tasting their wares at a fraction of the price.

MAP 2: 73 rue du Sault-au-Matelot, 418/692-1299, www.echaude.com; Mon.-Sat. 11:30am-2pm and 5pm-10pm, Sun. 10:30am-2:30pm and 5pm-10pm

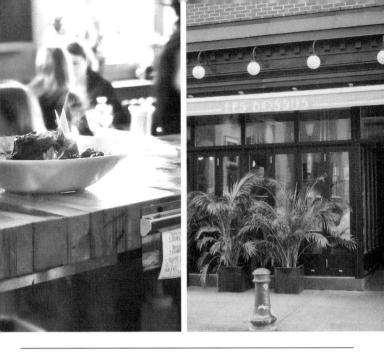

Clockwise from top left: Le Clocher Penché, Saint-Roch; French bistro Les Bossus, Saint-Roch; Le Café Buade, Vieux-Québec's Upper Town.

Laurie Raphaël $$$

At Laurie Raphaël it's all about infusing the flavors and aromas of the region into the cuisine. Dishes include scallops, beef with truffle dressing, veal with zucchini flower, and orange soufflé. But, of course, the menu changes depending on the season, so check before booking. Those on a budget should try the "Chef! Chef!," a three-course meal ($30 at lunch, $60 at dinner) improvised by head chef Daniel Vézina. The interior is luxurious and inviting thanks to the subtle color palette, with tones of grays and sand; floor-to-ceiling windows open onto the dining room, but gauzy, sheer curtains afford the perfect balance of privacy and light. Reservations are a must.

MAP 2: 117 rue Dalhousie, 418/692-4555, www.laurieraphael.com; Tues.-Fri. 11:30am-2pm and 6:30pm-10pm, Sat. 6:30pm-10pm

Panache $$$

Situated in the Auberge St-Antoine, this former 19th-century warehouse has been transformed into one of the most inviting dining rooms in the city, with exposed wood beams, stone walls, and original wood flooring. A wrought-iron staircase leads to a second dining level, with tables tucked away under the eaves for an intimate and romantic setting. Using local ingredients and taking much of his inspiration from the fresh produce available, chef Julien Dumas creates dishes that cater to the season and the palate. Foie gras, veal sweetbreads, and local Québec cheese, however, can always be found on the menu. Reservations are recommended.

MAP 2: 10 rue St-Antoine, 418/692-1022, www.restaurantpanache.com; Mon.-Tues. 6:30am-10:30am and 6pm-10pm, Wed.-Fri. 6:30am-10:30am, noon-2pm, and 6pm-10pm, Sat.-Sun. 7am-11am and 6pm-10pm

SSS $$

The latest endeavor from the people who brought you Toast!, SSS (Simple, Snack, Sympathique) is more relaxed and hipper (not counting the name) than its progenitor. Drawing a young, fashionable crowd, it has two different rooms: a small bar lounge with high tables, red accents, and lips on the wallpaper, and an adult dining room with stone walls, black-lacquered floors, and crisp white tablecloths. The main menu is French-influenced and heavy on the meat, with dishes like ribs, New York cut steak, and pasta with duck confit. The relaxed atmosphere, along with a late-night kitchen cooking up snacks like grilled chicken curry, gourmet hot dogs, and burgers, makes it a great choice for an evening cocktail or late dinner.

MAP 2: 71 rue St-Paul, 418/692-1991, www.restaurantsss.com; daily 11:30am-2pm and 5pm-midnight

Toast! $$$

Located in the heart of the Vieux-Port in the Priori hotel, Toast! offers modern cuisine in a picturesque setting. The atmosphere here is hip, with warm, orange-hued lighting illuminating the 200-year-old stone walls. Using French and Italian influences, dishes include vegetarian risotto with stuffed zucchini, salmon with smoked sour cream, and red deer bacon. For dessert, they offer a selection of cheeses, including a Québec cheese plate, *croque monsieur,* and a sheep's milk plate with figs and rye bread. In the summer, a large terrace is open out back, drawing everyone from young families to passing tourists and young professionals.

MAP 2: 17 rue du Sault-au-Matelot, 418/692-1334, www.restauranttoast.com; Mon.-Fri. 11:30am-2pm and 6pm-10:30pm, Sat. 6pm-10:30pm, Sun. 10:30am-10pm

SEAFOOD

La Cabane Lobster Shack ⑤⑤

It's all about low-key seafood at this casual and hip restaurant overlooking the Vieux-Port. As the name suggests, lobster, or *homard* in French, is the main attraction here, but it's not presented in the fussy way we once imagined. Instead it's served in typical Québécois dishes such as poutine or on a hotdog bun as a lobster roll. If you're not a fan of the lobster, there are a number of mussel dishes to try as well as bistro staples like steak and fries. No matter what you order, it's bound to taste pretty good if you can nab a seat on their sunny patio and wash the whole meal down with a local beer.

MAP 2: 115 Quai St-André, 418/692-1010; Sat.-Wed. 5pm-9pm, Thurs. 5pm-10pm, Fri. 11am-11pm

Café Riviera ⑤⑤

Located next to the Silo de la Bunge, this is the hangout for wannabe sailors and those who actually own boats docked in the marina. Even if you left your Breton shirt and Top Siders at home, a trip to Café Riviera is worth it for the outstanding view of the city alone. It's owned by Captain Bernier, and has the seafaring qualities—blue-checkered tablecloths, lanterns hanging from the ceiling, boat miniatures—you'd expect a restaurant owned by a captain would have. Dishes here range from classic (fries and pasta) to haute snacks (shrimp poutine, lobster sandwiches) and sophisticated meals (filet mignon). It's open throughout the summer.

MAP 2: 155 rue Abraham-Martin, 418/694-4449, www.riviera-quebec.com; May-Sept. Mon.-Fri. 9am-10pm, Sat.-Sun. 8am-10pm

Marie-Clarisse ⑤⑤⑤

There are only 12 tables, each set with a blue tablecloth and yellow flowers, in this cozy, romantic restaurant that occupies the ground floor of a 340-year-old house. Situated at the bottom of L'Escalier du Casse-Cou, the stone walls, wooden floors, and blazing fire in wintertime only add to the warm atmosphere. One of the top restaurants in the city for fish and seafood, it also offers fine meat dishes like chestnut and maple duck breast and calf's sweetbread. The menu changes daily according to the fresh fish available, but the specialty remains the *marmite de poisson sauce rouille* (fish soup with bouillabaisse).

MAP 2: 12 rue du Petit-Champlain, 418/692-0857, www.marieclarisse.qc.ca; winter daily 6pm-10pm, summer daily 11:30am-2:30pm and 6pm-10pm

Parliament Hill
and the Plains

Map 3

CAFÉS

Bügel Fabrique des Bagels ⑤⑤

Bügel Fabrique des Bagels makes the best Montréal-style bagels in Québec City—wood fired and smothered in sesame seeds. The small neighborhood staple is decorated with old church pews, and lively patrons give it a homey, comfy atmosphere. In the summer the tiny outdoor patio is the perfect place to chow down on one of their breakfast bagels, like *le poussin*, a bagel with an egg (served daily until 2pm), or dig in to one of their sandwich creations with smoked chicken and curried mayonnaise. Vegetarian meals are served, as well as soups, salads, and desserts.

MAP 3: 164 rue Crémazie W., 418/523-7666; Mon.-Wed. and Sat. 7am-7pm, Thurs.-Fri. 7am-9pm, Sun. 7am-6pm

Le Fastoche ⑤

This great *sandwicherie*, located in the Halles du Petit-Quartier on the upscale rue Cartier, has been turning sandwich making into an art since 2008. This take-away counter caters to workers on lunch or locals needing a quick bite. Creative sandwiches with a unique blend of ingredients include the baguette with duck, port, and blueberries and the prosciutto with two pestos. If you're looking for something more substantial try the *boite-à-lunch*, which comes with salad, dessert, and a drink. Close to the Plains of Abraham, it's a great place to pick up a last-minute picnic.

MAP 3: 1191 ave. Cartier (Halles du Petit-Quartier), 418/948-3773, www.sandwicheriefastoche.com; Mon.-Fri. 9am-7pm, Sat. 9am-6pm

DESSERTS

Glacier Aberdeen ⑤

This ice cream shop, tucked into a nook behind avenue Cartier, is one of the best in the city, and locals flock here from all over the city just for a scoop. It has just a slim, long hallway and a walk-up window, so customers savor their treats on the sunny terrace. Across the street, a statue by a local artist also attracts some ice cream eaters. Sundaes, sorbets, frozen yogurts, and milkshakes are all made here, but the place is especially known for its soft-serve ice cream coated with Belgian chocolate and a trickle of maple syrup.

MAP 3: 90 rue Aberdeen, 418/648-6366; mid-Apr.-mid-Sept. daily 10am-midnight

FRENCH AND QUÉBÉCOIS

Bistro B ⑤⑤⑤

Bistro B's large picture windows overlook avenue Cartier and the sleek yet overstuffed sofas of the restaurant's outdoor lounge area come summer. Opened in 2012, it's a great place to grab a fancy cocktail—they regularly post their latest creations on a chalkboard in the window to entice passersby—or a casual yet sophisticated meal. The interior is large and spacious, with the high wooden chairs and tables populating the open-concept restaurant. Even the kitchen is open for all to see, with the stools along the chef's counter being the most sought after in the place. Just as the atmosphere is casual, so is the menu. Hand-written daily above the kitchen, it features everything from veal in truffle oil to arugula risotto and Caesar salad with blood sausage and a poached egg.

MAP 3: 1144 ave. Cartier, 418/614-5444, www.bistrob.ca; Mon.-Fri. 11:30am-2pm and 6pm-11pm, Sat.-Sun. 10am-2pm and 6pm-11pm

Café Krieghoff ❸❸

No matter the time of day, this place is always packed with both locals and tourists. Named after a famous early-Canadian painter who lived in the area, Café Krieghoff serves everything from your basic breakfast (eggs, toast, potatoes) to bistro-style dinners (quiche lorraine, grilled salmon). Neither the food nor the coffee is out of this world, and, beyond the hustle and bustle, the ambience is lacking, but the prime real estate (on the popular avenue Cartier close to the Plains of Abraham and Fine Arts Museum) and the large front and back terraces keep customers coming back. They also have a small seven-room B&B, which occupies the top two stories, a great choice if you're looking for something cozy and intimate.

MAP 3: 1091 ave. Cartier, 418/522-3711, www.cafekrieghoff.qc.ca; Mon.-Fri. 7am-10pm, Sat. 8am-11pm, Sun. 8am-9pm

Graffiti ❸❸❸

This chic and modern restaurant—exposed brick, soft lighting, modern furnishings—serves dishes influenced by both Italian and French traditions. Chef Robert Saulnier is known for his personal touch, which includes creations like veal sweetbread in pastry with candied apples, and roast rack of lamb with sun-dried tomato risotto. Located in the food emporium Les Halles des Cartier, it's popular with neighborhood locals and especially young couples and groups of friends in their late twenties, early thirties. On Sunday, they serve a decadent brunch; pop in for the poached eggs and blintzes.

MAP 3: 1191 ave. Cartier, 418/529-4949; Mon.-Thurs. 11:30am-2:30pm and 5pm-10pm, Fri. 11:30am-2:30pm and 5pm-11pm, Sat. 5pm-11pm, Sun. 9:30am-3pm and 5pm-11pm

Restaurant du Musée des Beaux-Arts ❸❸

One of the first things you notice when you enter the Musée des Beaux-Arts is the restaurant, located just off the entrance hall. The clink of glasses and plates and wafting aromas immediately grab your attention (especially if you're hungry). Featuring regional cuisine and local, organic produce, mains include pork breast, halibut, and stuffed portobello mushrooms. The atmosphere inside is fairly subdued with sparsely designed chairs and simple white tablecloths. During the summer, however, the *terrasse* out back has a stunning view of both the St-Lawrence and the Plains. It's a perfect spot for lunch, and dinner is served once a week, on Wednesday nights when the museum is open late.

MAP 3: Parc des Champs-de-Bataille, 418/644-6780, www.mnba.qc.ca; Thurs.-Tues. 10am-5pm, Wed. 10am-8:45pm

INTERNATIONAL
Le Cosmos ❸❸❸

Right next to the Voo Doo Grill, Le Cosmos shares the same fusion spirit and exotic decor. Dishes here are international, from General Tao chicken to burgers and pastas. It's a trendy and hip restaurant. The decor has organic influences with a sort of *Space Odyssey: 2001* vibe and is a bold mix of neon tree-like columns, illuminated pictures of forests, and an aquarium that runs the length of the floor. The contemporary furniture is 1960s-inspired. Bordering on kitsch, somehow it all seems to work. They have a great selection of cocktails and a big *terrasse* on Grande-Allée on which to knock one back.

MAP 3: 575 La Grande-Allée E., 418/640-0606, www.lecosmos.com; Mon.-Thurs. 7am-midnight, Fri. 7am-1am, Sat. 8am-1am, Sun. 8am-midnight

Voo Doo Grill ❸❸❸

Part of a big complex that houses famous Le Maurice nightclub, the Voo Doo Grill serves international food that, despite the name, tends toward Asian and fusion. As if that weren't confusing enough, the decor, once Africa-inspired with roaming drum circles, has recently been replaced by an art deco look, full of cast iron, fur, and gilded mirrors. Specialties of the house, however, haven't changed, so you can still get the same filet mignon, tandoori shrimp, and snow-crab cakes, all of which are better than what you'd expect. They also have a great selection of wine, over 200 choices. Customers, from traveling businesspeople to twentysomething students, come for dinner and stay to burn off the calories on the dance floors of Le Maurice and Le Charlotte Ultra Lounge, where the door fee is waived with proof that you ate at Voo Doo.

MAP 3: 575 La Grande-Allée E., 418/647-2000, www.voodoogrill.com; Mon.-Fri. 11am-midnight, Sat.-Sun. 5pm-midnight

ITALIAN
Casa Calzone ❸❸

If you're looking for Québec City's Little Italy, look no further than Casa Calzone. The red-checkered tablecloths, postcards of Italy on the wall, Italian music, and bottles of chianti subtly let you know you've arrived. Pastas and homemade pizzas are always good, but the real standouts here are their famous calzones. The proud owner often makes the rounds of the tables just to make sure what you've ordered has sent you to food heaven. Don't forget to please him as much as he pleased you and leave your comments on the wall provided.

MAP 3: 637 La Grande-Allée E., 418/522-3000, www.casacalzone.com; winter Mon.-Sat. 11:30am-2pm and 5:30pm-10pm, summer daily 11:30am-11pm

Milano Pizza $$

This pizza joint's reputation as one of the best in Québec City has been cemented over the last 40 years, thanks to the neighborhood regulars who drop in at least once a week. Though it's not gourmet (black olives are the fanciest topping), it's always fresh and delicious, and the unpretentious attitude keeps bringing people back. It's just off avenue Cartier, and for late-night cravings, it's the perfect place, especially during the summer when they often close after 1am.

MAP 3: 194 rue Crémazie W., 418/529-2919; Mon.-Thurs. 11am-1am, Sat.-Sun. 11am-midnight

Morena $

Part specialty store, part casual restaurant, Morena is your go-to place for authentic and delicious Italian staples. Whether it's a creamy latte to go, fresh homemade linguine ready to be thrown in the pot, or a can of San Marzano tomatoes, this place has you covered. There are only about six tables in the store and they're nearly always filled with neighborhood locals who pop in for a quick bite of their lasagna Bolognese or eggplant Parmesan. A great place to grab lunch or dinner, it's also a popular spot for brunch on the weekends, serving everything from two eggs the way you like them to baked eggs in tomato sauce.

MAP 3: 1040 ave. Cartier, 418/529-3668, www.morena-food.com; Mon.-Wed. 8am-7pm, Thurs.-Fri. 8am-8pm, Sat.-Sun. 8am-6pm

JAPANESE
Métropolitan Eddie Sushi Bar $$$

This restaurant's name might be lost in translation, but they got everything else right at this authentic Japanese restaurant on Cartier. The large, open dining room is painted white with dark wood accents in the door and window frames. The rest of the decor is kept simple with the tables and chairs almost precisely matched to the existing wood, evoking a particularly Zen ambience. Though you can still order your California and kamikazi rolls here, the emphasis is on traditional Japanese sashimi and sushi with *unagi*, *tobiko*, and scallops featured on the menu.

MAP 3: 1188 ave. Cartier, 418/649-1096, www.eddiesushi.com; Mon.-Fri. 4:30pm-10:30pm, Sat. 5pm-11:30pm, Sun. 5pm-10:30pm

TEA
Sebz Thés and Lounge $

The interior of this teahouse makes up for the exterior on the busy and less than picturesque boulevard René-Lévesque. The vibe here is more relaxed than British afternoon tea, and the friendly atmosphere makes it popular with local residents and students alike. More than 150 teas from China, Japan, India, and Africa are available. Detox Tuesdays are popular with regulars, as are the infusion blends, which they roast and blend on the spot.

MAP 3: 67 blvd. René-Lévesque E., 418/523-0808, www.sebz.ca; Mon.-Sat. 10am-9pm, Sun. 10am-6pm

Saint-Jean-Baptiste and Saint-Roch

Map 4

BAKERIES

La Boîte à Pain ⑤

This artisanal bakery has freshly baked bread all day long and the smell lures in just about anyone who passes by. The pastries are also awesome, from the croissants to the *pains aux chocolates* to the brioche. They also serve sandwiches—try the tomato, mozzarella, and basil—delicious soups spiced with curry, and great salads. Though the interior is nothing fancy, it does have a few nondescript chairs and tables where locals and weary tourists recharge with a coffee and a treat.

MAP 4: 289 rue St-Joseph E., 418/647-3666, www.boiteapain.com; Mon.-Fri. 6:30am-8pm, Sat.-Sun. 6:30am-5:30pm

Le Pain Grüel ⑤

This self-proclaimed *"boulangerie creative"* makes its breads and pastries by hand and with some of the healthiest ingredients. All breads are made using sourdough, but a variety of flours and ingredients are added according to the season. The results: multi-grain bread, cheese bread, bread with nuts. They even have a bread with chocolate and dried pears. The ambience is all business, with a simple counter and not much else. This is a take-away place, so you can feel French and eat your baguette as you stroll the street.

MAP 4: 375 rue St-Jean, 418/522-7246; Tues.-Fri. 6am-6:30pm, Sat. 6am-5pm

CAFÉS

★ Brûlerie Saint-Roch ⑤

This is one of the best cafés in the city, and the line starts early in the mornings when regulars pop in to get their usual before heading off to work. Ideally located on a corner lot, it has two walls of picture windows with bars and seats along both that are usually occupied. If it's not too packed, try to grab a seat on the tiny second-floor mezzanine that looks out over the action. Front and center when you enter is the gleaming Nuova Simonelli (the espresso machine), backed by a wall of coffee beans ready to be ground. The lattes here are outstanding—it's all in the foam—and the sandwiches and pastries are mouthwatering. There is a second location on rue St-Jean (881 rue St-Jean, 418/614-3359).

MAP 4: 375 rue St-Joseph E., 418/529-1559, www.brulerie-st-roch.com; Sun.-Wed. 6:30am-11pm, Thurs.-Sat. 6:30am-midnight

Café Babylone ⑤

With different events happening here almost every night of the week, Café Babylone is a great place to take in a different kind of show. Local musicians hit the tiny stage to try out new material, and on Tuesday nights you can stop by to hear everything from slam poetry to storytelling. Most of these events are pay-what-you-can. During daylight hours, it's a cozy café serving

Turkish specialties as well as sandwiches, salads, and even breakfasts. The atmosphere is laid-back and so is the decor; most of the furniture has been salvaged from secondhand shops.

MAP 4: 181 rue St-Vallier E., 418/523-0700, www.cafebabylone.com; Mon.-Fri. 10am-10pm, Sat. 9am-10pm, Sun. 9am-3pm

Librairie St-Jean-Baptiste $

A bookshop and café in one, Librairie St-Jean-Baptiste is one of the latest additions to the street. Situated in a building that dates from the early 1900s, the bookstore, dealing in mostly used books, has quickly become a meeting point for local artists and students. There's also a small café, where you're invited to while away the afternoon in this inviting and relaxed atmosphere. Snacks, including sandwiches, soup, and grilled cheese, are also available.

MAP 4: 565 rue St-Jean, 581/999-0951, www.librairiesjb.com; daily 11am-9pm

Nektar $

At Nektar, coffee is an art. Baristas here are experts and will explain the ins-and-outs of a good cup of joe to you, all in a thinly veiled attempt to lure you into tasting their *grands crus,* the latest vintage of coffee. If they succeed in getting you to taste the Nektar, you'll have a hard time going back to your Starbucks Breakfast Blend. Despite their devotion to java, they also have pastries, crêpes, and pizzas on hand in the off chance you might want something solid. The interior is a bit of a letdown; chocolate brown walls give the place a cozy feel in winter, but in warmer months it all seems a bit too dark.

MAP 4: 235 rue St-Joseph E., 418/977-9236, www.lenektar.com; Mon.-Wed. 7am-11pm, Thurs.-Fri. 7am-midnight, Sat. 8:30am-midnight, Sun. 9:30am-9pm

Pain et Passion $

Located in what used to be a cookie factory, this Mediterranean grocery store offers pretty much everything. Alongside various kinds of homemade bread, you'll find deli, pastry, and cheese counters. They've also got hot meals, salads, pastas, and good coffee. Locals come here for special ingredients or for a quick and easy take-away dinner. Grab a seat at one of the few tables and eat among the old artifacts, imported European products, and old factory decor, and lounge in the laid-back, almost soothing atmosphere. They also offer nice breakfasts on weekends 10am-2pm.

MAP 4: 85 rue St-Vallier E., 418/525-7887, www.painetpassion.com; Mon.-Fri. 7am-7pm, Sat.-Sun. 9am-5:30pm

CRÊPERIES
★ Crêperie Le Billig $

This is the most authentic crêperie in Québec City—some even say it's better than the ones found in France. It was founded by a true Breton, and authentic *galettes* made of organic buckwheat flour and sweet crêpes made of sarrazin are both available. First-timers should try the classic crêpe suzette, flambéed with Grand Marnier. Don't forget to wash your sweet or savory crêpe down with a cider. The lively and boisterous ambience is palpable since the place is always full of locals packed into the seven tables or taking up the one or two outside tables in the summer. Reservations are a must.

MAP 4: 526 rue St-Jean, 418/524-8341; Tues.-Sat. 11am-9pm, Sun. 11am-3pm

DESSERTS

Tutto Gelato $

This 100 percent authentic Italian *gelateria* comes from the heart of a 100 percent authentic Italian. When owner Giacomo Donati moved to Canada he brought with him gelato recipes and lots of them. All the gelato here is homemade, and with over 100 recipes, there's always a different flavor to try, including matcha, saffron cream, ginger, sea-salt caramel, and all the classics. Modern and sleek, this slim take-away counter also has cakes, biscuits, coffees, and even homemade soy milk ice cream.

MAP 4: 716 rue St-Jean, 418/522-0896, www.tuttogelato.ca; late Apr.-early Oct. daily 10:30am-8pm or midnight depending on the weather

FRENCH

Au Bonnet d'Âne $$

Situated in what was once the local general store, this café and restaurant is a local favorite. It's not hard to imagine a shopkeeper behind the dark, heavy bar, or think of the long bay windows, now comfortable banquettes, as filled with stuff for sale. The relaxed, sometimes boisterous atmosphere is laid-back and inviting. Old artifacts line the shelves, the menu is written on the mirror behind the bar, and old photos hang on the walls. The burgers are some of the best. Their weekend brunch is always hearty, but refined. A small *terrasse* on the side is a great spot in the summer.

MAP 4: 298 rue St-Jean, 418/647-3031, www.aubonnetdane.com; Mon.-Fri. 11am-10pm, Sat.-Sun. 8am-10pm

Les Bossus $$

This is a classic French bistro, from its checkered-tile floor to the waiters in long black aprons to the menu that lists everything from breakfast to dessert. Simply decorated, the narrow restaurant has a long bar on the right, an entire wall with banquette seats on the left, and black-lacquered chairs and tables in the middle. All this might look very elegant, but everything here stays simple and relaxed. Not convinced? Bossus in English means "The Hunchbacks." The diners here are diverse—businesspeople, locals, and tourists. They come to eat bistro classics like tartare, *boudin noir,* duck confit, and filet mignon. Les Bossus also serves an excellent breakfast.

MAP 4: 620 rue St-Joseph E., 418/522-5501, www.lesbossus.com; Mon.-Fri. 11am-10pm, Sat.-Sun. 9am-10pm

Le Cercle $$

Defying all conventions, Le Cercle is a restaurant, a bar, a café, and a performance venue, and is the go-to place for the young and hip. With its concrete floors, light wood interior, and floor-to-ceiling windows, it is one of the city's coolest restaurants. Serving both tapas-style munchies (try the grilled sardines and rabbit shoulders—seriously) and mains (smoked salmon tartare and veal smoked ribs), it's also one of the more popular brunch places in town. It may not be surprising to learn that they serve up some of the most sought-after cocktails (at brunch you can order an entire carafe of mimosas), but one surprising twist about Le Cercle is the wine cellar. It blends in so well, you barely even notice the $1,600 bottles of Château Pètrus stacked up against the wall.

MAP 4: 228 rue St-Joseph E., 418/948-8648, www.le-cercle.ca; Tues.-Fri. 11:30am-3am, Sat. 10am-3am

★ Le Clocher Penché ❸❸

If you ask Québec City residents what their favorite restaurant is, or at least which one gives you the best bang for your buck, they'll tell you Le Clocher Penché. It's set in an old bank, and the washrooms are where the big safe used to be. The ever-changing menu includes dishes like roasted snails, scallops with spaghetti squash, and black pudding with apple chutney. They use all local, fresh products. It's called Clocher Penché (Leaning Belfry) because the church next door has a slanted bell tower. Large windows open onto the street in summertime and give the dining room lots of light no matter the time of year. The light wood chairs and tables give the whole atmosphere a delightful airiness. Reservations are recommended.

MAP 4: 203 rue St-Joseph E., 418/640-0597, www.clocherpenche.ca; Tues.-Fri. 11:30am-2pm and 5pm-10pm, Sat. 9am-2pm and 5pm-10pm, Sun. 9am-2pm

★ Le Moine Échanson ❸❸

First the translation—*échanson* means "cup-bearer," an officer whose duty was to serve the drinks at a royal table. *Moine* means "monk." The concept at this *bistro à vin* is to discover a new wine region of France every time you visit. The menu, using Québécois and French products, varies according to season and climate. For example, you'll be in Savoy and Alsace in winter, the Mediterranean in summer (including Greece, Portugal, Spain), and Québec in fall.

It's small and cozy with wood tables, a chalkboard menu, and lots of natural light; the ambience here transports you to France without crossing the Atlantic. In summer, prime tables are available outside to let you appreciate the vibe of Faubourg Saint-Jean-Baptiste. A favorite with couples or friends on dates, it can get packed, so reservations are a good idea.

MAP 4: 585 rue St-Jean, 418/524-7832, www.lemoineechanson.com; Sun.-Mon. 5pm-10pm, Tues.-Wed. 11:30am-2pm and 5pm-10pm, Thurs. 11:30am-2pm and 5pm-11pm, Fri. 11:30am-2pm

Versa ❸❸❸

One of the first restaurants to open in the revitalized Saint-Roch neighborhood, this oyster bar headed by young chef Christian Veilleux is the only one of its kind in the city. It looks just as much like a club as a fine dining establishment. The centerpiece of the dining room is a long communal table illuminated by a modern disco ball. The atmosphere is hip and young.

Aside from the oysters, mains include seared sweetbreads and baby-back ribs. In summertime the floor-to-ceiling window slides open and revelers mingle on the tiny, cobblestone street.

MAP 4: 432 rue du Parvis, 418/523-9995, www.versarestaurant.com; Mon. 11:30am-2pm, Tues.-Fri. 11:30am-close, Sat. 5pm-close

JAPANESE
Yuzu Sushi Bar ❸❸❸

This sushi bar is named after a small Japanese citrus fruit whose delicate grapefruit-meets-mandarin flavor is often found in fusion cooking. There could be no better symbol for what Yuzu does: blend traditional Japanese with North American flavors. The interior of this modern sushi bar is just peachy, with the color on the walls, the plush upholstery of the chairs, and even the pink hues of the wooden tabletops. It's frequented by young, chic professionals. Dishes like tempura, beef sashimi, and dragon rolls are all available here, but where Yuzu differs is with its specialties and tasting menus, which mix flavors like blue fin tuna with pesto and salmon tartare with quinoa salad.

MAP 4: 438 rue du Parvis, 418/521-7253, www.yuzu.ca; Mon.-Wed. 11:30am-2:30pm and 5pm-10pm, Thurs.-Fri. 11:30am-2:30pm and 5pm-11pm, Sat. 5pm-11pm

MIDDLE EASTERN
Le Carthage ❸❸

Named after the ancient African city, Le Carthage serves fine Tunisian cuisine. The atmosphere is laid-back and the surroundings majestic; the slightly curved ceiling and intricate moldings give the whole room an exotic feel. Seating here is North African as well, and low chairs and tables adorned with colorful plush cushions invite you to take your shoes off and relax. Bring your own wine to accompany dishes like tahini, royal couscous, or *merguez* and quail brochettes. On weekends, enjoy traditional music and belly-dancing as you sit back and finish your meal with some sticky baklava.

MAP 4: 399 rue St-Jean, 418/529-0576; Tues.-Fri. 11am-2pm and 5pm-11pm, Sat.-Mon. 5pm-10pm

Le Sultan ❸

Decorated with hookahs and gilded tea pots, Le Sultan looks like something out of *Arabian Nights*. It's super casual; you can get takeout or eat in one of their brightly decorated rooms. It's the perfect place for a Moroccan mint tea. Their simple food is fresh, healthy, and delicious, and their *shish taouk "gigot d'agneau"* is not to be missed. A salon at the back is welcoming; leave your shoes at the door and let yourself sink into the cushions. They accept cash only.

MAP 4: 467 rue St-Jean, 418/525-9449; Mon.-Thurs. 11:30am-11pm, Fri. noon-midnight, Sat.-Sun. noon-11pm

QUÉBÉCOIS

Chez Victor $

The ambition of this self-proclaimed burger gourmet is to make a hamburger a "piece of art." And so far, everybody in Québec—artist or not—would agree that they make the best burgers in town. The salmon burger, duck burger, and wild boar burger are interesting takes on the old standard. Vegetarians get choices as well, a rarity in Québec, with tofu, nut and spinach, and cereal burgers available. The success led them to open new restaurants, including one in the Vieux-Port (300 rue St-Paul, 418/781-2511), but the one on St-Jean remains the best and definitely worth the walk, with its stone walls, low ceiling, and casual atmosphere.

MAP 4: 145 rue St-Jean, 418/529-7702, www.chezvictorburger.com/st-jean; Sun.-Wed. 11am-9pm, Thurs.-Sat. 11am-10pm

Le Comptoir $

One of the main things about Québécois food—be it at one of the best restaurants in the country or a typical neighborhood diner—is that it always comes back to comfort. And that's what Le Comptoir (the Counter) serves up: satisfying comfort food in a comfortable setting. Located on St-Jean, this cute restaurant—it's all red and white banquettes and bar stools line the windows—offers two stories of cozy charm for you to settle in with your friends and family. Most of the clientele can be placed in three categories: locals, journalists (the offices of the Francophone version of Canada's national broadcasting network is just across the street), and families (what kid will say no to a burger?). The menu, too, aims to please. They have two specialties here, the very British fish and chips and smoked meat. The fish is as fresh as anything you'd find on the coast of Maine, while the smoked meat comes directly from Montréal's Lester's. Of course, their burgers and club sandwiches hit the spot too.

MAP 4: 849 rue St-Jean, 418/614-5522; daily 11am-10pm

Snack Bar St-Jean $

Snack Bar St-Jean is a rare find: a place that can satisfy your craving for burgers and fries just as easily at 4am in the morning as at noon. Open till 5am seven days a week, this snack bar is all about being here for you when that craving for grilled cheese hits. This modern diner is nicely, if not overly, decorated with low sturdy wooden tables and chairs that can stand up to a lot of abuse. There's even a backyard patio come summertime, the perfect place to kick back with your enormous and ingenious poutine club (a club sandwich dumped on a pile of fries and covered in gravy, essentially). Everything here is over the top and that's part of the charm. If you're watching your calories, this place is best to be avoided (though they do have a rather demure toasted tomato sandwich on the menu). This is a place to revel in your love of the fatty and fried. Come for the "Gangbang Burger," featuring both a beef and chicken patty, but stay for the other crazy creations that come out of the kitchen.

MAP 4: 780 rue St-Jean, 418/522-4727, www.snackbarsaintjean.com; daily 10am-5am

Taverne Steakhouse Le Tonneau ⑤

Opened in 1939, Taverne Steakhouse Le Tonneau, one of the oldest restaurants in the city, has witnessed a lot of history. Rumor has it that the first separatist powwows were held here, when St-Joseph was still slightly unsavory. Most recently, it's witnessed the cleanup of the area, and though it's been cleaned up itself, it has managed to retain its unique personality and clientele. The Formica tables and refrigerators in imitation wood, paired with the long bar, give it the air of an urban saloon. The regulars are still here, but they're surrounded by a younger, hipper generation. Smoked meat, liver, poutine, and blood pudding are popular, as are new additions like beef and salmon tartare. If you manage to eat the hulking 72-ounce sirloin steak in less than an hour, the boss picks up the tab. You have been warned.

MAP 4: 732 rue St-Joseph E., 418/525-9337; daily 11am-3am

TEA
Camellia Sinensis ⑤

Québec City deserves its own branch of this great Montréal-based teahouse and it's no surprise to find it here on St-Joseph. Tea tasters travel the world to find the best and rarest of teas. More than 180 fresh teas are kept in store, and they come from as far way as Japan, India, China, and Taiwan. This small store is set up like an old sweet shop with a counter, and the soft green walls are filled with silver tea tins. The shelves in heavy dark wood give it a feel of gravitas. Tea being a serious business for them, the owners organize a number of tea-centered activities, including tastings, workshops, and even classes on traditional tea ceremonies.

MAP 4: 624 rue St-Joseph E., 418/525-0247, www.camellia-sinensis.com; Mon.-Wed. and Sat. 10am-6pm, Thurs.-Fri. 10am-8pm, Sun. 10am-5pm

VIETNAMESE
La Petite Boîte Vietnamienne ⑤

The brainchild of young chef Thi Cam Nhung Lê, La Petite Boîte Vietnamienne brings together Western and Eastern influences. Vietnamese classics, like *phô*, the national soup, alternate with Québécois dishes that Nhung Lê then revisits, like duck breast with Hanoi spices and mussels in Vietnamese spices. It's a must among local adventurous eaters and those wanting a change from bistro fare. The tiny dining room is simply decorated with rich red walls and paper lanterns; seats are also available at the bar, where you can watch the chef at work and sip a mojito, her own drink of choice.

MAP 4: 281 rue de la Couronne, 418/204-6323; Tues.-Fri. 11am-10pm, Sat. 4pm-10pm

Nightlife

Highlights

★ **Best Place to Find Your Sea Legs:**
With 50 different cocktails and an interior that makes you feel like you're drinking in the captain's cabin, **Bar Ste-Angèle** will soon have you swaying with the ship (page 88).

★ **Best Terrace:** With cocktails in mason jars, imported beer on tap, and a large patio that looks onto the old walls, **Le Sapristi** is your go-to for alfresco drinks (page 89).

★ **Most Incomprehensible Good Time:** You might not understand the lyrics to the songs sung at **Le Pape-Georges,** but the energy at this *boîte à chansons* is infectious (page 92).

★ **Best Dance Club:** The sheer size of the dance floor and variety of music at **Le Maurice** will keep you dancing all night long (page 93).

★ **Best (and Only) Place to Smoke Indoors:** With its walk-in humidor and selection of over 200 cigars, **Société Cigare** lets smokers enjoy their stogies in dignified surroundings (page 94).

★ **Best Microbrew: La Barberie** is socially and environmentally conscious, so you can down your tasting selection of eight beers guilt free (page 95).

★ **Best Place to Skip the Meal:** Pitchers of beer are served in watering cans at **La Cuisine,** which cooks up full-on dance parties that rage on well into the night (page 96).

★ **Most Authentic Québécois Tavern: Taverne Jos Dion** is one of the oldest bars in the city. Head here for the live accordion music and stay for the cheap beer (page 98).

★ **Best Drag Show:** Gay bar and night-club **Le Drague** is nothing but unadulter-ated fun, and the dance floor is always packed with people letting loose (page 100).

★ **Best Game Selection:** Head down-stairs to the Game Bar at **Le Boudoir** for some old-school Pac-Man and new-school sounds (page 100).

Québec City might be known for its historic sights but it also has some worthwhile night-life. Though the rejuvenation of the Saint-Roch neighborhood has led to new hipster venues and interesting bars, La Grande-Allée remains the epi-center of the city's nightlife, with dance clubs and

bars chockablock along the strip. The late-night scene, however, still lacks a certain amount of diversity. Sure, you can always catch a band or find a place to dance the night away, but the selection can feel limited compared to most major North American cities. Nightlife here tends to stick to the neighborhood bar, and it is in these small establishments that you'll find the city's true ambience.

One facet of nightlife specific to Québec is *chansonniers* (singer/songwriters). These folk singers perform in *boîtes à chansons* ("music boxes"). These venues, deeply entrenched in Québécois identity, give singers and songwriters a platform to sing about their heritage and experience and were first popular shortly after World War II. Famous *chansonniers* have included Félix Leclerc and Raymond Lévesque, who helped popularize this new form of folk music in the 1950s. It's still popular today, and there are venues in the city dedicated solely to supporting emerging songwriters, who sing both old classics and new material. Those looking for a uniquely Québécois experience should make time to check out one of these performances, even if the lyrics remain something of a mystery.

Montréalers love to antagonize Québeckers by calling it a "town," rather than a city, and though it can feel small at times, that isn't always a bad

Previous: Québec City at night; drinks at a Québec City bar.

thing. When the city comes alive at night, it's in the numerous bars and taverns in neighborhoods all over the city. Even in the deepest of winter the bars are packed with men and women downing pints from local breweries. Many of the bars also feature regular live music that ranges from jazz trios to local rock acts, and if you feel like dancing, chances are you aren't alone. Québeckers are always up for a good time, so it doesn't take much to get the city's population out of their seats, even if there's no actual dance floor.

Those in the mood for neon lights, thumping bass, and big crowds should head to La Grande-Allée, the city's biggest boulevard, which is full of historical buildings that have been converted into bars and dance clubs. The legal drinking age is 18 throughout the province, and this is the place where teens can be found reveling in their newfound freedom. If you're looking to dance but want something more *branchée* (trendy), head over to Le Drague, the city's gay club, for some guaranteed fun.

When looking for a place to pop in for a nightcap or hear some local music, don't be afraid to wander along quiet side streets or go beyond the old city walls—it's in these places that you'll find the most authentic ambience and the most affordable beer.

Vieux-Québec's Upper Town

Map 1

BARS

★ Bar Ste-Angèle

Cocktails here come in a rainbow of colors and a multitude of flavors, including Red Devil, Blue Angel, and Kamikaze. With 50 cocktails to choose from, which you can get by the pitcher, they all start to become tempting after a while. They also have an extensive selection of imported beers and scotch. The bar is designed to resemble the cabin of a ship; there's a lot of heavy woodwork, tiny windows, and mini tables. Small and often packed, it's the perfect retreat when it's super cold or rainy out. Live jazz plays Thursday, Friday, and Saturday nights.

MAP 1: 26 rue Ste-Angèle, 418/692-2171; daily 8pm-3am; no cover

L'Ostradamus

It's not every day that a popular student bar is found in a historic building. Designed by Eugène-Étienne Taché and built in 1890, L'Ostradamus takes up two floors of this impressive Victorian structure, which is hidden on the twisty-turny rue Couillard. The all-wood interior gives it a warm though distinctly bar-like feel. The young and hip have been flocking here for the cheap drinks and fun atmosphere since it opened in 1973. The top floor is a show lounge dedicated to showcasing new music, stand-up comedy, and other events, while the vibe on the first floor is more relaxed, perfect for beer with friends.

MAP 1: 29 rue Couillard, 418/694-9560; daily 4:30pm-3am; no cover

★ Le Sapristi

Owned by the team behind burger joint Les Trois Garçons, brand new bar Le
Sapristi is a much needed breath of fresh air. Taking over the coveted corner
spot on St-Jean just inside the old walls, Le Sapristi serves up delectable mixed
drinks made all the more desirable because they're casually served in old
mason jars. On tap you'll find a number of local brews alongside European
staples like Newcastle Brown Ale and 1664 Blanc. The crowd is mostly full
of twentysomethings and thirtysomethings, many of whom stop off for an
after-work drink and bite. Stone walls, rustic but nicely finished wood tables
and chairs, and a newly refurbished copper ceiling pull the whole casual vibe
together. If you get hungry, they also serve some mean pizzas and charcuterie
plates. In the summer there's not one but two *terrasses* to choose from, one
out front offering a great view of the St-Jean gate and a larger one around the
side that's perfect for whiling away the hours with friends.
MAP 1: 1001 rue St-Jean, 418/692-2030, www.sapristi.ca; daily 11am-3am; no
cover

LIVE MUSIC
Boîtes à Chansons
Les Yeux Bleus

If you want to experience the peculiarly Québécois institution of *boîtes à chansons*, this is the place to do it. It was in these small filled-to-capacity rooms that
emerging Québécois singers first got their start in the 1950s, and the tradition
continues to this day, especially at Les Yeux Bleus (The Blue Eyes), the most
popular venue for *chansonniers* in the city. Situated at the end of a courtyard
off of St-Jean, the room here gets packed early with audiences of all ages. Even
if you don't understand a word of what the musician three feet from your table
is singing, you'll witness the magical effect it has on the audience.
MAP 1: 1117½ rue St-Jean, 418/694-9118; daily 8pm-3am; no cover

Jazz Bars
Le Charles Baillairgé Jazz Bar

Situated in the Hotel Clarendon, the Charles Baillairgé Jazz Bar continues
the 30-year tradition originally started here by L'Emprise. Found on the
street level of the hotel, the large, open-concept bar with low lights, bucket
chairs, and a small stage makes for an intimate atmosphere. With jazz
groups playing almost every night, the stage has hosted such legendary
names as Diana Krall and John Zorn and continues to be a showcase for
Québec's emerging and established jazz musicians.
MAP 1: 57 rue Ste-Anne, 418/692-2480, www.hotelclarendon.com; daily
7pm-10:30pm; no cover

LOUNGES
St-Laurent Bar and Lounge

Like its sibling establishments Le Champlain and Café de la Terrasse,
Château Frontenac's St-Laurent Bar affords the same great views of
the St-Lawrence River. Unlike its siblings, however, this is the only establishment that is exclusively a bar (though light meals are available

from the restaurants). The circular, rich wood bar is the centerpiece of the St-Laurent, with massive picture frame windows that look out onto the *terrasse* and river beyond. The seating is placed around the bar, and old wingback-style chairs are the standard. Evening or afternoon, the cocktail reigns supreme, with a number of classics on the menu like whiskey sours, gin fizz, and Tom Collins, as well as a list of martinis like the Winston Churchill or F. D. Roosevelt, all named after illustrious guests. Dress code is smart casual. Men in sleeveless shirts will be turned away.

MAP 1: 1 rue des Carrières, 418/266-3919, www.fairmont.com/frontenac; daily 11:30am-1:30am; no cover

PUBS
Pub St-Alexandre
If you like beer, then you'll love Pub St-Alexandre. It's the English pub of Québec City, with mahogany paneling, big mirrors, and an "olde British pub" facade to prove it. Pub St-Alexandre has been here for more than 20 years and offers the largest selection of beer in the province. More than 250 beers are available, mostly from Ireland, Britain, Germany, and Belgium. They also carry a selection of 40 single malts. It's a hangout that attracts both locals and tourists. If you find yourself confounded by choice, the servers are all beer experts.

MAP 1: 1087 rue St-Jean, 418/594-0015, www.pubstalexandre.com; daily 11am-3am; no cover

Pub St-Patrick
Pub St-Patrick is hard to miss, with its ideal location and large, usually packed *terrasse* full of students, tourists, and professionals still in their suits after work. Inside this bustling pub is some of the most fascinating architecture. The building dates back to 1749, and several of the rooms are made completely of stone, and feature vaulted ceilings. Once used as barracks during the French regime, they are now some of the coziest places to sip a pint of Guinness. Imported beer is a specialty here and you'll find Harp, Kilkenny, and Smithwick's on tap, as well as an outstanding scotch selection.

MAP 1: 1200 rue St-Jean, 418/694-0618; daily 11:30am-3am; no cover

Vieux-Québec's Lower Town
Map 2

BARS
L'Oncle Antoine
Right next to Place Royale, L'Oncle Antoine is one of the coolest looking bars in the city. Located in the cellar of one of the oldest buildings in the city, it dates back to 1754, and the vaulted brick ceilings and walls make you feel like you're hanging out in an old bunker. In wintertime, a raging

Clockwise from top left: Le Pape-Georges, Upper Town; Pub St-Patrick, Upper Town; LGBT hot spot Le Drague, Saint-Jean-Baptiste and Saint-Roch.

fireplace gives a unique ambience and keeps things cozy. Fifty different beers are on tap, including local specialties like Fin-du-Monde, and bar snacks like hot dogs and nachos are also available.
MAP 2: 29 rue St-Pierre, 418/694-9176; winter daily 11am-3am, summer daily 10am-3am; no cover

Taverne Belley

Located in a hotel of the same name, Taverne Belley looks out over the marina and the farmers market. In the summer, the outdoor *terrasse* attracts everyone from office workers to cyclists looking for a refreshing drink and a rest. Opened in 1933, it also has a popular *pétanque* court just in front of the *terrasse,* to which players flock daily in the summertime. True to its name, the Belley is really all about the beer, and there are a number of imported and local microbrews available. There's also a large selection of wines and port to sip next to the fireplace as you take in the warm wintertime ambience.
MAP 2: 249 rue St-Paul, 418/692-4595; daily 8am-midnight; no cover

LIVE MUSIC
Boîtes à Chansons
★ Le Pape-Georges

It's easy to miss Le Pape-Georges, one of the best and only *boîte à chansons* bars in Vieux-Québec's Lower Town; it's hidden down a little back lane, off the popular rue Petit-Champlain. Though it calls itself a wine bar, the crowds don't come here for the selection of wines, ports, and microbrewery beers alone. They come instead for the ambience of this welcoming bar, located in a historical house built in 1790. The patrons gather around small tables and huddle up against the stone walls to hear the songs of *chansonniers* (folk singers) and jazz bands. While you listen, snack on some Québec cheese and charcuterie, or a pot-au-feu in the winter.
MAP 2: 8 rue du Cul-de-Sac, 418/692-1320; summer daily noon-3am, winter Mon.-Wed. 4pm-3am, Thurs.-Sun. noon-3am; no cover

Parliament Hill and the Plains   Map 3

BARS
L'Inox

Founded in 1987, L'Inox is the beer institution of Québec. Formerly located in the Vieux-Port, it recently moved up to the nightlife mecca of the Grande-Allée. Its new interior is modern with high ceilings and basic bar seating. In respect to the forefathers of New France, L'Inox tries to hold up the long tradition of brewing and drinking beer, which has existed in Québec since the early days of the colony. The big vats are visible at the back of the bar and patrons are more than welcome to go downstairs for a more personal visit. Come and savor a Viking or a Trouble-Fête (with

coriander and citrus flavors), brewed on the spot, and enjoy it with one of
their famous European hot dogs.

MAP 3: 655 La Grande-Allée E., 418/692-2877, www.inox.qc.ca; Apr.-Oct. daily noon-3am, Nov.-Mar. daily 3pm-3am; no cover

Le Jules et Jim

Just like the famous François Truffaut film from which it took its name, this little *bar de quartier* has become a classic. Since it's a popular neighborhood bar, the patrons are mostly locals, and there's no better place to soak up the city's authentic atmosphere. Clearly stuck on the notion of French classics, music here tends toward Edith Piaf, Jacques Brel, Georges Brassens, and the like. The low wooden tables and deep red velvet banquettes give it an added Old-World charm.

MAP 3: 1060 ave. Cartier, 418/524-9570; daily 3pm-3am; no cover

DANCE CLUBS

Le Charlotte Ultra Lounge

This club is in what used to be the attic of this grand old house, which is now a nightlife complex. It's named after former premier Maurice Duplessis's secretary, Charlotte, with whom he is suspected of having an affair—in this very attic! Québec political scandal aside, the ambience here tends toward chill, compared to the dance floor action in the main bar. Retro and pop nights are popular here. Appealing to a mid-twenties to late-thirties crowd, the interior is refined and rich with padded walls, velvet couches, and fur throws.

MAP 3: 575 La Grande-Allée, 418/647-2000, www.mauricenightclub.com; Sun.-Tues. 9pm-3am, Wed.-Sat. 8pm-3am; $5 cover

Le Dagobert

Set in a huge castle-like house on the Grande-Allée, the "Dag" as it's known has been an institution for more than 30 years. Inside there are two distinct sounds: The first floor has a rock vibe with regular live shows by cover bands, while the second floor is a full-blown club with a huge dance floor, neon lights, and a mezzanine running along its edges. It's here that you'll catch sets by some of the world's best DJs. The crowd is younger than what you'll find at Maurice, with many of them barely over the drinking age. During the summer, a line forms quickly for entrance onto the *terrasse,* so get here early to avoid it.

MAP 3: 600 La Grande-Allée E., 418/522-0393, www.dagobert.ca; daily 9pm-3am; no cover

★ Le Maurice

Le Maurice is housed in the former headquarters of the Union Nationale, a conservative political party headed by Maurice Duplessis (hence the name), which governed the province throughout the 1940s and '50s. The epicenter of a good 70 percent of the city's entire nightlife, this complex includes Le Charlotte Ultra Lounge, Voo Doo Grill, and Société Cigare. The complex's main attraction remains Le Maurice, with its immense dance floor and eclectic music, everything from electro to salsa and rock to R&B. It is a good place to lose yourself in the beat. Come winter don't miss the famous Iceothèque, the ice disco that takes up the entire front *terrasse*.

MAP 3: 575 La Grande-Allée E., 418/647-2000, www.mauricenightclub.com; Sun.-Wed. 8pm-3am, Thurs. 11pm-3am, Fri. 8:30pm-3am, Sat. 10pm-3am; $5 cover Wed.-Sat.

LIVE MUSIC
Boîtes à Chansons
Rideau Rouge

This former lounge has since transformed itself into a *boîtes à chansons*, complete with makeshift stage and stage lights bright enough to make even the most amateur of open mic performers feel like a burgeoning star. It's a few steps down into this club; luckily, there's usually a hostess waiting to usher you down from the street. Once in the club, it's all neon lights and slate walls. Chandeliers hung over the bar illuminate the suspended glasses like so many crystals. There's also ample floor space for spectators to stand and watch the show, or you can take a seat at one of the many tables that line the walls. If live music makes you hungry, you're in luck. They also have a menu populated with a variety of burgers.

MAP 3: 1147 ave. Cartier, 418/977-6843, www.rideaurouge.ca; daily 11am-10pm; free-$20 cover

Les Voûtes Napoléon

With its stone arches and low ceiling this *boîte à chansons* has a cozy albeit cave-like feel. Located in the basement of what used to be Restaurant Bonaparte (and is now the Savini), it's a great place to listen to some traditional Québécois music. The stage is so tiny, there's little room for a backup band for the singers who pass through here, so instead they're backed by a modest-sized sound system. It's busy from the moment it opens to the moment it closes, so don't be surprised if the crowd ends up singing louder than the musician. Shows usually start around 10pm.

MAP 3: 680 La Grande-Allée E., 418/640-9388, www.voutesdenapoleon.com; daily 8pm-3am; no cover

LOUNGES
★ Société Cigare

If you're nostalgic for the days when you used to be able to light up as you sipped your vintage cognac, then Société Cigare is sure to put a smile on your face. The only place in Québec City where you're allowed to smoke indoors, Société Cigare is part of the huge nightlife complex on Grande-Allée that includes Le Maurice and Voo Doo Grill. Customers can choose from a selection of over 200 brands of cigars, including Cuban Cohibas and Dominican Ashtons, from the Société's walk-in humidor. The soft lighting, all-wood bar, and leather club chairs give the bar a distinctly masculine feel. Smokers can choose from a range of scotch, port, and cognac to go with their cigars, and those with their own stogies are free to cut and light them here, as long as they get a drink to go with them.

MAP 3: 575 La Grande-Allée E., 418/647-2000; daily 1pm-3am; no cover

PUBS

Blaxton Pub and Grill

A former sports bar, Blaxton has reinterpreted itself as a classy neighborhood joint with the logo to prove it. If you want to see the game, however, this is still your best bet. Big-screen TVs are scattered throughout the wood and brick bar, which is populated with high stools and tables. Always a lively place, things get especially busy during weekday happy hours; this is an ideal spot to catch the game. The crowd tends to be younger, with most clients in their twenties or thirties. Shunning pub fare for more standard American food, they serve pizza, burgers, chicken, New York-style steaks, and ever-so-elusive chicken wings.

MAP 3: 1179 ave. Cartier, 418/522-9955, www.blaxton.com; Mon.-Fri. 11:30am-3am, Sat.-Sun. 3pm-3am; no cover

Pub Galway

This charming Irish pub in what was traditionally the English-speaking part of town is a little slice of Ireland, full of wood paneling, stained-glass windows, and smaller tables and chairs. It's not hard to imagine yourself in a country pub some 3,000 miles away. With a selection of 15 different whiskeys and over 20 different kinds of (mostly imported) beer, they also serve up pub classics like Irish poutine (it involves whiskey), fish and chips, and Irish stew with Guinness. The staff knows the regulars by name but still gives newcomers the same warm welcome.

MAP 3: 1112 ave. Cartier, 418/522-5282, www.pubgalway.com; daily 10am-3am; no cover

Saint-Jean-Baptiste and Saint-Roch

Map 4

BARS

★ La Barberie

This artisanal microbrewery started out as a small co-op in 1996 and now exports its beer to bars throughout the province. Situated in the heart of Saint-Roch, the brewery and bar—technically their tasting salon—are right next door to each other, so you know exactly where your pint is coming from. The owners, who are passionate about their beer but also dedicated and involved in the local community, made just about every inch of the bar and the rustic interior—wood tables, lots of light—to feel welcoming. First time visitors should try the tasting carousel featuring eight different draft beers. And if the weather is nice, drink them out on the sidewalk *terrasse*.

MAP 4: 310 rue St-Roch, 418/522-4373, www.labarberie.com; daily noon-1am; no cover

★ La Cuisine

Started in 2006, this brightly decorated spot with a retro feel is a daytime restaurant and nighttime hot spot. The restaurant formula goes like this: five meals per night (changing every week), all at the same price and all home-cooked. Québécois classics like *pâté chinois* and lasagna are staples on the menu, which is all made to reproduce home-cooked comfort food. Truth be told, however, most people who go to La Cuisine (The Kitchen) have likely never eaten here. It's a place to drink and dance the night away, especially among *branchée* twenty- and thirtysomethings. Music here tends toward popular indie hits and classic '80s (we're talking Blondie, Elvis Costello, the Jesus and Mary Chain) with a few Top 40 tunes thrown in for good measure.

MAP 4: 205 rue St-Vallier E., 418/523-3387, www.barlacuisine.com; Mon.-Thurs. 11am-1am, Fri. 11am-3am, Sat. 2pm-3am, Sun. 2pm-1am; no cover

Fou-Bar

Open since 1984, Fou-Bar is a veritable institution in the Faubourg Saint-Jean-Baptiste area, hosting everything from art exhibitions and vernissages to comedy nights, musical improv events, and concerts. People of all ages meet up here. Many musicians have regular nights here and the beer on tap is almost all from local breweries. Like all bars worth their weight, it also has a foosball table at the back.

MAP 4: 525 rue St-Jean, 418/522-1987, www.foubar.ca; daily 3pm-3am; no cover

Mo

In Japan, sushi bars have built-in taps that spout hot water; at Mo's in the hip Saint-Roch region, the built-in taps spout beer. This new breed of urban tavern mixes a minimalist design aesthetic—cream leather couches, geometric light fixtures—with classic cheap beers, and attracts hip young professionals and beer lovers. Local Québec brew Belle Gueule is available from the taps, and Mo stays true to its tavern roots and offers big 325-milliliter bottles of Tremblay and Labatt 50, a particularly Québec phenomenon. A large sidewalk *terrasse* is an inviting place in the summer, though sadly, no table taps here.

MAP 4: 810 blvd. Charest E., 418/266-0221, www.moresto.ca; Sun.-Tues. 11:30am-midnight, Wed.-Sat. 11:30am-1am; no cover

La Ninkasi

This two-floor bar in the middle of the action on St-Jean has a nice terrace out back with a view of the St-Matthew cemetery next door. A popular student hangout, with a boisterous vibrant atmosphere, it's dedicated to promoting Québec music and local beer, making it one of the best spots to catch emerging bands in the city. DJs take over the sound system on Thursdays and Fridays, so stop by if you're in the mood for a dance or two. With big-screen TVs, foosball, and pool tables, it's also a great place to watch hockey or any other big-time sports game.

MAP 4: 811 rue St-Jean, 418/529-8538, www.laninkasi.ca; Mon.-Fri. 2pm-3am, Sat.-Sun. noon-3am; no cover

When you order a beer in Québec, there's a decent chance the beer you're ordering hasn't traveled more than 300 kilometers—the distance between Québec City and Montréal. Even brands that after a while start to feel as commonplace as Labatt and Budweiser come from some local, Québec-owned and -run brewery. There's a proud history of beer in the province, and the more time you spend in bars, the more you notice it.

Beer has been a part of Québécois culture for as long as Québécois culture has existed. When the first colonists arrived in Québec City from France at the beginning of the 17th century, they brought with them the tradition of brewing and were soon replicating century-old production techniques in the new world. In Québec though, they replaced hops with spruce, which made the particularly tangy spruce beer. An integral part of their diet, beer was full of important vitamins and nutrients that helped the colonists fend off scurvy. By the late 1640s, the Jesuit priests, headed by brother Ambroise, were brewing their own for themselves and the community.

People carried on brewing their own throughout the colony, and it wasn't until 1671 that Intendant Jean Talon opened the Brasserie du Roi, the first brewery in Québec City. Made entirely of Québec products, it was shipped as far away as the Caribbean and Europe. After that, home brewing started to die out in the French regime for one reason or another and only started to resurface again in the late 1700s with the arrival of British rule. With the Brits came true life-long brewers who were making beer here as early as 1791.

It's this mix of British and French (as well as some Belgian) brewing techniques that makes Québec beer so unique. Each micro- and independent brewery has its own distinct flavors and blends that can be traced back to brewing practices from one tradition or another. Some well-known local breweries include: La Barberie, Microbrasserie de l'Ile d'Orléans, and L'Inox.

Le Sacrilège

This popular bar on St-Jean draws a range of clients, from *fonctionnaires* (civil servants) and drunkards in the afternoon to university students at night. Everybody mixes here for the famous 5 à 7—Québec's version of happy hour. They have a good choice of microbrewery beers on tap. Thanks to stone walls, long, almost pew-like seats, and small round tables, the entire atmosphere is welcoming and unpretentious. Out back you'll find one of the biggest and best terraces in the city. Music here tends toward rock and indie music with particular DJs taking over the decks and switching things up.

MAP 4: 447 rue St-Jean, 418/649-1985, www.lesacrilege.com; daily noon-3am; no cover

Les Salons d'Edgar

Part billiard room, part bistro, part tango club, Les Salons d'Edgar wears a number of different hats. Once a theater, it has since been converted into one of the most diverse bars in the city, though it's still the hangout of choice for established Québécois actors and up-and-coming stars. Located in the front of the house, the bistro is fairly typical with heavy velvet curtains adorning the windows and candles on each table. In the second room, however, it's a whole different story. The electric blue walls of the billiard room are in striking contrast to the restaurant, but somehow it works. The five pool tables are never free for long, so make sure to grab a drink while you wait your turn. On Sundays, from 6pm onward, it turns into a tango club for amateurs and old pros alike.

MAP 4: 263 rue St-Vallier E., 418/523-7811, www.lessalonsdedgar.com; Sept.-June Wed.-Sun. 4:30pm-2am; no cover

Scanner

This punk-edged alternative bar is quiet in the afternoon but gets wilder at night when the garage-rockers, punks, indie-kids, and rockabillies come to hang out. It's a no-nonsense bar with screens projecting videos and artwork, loud music on the stereo, arcade games, pool tables, and two different kinds of foosball—European and North American. They have some of the best-priced microbrewery beer in the city and typical Québécois snack foods like nachos and hot dogs to go with it. Bands play here most weekends—think metal, punk, country—so check the site. They also have free Wi-Fi, if you're looking for an afternoon beer but still need to get some work done.

MAP 4: 291 rue St-Vallier E., 418/523-1916, www.scannerbistro.com; Mon.-Sat. 11am-3am, Sun. 3pm-3am; no cover

★ Taverne Jos Dion

Set in the heart of the working-class district of Saint-Sauveur, Taverne Jos Dion stands as a testament to taverns of a bygone era. Opened in 1933, it is the oldest tavern in Québec and, according to some, in North America. In fact women have only been allowed since 1986, when the government forced their hand, telling them to either accept women or close. Wanting to be democratic, they put it to a vote and *les habitués* (the regulars) voted to keep the bar open, and subsequently let the women in. It remains, however, decidedly masculine and is a good place to watch sports games as well as drink your weight in beer, which is ridiculously cheap. Live accordion music is featured on Thursdays and Fridays to give it an even more authentic touch.

MAP 4: 65 rue St-Joseph W., 418/525-0710; Mon.-Sat. 8am-3am, Fri. 11am-3am, Sat. 2pm-3am, Sun. 2pm-1am; no cover

Le Temps Partiel

Run as a co-op, this is Québec City's alternative bar, as the website says: *une place différente pour des gens différents* (a different place for different people). In a past life, it was known as the Fourmi Atomique, a mythic place located in Old Québec whose walls collapsed in 2001. The bar relocated to the current location while waiting for a reconstruction that never came, hence the name Temps Partiel—it was supposed to be temporary. In many ways, the big square room with artwork occasionally on the wall still looks temporary, but the music (punk, indie, and electro), cheap beer, and alternative events like video projections, concerts, DJs, and exhibitions keep customers coming back. They also have free pool on weekends.

MAP 4: 698 rue d'Aiguillon, 418/522-1001, www.letempspartiel.com; daily
noon-3am; no cover

GAY AND LESBIAN
Bar Le St-Matthew

Two former gay bars, Taverne 321 and the 889, have come together to create
the Bar Le St-Matthew, a small, welcoming bar in Upper Town. Located on
a small side street, the gay-friendly bar is popular with both gay and straight
locals who pop in for affordable drinks. The atmosphere is laid-back with
simple decor, pool tables, and a friendly staff. During the summer, the *terrasse* is open for cocktails alfresco.

MAP 4: 889 Côte Ste-Geneviève, 418/524-5000; daily 11am-3pm; no cover

★ Le Drague

Le Drague takes up most of the real estate on this small cobblestone street
that constitutes the city's Village Gai (gay district). It's divided into four
different sections, and each area of the club has its own vibe, from the quiet
bar Verrière to the dance floor intensity of the main room, from the men-
only vibe of Zone3 to the Cabaret with almost nightly performances. The
events calendar is packed and includes weekly drag acts, karaoke, quiz
games, and country dancing. Most people, though—gays, straights, lesbi-
ans, and transsexuals—come to dance like fools to the house and Top 40
hits that blare out over the crowded dance floor.

MAP 4: 815 rue St-Augustin, 418/649-7212, www.ledrague.com; daily 10am-3am;
no cover

LIVE MUSIC
Jazz Bars
Le Largo

This Mediterranean restaurant turns into a jazz club later in the night.
Long and narrow, with floor-to-ceiling picture windows that open out onto
the street in the summer, the interior is exuberantly decorated with plush,
bright-red banquettes, blond-wood floors, and lots of light from exquisite
chandeliers. Live jazz is played here almost every night of the week, with
bigger-named musicians taking the Thursday through Saturday evening
time slot. Many of the musicians are local, but well-known bands are also
known to pass through. You don't have to eat here to enjoy the music;
those solely interested in the performance should head here around 10pm.

MAP 4: 734 rue St-Joseph, 418/529-3111, www.largorestoclub.com; daily
noon-1am; free-$20 cover

LOUNGES
★ Le Boudoir

This two-floor lounge in the heart of Saint-Roch has multiple personali-
ties, each attracting a diverse clientele. Upstairs, it's a restaurant by day
and a lounge by night; most people skip the meals, however, and come
solely for the ambience. Windows roll open in the summer onto the tiny
rue du Parvis, giving the dark bar a bit of ambient lighting when the sun

sets. Mixing the feel of a gentleman's club with 1960s futurism, the decor is distinctly modern and perfectly suited to the clientele of young professionals. Downstairs it's a different story. Called the Game Bar, it features 1980s arcade games like Pac-Man and Donkey Kong as well as foosball and darts. Wii and Playstation 3 can also be found, hooked up to a screen on the dance floor. This venue draws a younger, hipper crowd; nights here include iPod battles and DJ sets by international DJs as well as popular musicians.

MAP 4: 441 rue du Parvis, 418/524-2777, www.boudoirlounge.com; Mon.-Fri. noon-3am, Sat.-Sun. 4pm-3am; free-$20 cover

PUBS
Pub Nelligan's

A little known fact about Québec: It has quite a bit of Irish heritage. In fact, an estimated 40 percent of French-speaking Québecers have Irish ancestry, and Nelligan's is here to help celebrate that ancestry. Located on an unassuming side street, it's easy to miss the 200-year-old building that houses this cozy local. Like all Irish pubs, the atmosphere here is inviting, with the bar stools taken up by pub regulars. The decoration is fairly bare-bones, but there's no lack of wood or handwritten Jameson signs. Take a seat near the window and down pints of Irish beer to your heart's content. They've got a number of Irish brews on tap, including Guinness, Kilkenny, Smithwick's, and Harp.

MAP 4: 789 Côte Sainte-Geneviève, 418/704-7817, www.pubnelligans.ca; daily 4pm-3am; no cover

Greater Québec City

Map 5

BARS
Le Pub de l'Université Laval

If you're a student looking for a place to party, hop the bus out to Université Laval to find your kindred spirits. Barely 15 minutes by bus, Le Pub de l'Université Laval is the campus hot spot. Located in the Pavillon Alphonse-Desjardins, it has the usual student bar vibe, nondescript tables and chairs, and TVs mounted on the walls. What it lacks in ambience, however, it makes up for in cheap beer. Drink specials are available throughout the week, including weekends, when the entire bar turns into one gigantic dance floor.

MAP 5: 1312 Pavillon Alphonse-Desjardins, Cité Universitaire, Sainte-Foy, 418/656-7075, www.cadeul.ulaval.ca/pub; Mon.-Fri. 11am-2am, Sat. 5pm-2am; no cover

DANCE CLUBS
L'Ozone Laurier

Outside of the city center, close to the malls of Sainte-Foy and the campus of Université Laval, is L'Ozone. Situated in a hotel of the same name, this lounge and dance club has become a popular place thanks to a number of cool after parties—this is where the Black Eyed Peas came after their performance at Festival d'Été, and French rap group TTC has also made an appearance. Appealing to university students and twentysomething Sainte-Foy residents, the vibe is youthful and energetic. The decor is minimalist chic, with stone walls, low leather couches, and neon lights. With hip-hop, house, Top 40, and hits from the '80s and '90s on rotation, the two dance floors are always bumping when the party gets underway around 10 at night. A second Ozone can be found on the Grande-Allée (270 La Grande-Allée E., 481/529-7932, www.ozonehotelbar.com), but it is more of a bar than a club.

MAP 5: 2810 blvd. Laurier, Sainte-Foy, 418/652-2020, www.ozonehotelbar.com; daily 7pm-3am; $5-20 cover

Arts and Culture

Highlights

★ **Best Place to Get Bookish:** The library at the **Morrin Centre** is well stocked and cozy (page 106).

★ **Most Intimate Venue:** Catching a show at **Le Théâtre du Petit Champlain,** with its 140-seat capacity, means you're practically in on the act (page 108).

★ **Best Art Complex:** Home of the opera, the orchestra, the ballet, and theater company Théâtre du Trident, **Grand Théatre de Québec** is the center of all things high culture in Québec City (page 112).

★ **Best Mix of Art and Culture:** **Méduse** is a hub for all things cultural, from photography galleries to multi-disciplinary acts (page 114).

★ **Best Contemporary Gallery:** **Morgan Bridge** focuses on emerging artists whose work is often illustrative, street-inspired, and humorous (page 114).

Nowhere is the spirit of Québec culture more evident than in its arts. Though the province counts for just over 24 percent of the entire Canadian population, the cultural community is diverse and thriving. Québec City is the center for Francophone arts in the country, and the latest in theater and performing arts can be found here, as well as a strong visual arts community. There is an emphasis on homegrown talent, and though you'll often find European influences and artists, the Québec artist is championed. And why not? The culture here is so rich and unique, it doesn't need to depend on outside sources.

Since Québec is a predominantly Francophone city, English productions are rarely mounted, and it's in music, visual art, and dance that the language barriers come tumbling down. And with many of the most cutting-edge producers creating and exhibiting in cultural hot spot Méduse, you barely have to leave the building to catch it all. Once almost exclusively defined by traditional and artisinal work, the contemporary art scene has grown over the past decade. There are now a number of cool, boundary-pushing galleries that feature the more experimental works by local and international visual artists.

Tradtional arts and crafts still play a major role in the city's visual arts scene. Take the opportunity to explore the many galleries that showcase traditional Québécois and First Nations artwork, as it's some of the finest in the province.

Previous: Palais Montcalm on the Place d'Youville; Le Capitole, Upper Town.

Vieux-Québec's Upper Town

Map 1

CONCERT VENUES

Le Capitole

Opened in 1903, this playhouse retains many of the architectural charms
that made it so illustrious back then: a sweeping marble staircase, gold
trimmings, and balustrades. Originally the place to see the biggest music
hall and vaudeville acts, Le Capitole is mainly a venue for movie screen-
ings and concerts. Tributes to bands like Emerson, Lake, and Palmer
and Supertramp are popular, as are classic French singers like Charles
Aznavour. It's here that you'll also catch long-running performances like
the *Elvis Story* and *Ring of Fire* (the Johnny Cash musical), often shown
with English subtitles.

MAP 1: 972 rue St-Jean, 800/261-9903, www.lecapitole.com; $30-120

Palais Montcalm

Built in 1932, this art deco building just outside of the walls was originally
a public pool before being converted into a concert hall. After undergoing
major reconstruction in 2007, Palais Montcalm has emerged as one of the
main centers for artistic life in the city. Seating close to 1,000, this is the
home stage of chamber orchestra Les Violons du Roy (the King's Violins)
as well as the site of many jazz, classical, and world music concerts.

Along with the large auditorium, it also has a multipurpose café/the-
ater and café/bar.

MAP 1: 995 Place d'Youville, 877/641-6040, www.palaismontcalm.ca; $20-60

GALLERIES

Galerie d'Art Brousseau and Brousseau

Founder Raymond Brousseau first started collecting Inuit art in 1956 after
receiving a sculpture as a present. In 1974 he opened his first gallery, and it
has since become one of the most respected commercial galleries dealing
in Inuit art. The large, open space with carpeted floors is a blend between
store and gallery, but the aim here is to display the works in the best light
possible. Works from four specific regions (Kitikmeot, Kivalliq, Nunavik,
and Baffin) are available, each with their own style and materials. The staff
here are all expertly qualified in specific fields.

MAP 1: 35 rue St-Louis, 418/694-1828, www.sculpture.artinuit.ca; daily
9:30am-5:30pm; free

MUSEUMS

★ Morrin Centre

Military barracks, city jail, and an English college make up the past lives
of this cultural center dedicated to preserving and sharing the history of
Anglophone culture in Québec. Built during the French regime in 1712, the
original structure was used to house French troops and eventually prisoners

of war. The current neoclassical structure was built in 1808 and was the first jail in Canada based on the ideas of prison reformer John Howard. Converted in 1868, it became the first English college in the city. Today, visitors can see remnants of these histories as they tour the Victorian library and head down to the old jail cells.

MAP 1: 44 Chaussée des Écossais, 418/694-9147, www.morrin.org; Tues. noon-9pm, Wed.-Fri. and Sun. noon-4pm, Sat. 10am-4pm; tours June-Sept. Mon.-Sat. 11am and 3pm, Sun. 1:30pm; tours $9 adult, $7 student, children under 8 free

Musée Bon Pasteur

This congregation of nuns, the Good Shepherd Sisters of Québec, was established by a mother of three, Marie Fitzbach, in 1856. Started as a women's shelter, it soon became a place of refuge for marginalized women and abandoned children in the 19th and 20th centuries. Housed in a structure that was built in 1878, the museum takes up three floors. Exhibits look at the past and future of the congregation, with many personal artifacts of the founders and their predecessors as well as a trip through the trials and tribulations facing Québec women throughout the congregation's history.

MAP 1: 14 rue Couillard, 418/694-0243, www.museebonpasteur.com; Tues.-Sun. 1pm-5pm; $3 adult, $2 senior, $2 student, children 12 and under free

Musée du Fort

Situated in the shadow of the Château Frontenac, the Musée du Fort, located in a historic house, features a 30-minute multimedia show that recreates the six sieges of Québec City and the Battle of the Plains of Abraham. Other highlights include a model of the city as it was in 1759 at the time of British conquest, as well as a small exhibit of weapons, uniforms, and military badges.

MAP 1: 10 rue Ste-Anne, 418/692-2175, www.museedufort.com; Feb.-Mar. and Nov. daily 11am-4pm, Apr.-Oct. daily 10am-5pm, Dec.-Jan. closed; $8 adult, $6 senior, $6 student

Québec Experience

As the name suggests this exhibit invites you to experience the history of Québec City—but in 3D. Admittedly, the technology is in need of an update, and what was once state-of-the-art now feels like a throwback to the late-1980s. Still, if you're into a bit of kitsch (which is a must in Québec), this show presents all the major events, from the falling bridge to rifle crossfire, and real falling water.

MAP 1: 8 rue du Trésor, 418/694-4000, www.quebecexperience.com; mid-May-mid-Oct. daily 10am-10pm, mid-Oct.-mid-May daily 10am-5pm; $9.50 adult, $7 senior and student, children under 6 free

Vieux-Québec's
Lower Town

Map 2

CONCERT VENUES
L'Agora du Vieux-Port

Looking out on to the St-Lawrence River, this outdoor theater couldn't be better located. Built down into the ground, the sunken stage and raised seating give it the air of a natural amphitheater. With seating for just over 4,000 (22 reserved for wheelchairs), it is one of the largest venues in the city, and its location near the Champlain bike path means an audience of passersby. It's open throughout the summer season from June to September, and shows here include everything from rock concerts to comedy shows and have included performers like Green Day and Bill Cosby. Events are cancelled when it rains.

MAP 2: 84 rue Dalhousie, 418/691-7211, www.agoraportdequebec.ca; free-$120

★ Le Théâtre du Petit Champlain

Situated in the pretty Quartier du Petit-Champlain, this small venue was built in the mid-19th century and was originally used as a theater, but since 1994 it's become a mecca for emerging and established artists. It consists of two smaller stages: La Salle Ulric Breton, which seats 140, and the Mezzanine, which seats 90. The shows are always intimate. The exposed brick walls and balcony seating give both rooms a cozy, cavern-like atmosphere. Many popular, and cool, French-language performers play here as well as the occasional English-language band. They also host shows by the Québec Gospel Choir come the holidays (it's a lot rockier than it sounds) as well as comedy acts.

MAP 2: 68 rue du Petit-Champlain, 418/692-2631, www.theatrepetitchamplain. com; free-$25

GALLERIES
Atelier Guy Lévesque

Self-taught artist Guy Lévesque takes inspiration from traditional theater like Commedia dell'Arte, Japanese nô theater, and the Venice Carnival to create his leather masks. Using a mold technique that dates back to the Middle Ages, the masks consistently take on a personality of their own. Entering his gallery and workshop, visitors are able to see the work in process, and it gives them a better understanding of how his vision comes together. Though masks are his specialty, he also creates sculpture and chairs, mostly out of metal and leather.

MAP 2: 79 rue du Sault-au-Matelot, 418/694-1298, www.guylevesque.com; Mon.-Sat. 10am-5pm; free

Galerie Madeleine Lacerte

Housed in an old car garage on a corner lot in the Vieux-Port, Galerie Madeleine Lacerte is one of the most prominent contemporary art galleries

Open-Air Gallery Rue du Trésor

Back in the 1960s, a group of art students looking for a place to show their work got together and started hanging their pieces on the walls of a narrow alleyway not far from Château Frontenac.

Called **Rue du Trésor** (Treasure Street, www.ruedutresor.qc.ca), it is one of the oldest streets in the city and has been around for three centuries. At the time of the French regime it was along this street that the colonists would pass in order to reach the Royal Treasury, where they paid their taxes. After the British conquest, the street was no longer so important and instead served its purpose as a service alley.

In fact, when the students started using it as an open-air art gallery, it was little more than a shortcut. Today, 36 different artists exhibit their work, and some of those original students are still here, selling their picturesque watercolors of Québec City scenes or abstract etchings of something completely indefinable. What started out as a ballsy venture has turned into a popular spot for emerging and established artists to show off and sell their work. Locals and tourists alike come here looking for a little piece of the city to take home with them.

in Québec City. It was founded by Madeleine Lacerte in 1986, and her son Louis Lacerte is now the gallery director. It's dedicated to supporting Québec and Canadian artists on both national and international levels. The artists they represent are all based in Canada. Exhibits range from painting and photography to installation and conceptual pieces and feature both established and emerging artists. They continue to be on the forefront of contemporary art.

MAP 2: 1 Côte Dinan, 418/692-1566, www.galerielacerte.com; Mon.-Wed. 9am-5pm, Thurs.-Fri. 9am-6pm, Sat.-Sun. noon-6pm; free

Galeries d'Art Beauchamp and Beauchamp

Six commercial galleries make up this large collection of exhibition spaces located in the Vieux-Port. Each gallery has its own mandate, allowing for a huge variation in the types and the prices of work, as well as its own layout; some galleries have so many pieces on the walls you can barely see the wall. The galleries represent over 140 artists, particularly local ones. Both classical and contemporary works are on view here, as well as photography. Though typical closing time is 6pm, they often stay open much later in summer.

MAP 2: 10 rue du Sault-au-Matelot, 877/694-2244, www.galeriebeauchamp.com; daily 9:30am-6pm; free

MUSEUMS

Maison Chevalier

Built by trader and ship owner Jean-Baptiste Chevalier in 1752, the Maison Chevalier incorporates other buildings that date back to 1675 and 1695. A great example of early New France architecture, the house features firewalls, high chimneys, and vaulted cellars. Ravaged by fire, the house was

ARTS AND CULTURE
VIEUX-QUÉBEC'S LOWER TOWN

Top: Le Capitole, Vieux-Québec's Upper Town. **Bottom:** Rue de Tresor.

rebuilt in 1762 and was run as an inn throughout the 19th century. Inside, you'll find exposed wood beams, wide wooden floorboards, and stone fireplaces. The permanent exhibit A Sense of the Past focuses on life in the 18th and 19th centuries, and English guidebooks are available at the front desk. One weird fact: The facade, which looks out on the St-Lawrence River, was originally the back of the house.

MAP 2: 50 blvd. Champlain, 418/646-3167, www.mcq.org; Tues.-Sat. 10am-5pm; free

Musée Naval de Québec

This small museum in the Vieux-Port is dedicated to the city's naval history. The new permanent exhibit Meanders looks at the major historic events that have taken place on the river, from the first Amerindian settlements to the numerous invasion attempts by the British to the German U-boat attacks that happened in her waters.

Personal stories add a human face to the history, and objects include bows and arrows, 18th-century muskets, and a model of the hull of a World War II warship. It also hosts various traveling exhibitions.

MAP 2: 170 rue Dalhousie, 418/694-5387, www.museenavaldequebec.com; July-Aug. Tues.-Fri. and Sun. 10am-noon and 1pm-4pm, Sept.-June Tues.-Fri. 1pm-4pm; free (donations accepted)

THEATER
La Caserne Dalhousie

This center for the multidisciplinary arts was established by Robert Lepage and his creative collaborators—actors, writers, set designers, technicians, opera singers, and puppeteers—in 1997. The ultramodern venue looks almost mechanical, with visible pipes, scaffolding, and stairs. It's used primarily as a workspace for the company, called Ex Machina, to try out and create new performances. They occasionally hold public events to show off new works.

MAP 2: 103 rue Dalhousie, 418/692-5323, www.exmachina.qc.ca; cost varies

Parliament Hill and the Plains
Map 3

CINEMA
Cinéma

This repertory cinema, located above a pharmacy, might bring you back to your adolescence if you grew up watching unlikely films in unlikely places. It's devoted to screening original films that have never before been screened in Québec City, and the emphasis here is on classics, modern-day masterpieces, and of course, independent features. With 117 seats, it's intimate without being uncomfortable. English films are screened with French subtitles, but no matter the language, this place is for film buffs.

MUSEUMS
Maison Henry-Stuart

Take afternoon tea and cake in this charmingly authentic 19th-century cottage. Built in 1849 for Mrs. William Henry, the wife of a rich wood merchant, the house today is found on one of the biggest boulevards in the city, but inside it has retained its elegant and rich decor. Tours of the garden and house give visitors an idea of what life was like for well-to-do English families in Québec at the turn of the 20th century, and tea time is part of the hour-long tour.

MAP 3: 82 La Grande-Allée W., 418/647-4347, www.actionpatrimoine.ca; tours mid-June-early Sept. daily on the hour 11am-4pm; $8 adult, $3 child 6-12

THEATER
★ Grand Théatre de Québec

The largest arts complex in Québec City, the Grand Théatre was built to commemorate the country's centennial in 1967. Designed by Montréal-based architect Victor Prus, the large concrete structure opened in 1971. Home to the Québec Symphony Orchestra, l'Opéra de Québec, and the Théâtre du Trident, it's here that most large-scale performances happen, whether it's a dance piece by the Ballet du Québec, a rock extravaganza like Jason Bonham's Led Zeppelin Experience, or a concert by Québec indie rock kings Karkwa.

MAP 3: 269 blvd. René-Lévesque E., 877/643-8131, www.grandtheatre.qc.ca; $20-120

Saint-Jean-Baptiste and Saint-Roch   Map 4

CONCERT VENUES
Le Cercle

Not only does Le Cercle serve up a mean meal and cool bar atmosphere, but it's also the place where you'll find the coolest music shows. This St-Roch staple is all concrete floors, high ceilings, great acoustics, and even better acts. If you want to dance the night away to the sounds of Berlin's latest electro sensation, this is your destination. Since it's one of the few places to catch new music in the city, it's become quite popular. Get your tickets ahead of time and if you want a decent view, arrive early. In addition to live music, they also host a number of film and art events.

MAP 4: 228 rue St-Joseph E., 418/948-8648, www.le-cercle.ca; $10-30

Impérial de Québec

This theater and concert hall in Saint-Roch has a long history. Originally the site of the neighborhood's cemetery, this was a factory before becoming a theater with a second-floor art gallery in 1912. Rebuilt under new

ownership in 1917, in the style that was popular at the time—a flat, square
marquee, and the Imperial's sign illuminated and protruding from the
center of the building—it's this facade that still exists and is one of the few
theaters in Québec that recall the golden age of silent films. Inside, the
old-time charm remains, with balustrades adorned with winged cherubs
and moldings framing the stage. It's a midsize venue; bands like Gwar and
Broken Social Scene have hit the stage along with cabaret acts and the occasional movie screening.

MAP 4: 252 rue St-Joseph E., 418/523-2227, www.imperialdequebec.com; $15-50

GALLERIES

Centre Materia

This artist-run center is dedicated to the field of fine crafts. With an aim
to broaden the public's familiarity with and recognition of this art form,
they host a number of openings and exhibits by diverse artists, everything
from glasswork to textiles. Both emerging and established artists exhibit
here, but unlike conventional galleries, Materia doesn't represent the individual artists. Located in a bright, open space on the busy boulevard
Charest, the gallery has an industrial feel with white walls and exposed
pipes and ceiling beams.

MAP 4: 395 blvd. Charest E., 418/524-0354, www.centremateria.com; Wed. and
Fri.-Sun. noon-5pm; Thurs. noon-8pm; free

Galerie d'art Factory

Representing both established and emerging local talent, Factory has a
distinctly contemporary edge, in both the artwork hanging on its walls
and in the surroundings themselves. Large picture windows showcase the
many large-scale works suspended in front of rough brick walls above a
polished concrete floor. A pristine white couch located in the middle of the
room invites visitors to linger and contemplate the metal sculptures and
day-glo paintings. It's also perfect for lounging and sipping during one of
the gallery's vernissages.

MAP 4: 837 rue St-Joseph E., 418/561-2558, www.galeriefactory.com; Wed. and
Sat.-Sun. noon-5pm; Thurs.-Fri. noon-8pm; free

Le Lieu

Situated in Saint-Roch, this artist-run center was established in 1982 and
focuses on multidisciplinary arts. The floor-to-ceiling windows of the
sparse space look out onto the street—perfect for catching the attention
of passersby. Le Lieu works with artists both at home and abroad, and
the contemporary work shown here focuses on practices like installation,
performance, and audio and visual art. It's often quite conceptual. It's rare
that you'll see a painting hanging on these walls. They also host Rencontre
Internationale d'Art Performance (RAIP), a yearly international festival
dedicated to performance art.

MAP 4: 345 rue du Pont, 418/529-9680, www.inter-lelieu.org; daily 1pm-5pm;
free

★ Méduse

Established in 1995, Méduse is an arts complex filled with galleries, studios, and offices dedicated to arts and culture. Made up of linked buildings, some of them modern, others refurbished historical structures, it's the home of 10 different businesses, from a radio station to art galleries. L'œil de Poisson, which exhibits contemporary works, and VU, the only gallery in the city dedicated to contemporary photography, are always worth checking out. Dance company La Rotonde often performs in the center's *salle multi*. This hub has become integral to all forms of the city's contemporary arts scene, and if you want to check out a specific space, check the times before you leave since they often vary.

MAP 4: 541 rue St-Vallier E., 418/640-9218, www.meduse.org; Wed.-Sun. noon-5pm; free

★ Morgan Bridge

Morgan Bridge takes the idea of what we perceive an art gallery to be and turns it on its head. With a strong connection to graffiti and skateboard culture—spray paint is sold in the gallery, along with zines, and many of the artworks are created on skate decks—the work is subversive, exciting, and out of the ordinary. It's not all street art though; throughout the space you'll find art naïf and work that tows the line between graphic and street art. In short, this is where you'll find the work of emerging underground artists in Québec.

MAP 4: 367 rue du Pont, 418/529-1682, www.morganbridge.ca; Wed. and Fri. noon-6pm, Thurs. noon-7pm, Sat.-Sun. noon-5pm; free

THEATER

Théatre La Bordée

Established in 1976 by a group of young actors directly out of theater school, this independent theater company situated in Saint-Roch mounts four productions a year. Walking the line between classical and experimental, their aim is to produce excellent theater that is also accessible to a large public. They focus on plays from Québec, but there is also a variety in their programs, and past seasons have included productions of Shakespeare's *Richard III*, Dumas' *Le Reine Margot*, and *The Pillowman* by Irish playwright Martin McDonagh. Consisting of two presentation halls, an Italian-style theater that seats 350 and one that seats 60, the settings are decidedly intimate. All productions are in French.

MAP 4: 315 rue St-Joseph E., 418/694-9721, www.bordee.qc.ca; $35 adult, $30 senior, $25 under 30

Greater Québec City Map 5

CINEMA
Le Clap

If you can get past the unfortunate name, Le Clap is a great repertory cinema that plays films that don't always get wide distribution in the province. It plays English movies with French subtitles. Fans of international and art-house cinema will enjoy their selection of festival hits from festivals like Cannes, TIFF, and Festival Nouveau Cinéma. With none of the bells and whistles you find at bigger name cinemas, the smaller auditoriums and intimate setting aren't for everyone.

MAP 5: 2360 chemin Ste-Foy, 418/653-2470, www.clap.qc.ca; $12 adult, $9 senior and student, $8 child

Sports and Activities

Québec City was blessed with huge green spaces, a waterfront, and a cliff face perfect for scaling. In fact, the city is so hilly that sometimes even a trip to the local store can feel like a hike. Blame the instense inclines, the promise of mountains looming to the north, and the beauty of one of the world's largest rivers. This is city that embraces its proximity to nature. Quebeckers are no strangers to the sporting goods store and they bring their partiuclar love of sports, like canoeing and skiing, to an urban environment.

Québec has a strong connection to the outdoors, even when the ground is buried under four feet of snow. Cross-country skiing and snowshoeing are part of getting around in the city. What better way to see the historical sights than skiing from one place to the next? There's no shortage of outdoor skating rinks, many of which are frozen rivers and ponds. Ice-skating is an idyllic and truly Canadian pastime. Not far from the city center are a number of mountains, pefect for exploring with snowboards and downhill skis.

The city is on one of the largest waterways in North America, so boating is a popular sport, and in summer the St-Lawrence is dotted with white sails and even the occasional sea kayak.

Though it's one of the hilliest cities in Canada, Québec City is also home to two of the longest bike paths in the country, running alongside the river; a trip down the Promenade Champlain is like a mini-break from the city. And, of course, come winter the bike path becomes one of the best ski trails.

Previous: Québec City skyline; Parc du Musée, Parliament Hill. **Next:** Parc des Plaines d'Abraham.

Highlights

★ **Best Winter Sledding:** At 250 meters high, the **Glissades de la Terrasse Dufferin** is the biggest (and only) winter slide in Québec City; speeding from the top down to the *terrasse* at speeds of up to 70 kilometers per hour has been a tradition since 1884 (page 119).

★ **Best Bike Path:** Running alongside the St-Lawrence River and through Cap Blanc and various parks, **Corridor du Littoral** is a great path for exercise and to see some of the lesser-known parts of the city (page 120).

★ **Best Place for Snow Sports:** With everything from cross-country skiing to ice-skating and snowshoeing available, **Parc des Plaines d'Abraham** is your outdoor sports paradise (page 122).

★ **Best Place to Have a Picnic:** Once the grounds of the governor-general's residence, **Parc du Bois-de-Coulonge** boasts groomed gardens and amazing views of the St-Lawrence that are still worthy of royalty (page 125).

★ **Best Summer Activity:** Nothing says summer like a game of baseball. **Les Capitales de Québec** are among the best in the Can-Am league (page 126).

Vieux-Québec's
Upper Town

Map 1

BOAT TOURS
Croisière Dufour

This company offers two different cruises in and around Québec. La Touristique is a 90-minute historical tour that will take visitors from the Vieux-Port along the coast of the Île d'Orléans and Montmorency Falls and allows for waterfront views of Château Frontenac and Cap Diamant. The Image Mill cruise allows you to take in Le Moulin à Images multimedia event from the water; with panoramic windows and three terraces, it gives you a different take on the spectacle. They also offer longer cruises into the Charlevoix region to see the whales and the fjords.

MAP 1: 57 rue Ste-Anne, 800/463-5250, www.dufour.ca; May-Oct. daily 1:30pm, mid-July-mid-Aug. daily 1:30pm and 3:30pm; $64 adult, $59 senior and student, $29 child, children under 6 free for 90-minute cruise

ICE-SKATING
Patinoire de la Place d'Youville

Located directly in front of the Palais de Montcalm, this outdoor skating rink is a veritable winter wonderland once the snow has settled. A great place to bring the kids, it is frequented by tourists and locals alike who want to go for a skate in the shadow of the old city walls. Skate rental and sharpening are available during opening hours, as is a warm changing room fitted out with lockers, but visitors have to bring their own padlock.

MAP 1: 995 Place d'Youville, 418/641-6256; late Oct.-mid-Mar. Mon.-Thurs. noon-10pm, Fri.-Sat. 10am-10pm; free

MINIATURE GOLF
Golf Touristique de Québec

Sign in at the clubhouse to receive your specialized club and ball before hitting the Upper Town links. A way of combining history with golf, this nine-hole course (rumor has it, it's a par 4) has you teeing off at various points around the city's fortifications (which are for the most part covered in grass), through its historic back streets, and even up along the walls of the Citadelle. A round takes approximately two hours and the course is open come rain or shine.

MAP 1: Parc-de-l'Artillerie, 2 rue d'Auteuil, 418/977-2453, www.golftouristique. com; June-Sept. daily 10am-5pm; $15 adult, $13 senior, $13.50 youth, children under 8 free

SLEDDING
★ Glissades de la Terrasse Dufferin

This entertainment of sliding down a steep 250-meter run at speeds of up to 70 kilometers per hour has been around since 1884. The Glissades de la Terrasse Dufferin (*les glissades*) are a Québec tradition. In front of the

Château Frontenac, with great views of the St-Lawrence, families line up in full winter regalia to ride a toboggan down to the base of the wooden structure. Up to four people can ride down on a single toboggan, though you're also allowed to try it solo and in pairs. A mini-sugar shack full of refreshments is available on the spot. Lines can be long, especially on weekends, so be prepared to wait.

MAP 1: Terrasse Dufferin, at rue des Carrières and Place d'Armes, 418/829-9898; mid-Dec.-mid-Mar. daily 11am-11pm; $2 pp per ride

SWIMMING
Parc de l'Esplanade
This children's wading pool is in the heart of Vieux-Québec's Upper Town. Situated in the shadow of the Fortifications, the wading pool is simple, with hardly any bells and whistles; still, it's the perfect place to let the kids cool off and let off some steam in the middle of the day. A children's playground can be found just a little further along.

MAP 1: Parc des Plaines d'Abraham, 418/523-5695; mid-June-mid-Aug. daily 11am-4pm; free

Vieux-Québec's Lower Town
Map 2

BIKING
Bike Paths
★ Corridor du Littoral
This 48-kilometer bike path stretches all the way from Saint-Augustin-de-Desmaures west of Québec City way to Chute Montmorency to the east. Running alongside the St-Lawrence, the path includes the Promenade Samuel Champlain; redone for the city's 400th anniversary in 2008, this section of the path is located below the Plains of Abraham and includes various parks and rest stops. It takes you along Cap Blanc, a charming working-class area built directly against the cliff.

Though it's mainly a bike path, runners, walkers, in-line skaters, and those in wheelchairs are free to use the path for both recreation and mobility. Open throughout the year, it becomes an ideal place to snowshoe and cross-country ski in winter.

MAP 2: St-Augustin-de-Desmaures to Chute Montmorency, 418/641-6290, www.routeverte.com; free

Bike Rentals and Tours
Cyclo Services
Offering both rentals and tours, Cyclo Services has different types of bikes on offer, including hybrids, road bikes, tandem, and children's bikes. All rentals come with a helmet, lock, and a map. Located across the street from the Corridor du Littoral, it couldn't be easier to jump on your bike and go. Five bike tours are available throughout the summer season; some, like the

one through Lower Town and the Vieux-Port, stay closer to home, while others, like Huron-Wendake, take you farther afield. Prices vary and times change often, so call or email ahead. For those with their own wheels, an on-site mechanic is available seven days a week.

MAP 2: 289 rue St-Paul, 418/692-4052, www.cycloservices.net; daily 9am-9pm; tours May-Oct. 9am-9pm; $35 per day

Écolocyclo

Located at the Marché du Vieux-Port, Écolocyclo is perfectly situated on the Corridor du Littoral, the longest bike path in the city. The majority of their rental fleet bikes are mountain and city bike hybrids, with at least 21 speeds, perfect for those steep Québec streets. They also offer electric bikes to help give your pedaling a bit of a push, as well as tandems, trail-a-bikes for children, and recumbent bikes for those who want to give laid-back riding a try. Though they don't offer tours, they will give you suggested routes to try, and all of their bikes are available for rentals of up to three days, at reasonable prices—perfect for getting around.

MAP 2: Marché du Vieux-Port, 160 Quai St-André, 418/692-2517, www.ecolocyclo. net; May-Oct. daily 9am-6pm; $17-45/hour

BOAT TOURS

Croisière AML

Cruises are available on the *Louis Jolliet,* a restaurant boat that can take you as far north as the Charlevoix region. Divided into day and night cruises, options include the brunch cruise with activities for kids, a tour of Île d'Orléans, a fireworks cruise, and a five-course dinner cruise. The captain's lounge, three dining rooms, and terraces are on board as well as a gift shop and a bistro. Entertainment is part of every cruise and guide Louis Jolliet—an early Canadian explorer—will reveal all the area's secrets. An orchestra plays in the evenings; passengers can dance the night away.

MAP 2: Quai Chouinard, 10 rue Dalhousie, 866/856-6668, www.croisieresaml. com

Croisières Coudrier

Departing from the Vieux-Port, Croisières Coudrier offers some unique and interesting tours. Many of the cruises are also educational. Learn about Québec's own Ellis Island, Grosse-Île, a quarantine station between 1832 and 1937 and the home of Irish immigrants; passengers will have a chance to visit the island. Or experience the charms of Isle-aux-Grues by bike and taste their well-known cheese. Apple-picking and five-course dinner cruises are also available, as is a sightseeing tour, which lets you see the city from the river.

MAP 2: Bassin Louise, Pier 19, 180 rue Dalhousie, 888/600-5554, www. croisierescoudrier.qc.ca; May-mid-Oct. Sat.-Sun. 1:30pm, July-Aug. daily 3:30pm; $32 adult, $30 senior and student, $15 child, children under 5 free for 90-minute cruise

GYMS

Planète Fitness Gym

This 24-hour gym is open seven days a week and offers à la carte memberships that allow up to 10 visits. Longer memberships are available for three months up to a year. Along with a weight and cardio room, they also offer a number of classes, including crossfit, spinning, and toning, many of which start as early as seven in the morning.

MAP 2: 400 blvd. Jean-Lesage, 418/523-0284, www.planetefitnessgym.qc.ca; daily 24 hours

Parliament Hill and the Plains

Map 3

CROSS-COUNTRY SKIING AND SNOWSHOEING

★ Parc des Plaines d'Abraham

Come winter, this historical sight becomes an outdoor sport paradise. For beginners and pros, the 12.6 kilometers of cross-county trails and the 3.8-kilometer (round-trip) trails for snowshoers are the best place to experience winter in the city's own backyard. Four classic trails, made up of one easy trail and three intermediate ones, are open. Those without their own equipment—boots, poles, skis, and snowshoes—can rent them from the Discovery Pavilion. A waxing room and two heated rest areas are available around the plains, and they also offer cross-country ski lessons.

MAP 3: Discovery Pavilion, 835 rue Wilfrid-Laurier (equipment rental), 418/648-2586, www.ccbn-nbc.gc.ca; late Dec.-mid-Mar. daily 8:30am-4pm; free

ICE-SKATING

Parc du Musée

This outdoor skating rink, directly in front of the Musée des Beaux-Arts and right on the Plains of Abraham, is a great place to bring the kids. Easily accessible and popular with locals, it was completely renovated in 2011. Skaters should bring their own skates and equipment, since there are no rental facilities on the premises.

MAP 3: Parc des Champs-de-Bataille; late Oct.-mid-Mar. daily 11am-6pm; free

SWIMMING

Piscine Parc du Musée

Located on the Plains of Abraham, this public pool and wading pool were renovated in 2011, giving them a brand new look. Conveniently located right on the Grande-Allée, it's easily accessible from all points in the city. A haven for locals, this is a great place to bring the kids, especially to let them go a little wild after an afternoon at the museum.

MAP 3: Parc des Champs-de-Bataille; mid-June-mid-Aug. daily noon-7pm; free

YOGA

Ashtanga Yoga Québec

A number of different types and levels of classes are available at this
Ashtanga yoga studio located in a local community center. Guided classes
are available for beginners to intermediate and for regular practitioners.
Courses run throughout the day, seven days a week, typically starting at
6:30am and ending at 7:30pm. Those already comfortable with their yoga
and just looking for a place to practice are welcome to drop in; there are
free practice times available throughout the week.

MAP 3: Centre Culture et Environnement Frédéric Back, 870 ave. de Salaberry,
418/682-0654, www.ashtangaquebec.com; Mon.-Sat. hours vary by season; $16
per class for nonmembers

Greater Québec City   Map 5

AMUSEMENT PARKS

Mega Parc des Galeries de la Capitale

A child's paradise, this amusement park in the middle of a mall is designed
for toddlers through tweens. Twenty different rides are waiting for kids
to take them for a whirl, from physical fun like the Magic Castle's ball
pit, slides, and rope games and the Baby Jungle's plush obstacle course to
more traditional fairway staples like mini-bumper cars, a miniature train,
a merry-go-round, Ferris wheel, and a rollercoaster. For kids wanting a bit
more sport, there's also a climbing wall, an ice rink, and mini-putt. Each
ride requires a varying number of tokens, anywhere from two to six, with
each token costing 50 cents.

MAP 5: 5401 blvd. des Galeries, 418/627-5800, www.mega-parc.com;
Sept.-mid-June Mon.-Wed. noon-5pm, Thurs.-Fri. noon-9pm, Sat. 9:30am-5pm,
Sun. 11am-5pm; mid-June-Aug. Mon.-Wed. 10am-5pm, Thurs.-Fri. 10am-9pm, Sat.
9:30am-5pm, Sun. 11am-5pm

BIKING

Bike Paths

Corridor des Cheminots

Intersecting with the Corridor du Littoral just outside Saint-Roch, the
Corridor des Cheminots is 22 kilometers long and takes riders from the
city to Haute Saint-Charles in the north. Since it passes through various
areas, including the St-Charles River and Wendake Village, riders can view
a diverse landscape. Open to cyclists, walkers, runners, and inline skaters,
it becomes a popular place for cross-country skiing and snowshoeing in
the winter.

MAP 5: North of Estuaire de la Riviere St-Charles to Haute Saint-Charles,
418/641-6412, www.routeverte.com; free

CLIMBING

Le Champlain and Le Pylône

For experienced climbers only, this natural climbing wall can be accessed from rue Champlain. Located just outside of the city, near the Pont de Québec, are two cliffs perfect for climbing. This outdoor climbing area is a popular place with local climbers and caters to both learners and intermediate climbers. Le Pylône is the beginner area with 5.8 routes, while Le Champlain, 30 feet high by 200 feet long with lots of overhanging routes, is great for experts. Known as the "School of Rock," it's a great place to practice, especially since the rock face is made up of difficult gritstone.

MAP 5: Near Pont de Québec

Roc Gyms

Opened in 1993, Roc Gyms is a climbing school that offers indoor climbing lessons. Over 75 climbing lines are available in the main room, while two bouldering rooms are also available on-site, as are a number of indoor aerial courses. Those that are already experienced climbers can sign up for courses in outdoor and ice-climbing. Located in Limoilou, it's easily accessible from downtown and Vieux-Port.

MAP 5: 2350 ave. du Colisée, 418/647-4422, www.aventurex.net; Mon.-Sat. 10am-10pm, Sun. 10am-6pm; $18 day rental with equipment

GOLF

La Tempête

Situated across the water in the city of Lévis, La Tempête is one of the top courses in the metropolitan area (of course, the green fees reflect this). It hosted the World Skins tournament in 2009 and has been called the first 18-hole golf course of international caliber in the area. Designed by golf architect Darrell J. Huxham, the 7,203-yard course is topped with a luxurious clubhouse and high-class restaurant.

MAP 5: 51 rue des Trois Manoirs, Lévis, 418/832-8111, www.golflatempete.com; May-Nov. daily dawn-10pm; $95-155 for 18 holes

ICE-SKATING

Pointe-aux-Lièvres

When the St-Charles River, which separates Saint-Roch from Limoilou, freezes over, it becomes a natural skating rink, measuring 1.5 kilometers long. It's here that you'll find people playing pickup hockey and families teaching the youngest members how to skate. If you want a real Canadian experience, there's nothing like plopping your bum on a cold park bench to lace up your skates. Of course, a warm changing room and heated pavilion with hot chocolate and skate rental are also available.

MAP 5: 5 rue de la Pointe-aux-Lièvres, 418/641-6345; late Oct.-mid-Mar. daily 24 hours; free

Domaine Maizerets

Situated just across the St-Charles River, Domaine Maizerets is both a public park and a historic site. Bought by the church in 1705, the land served as a farm and some of the church's old buildings are still standing. Tours of the beautifully landscaped gardens and arboretum are available, and concerts are often held on the park grounds. Two bike trails, Corridor des Cheminots and Corridor du Littoral, cut through the park, and in the winter it's a popular place for skating, cross-country skiing, snowshoeing, and tobogganing.

MAP 5: 1248 ave. de la Verendrye, 418/660-7357, www.domainemaizerets.com; free

Parc Cartier-Brébeuf

South of Saint-Roch, this national historic site commemorates both the winter of 1535, when Jacques Cartier and his shipmates spent the season near the Iroquoian village of Stadacona, and the site of the Jesuit missionaries' first home in Québec. Commemorative monuments are set up around the park, which is divided into east and west by a small river. With 6.8 hectares, it's a popular place for outdoor sport and a bike path cuts through most of it. An interpretation center is open on-site from early May to early September, offering guided tours and various family activities.

MAP 5: 175 rue l'Espinay, 888/773-8888, www.pc.gc.ca; free

Parc de la Plage Jacques-Cartier

Located outside of the city, just on the other side of the Québec Bridge, this waterfront park gives visitors direct access to the St-Lawrence River. The winding paths and roads that take you to the shore, coupled with the boulders and pebbles that line the beach, make you feel as though you're somewhere else entirely. Since swimming is prohibited, boating is the summer's most popular sport, along with the 2.5 kilometers of hiking trails.

MAP 5: 3636 chemin de la Plage Jacques-Cartier, Ste-Foy, 418/641-6300; May-Oct.; free

★ Parc du Bois-de-Coulonge

The former home of the governor-general of United Canada, Spencer Wood was bought by the Québec government in 1870 and was home to the province's lieutenant-governors until 1966. Though a fire destroyed the main residence, the splendid gardens remain, including a park that runs along the St-Lawrence, offering great views of the city. The park is a favorite for picnicking, self-guided tours, and its three kilometers of hiking trails. There's also a children's playground and sledding in winter.

MAP 5: 1215 Grande-Allée W., 800/442-0773; free

Parc Linéaire de la Rivière St-Charles

Starting at the Vieux-Port and running on for a total of 32 kilometers, this park runs along the banks of the St-Charles River, covering both urban and natural environments. Open year long, it has 4 kilometers of bike and rollerblade paths, ice-skating, snowshoeing, and 10 kilometers of cross-country skiing in winter. An interpretation center is located in the middle of the park.

MAP 5: 332 rue Domagaya, 418/691-4710, www.societerivierestcharles.qc.ca; free

Parc Victoria

Situated at the southern tip of Saint-Roch on the banks of the St-Charles River, Parc Victoria has been one of the few green spaces in the area since 1897. Almost completely surrounded by water, the small park was named after Britain's Queen Victoria. It provides excellent views of the river and it's here that you'll catch a baseball game by Les Capitales de Québec.

MAP 5: Rue Robert-Rumilly, 418/641 6654; free

SPECTATOR SPORTS
Baseball
★ Les Capitales de Québec

Members of the Can-Am Baseball League, Les Capitales are one of the most successful teams in the league. Making the playoffs almost every year since they entered the league in 1999, they garnered league titles in 2006, 2009, and 2010.

They play at the Stade Municipal, which seats approximately 5,000 and is located in Parc Victoria. The stadium opened in 1938 and has a long history within local baseball legend. This rich history and the affordable tickets ($10, $15 box seats) give you the feeling that you're still in touch with what sports used to be and should be.

MAP 5: Stade Municipal, Parc Victoria, 418/521-2255, www.capitalesdequebec.com

Football
Le Rouge et Or

This university football team has amassed a strong following in a city craving more spectator sports. Le Rouge et Or (the Red and the Gold, which are the school colors) won the Vanier Cup, the highest distinction for a Canadian university football team, four times in six years (2003, 2004, 2006, and 2008). They also hold the record for the longest winning streak in Canadian Interuniversity Sport football with 19 consecutive wins. If you happen to be visiting in the fall, a trip to Sainte-Foy to see a game is worth it; the bleachers are always packed and the energy is palpable.

Université Laval's outdoor stadium can hold up to 10,000 spectators it but fit double that in 2005 with standing room only. Their loyal fan base has also mastered the art of tailgating, getting to the stadium parking lot early on game day mornings.

MAP 5: PEPS de l'Université Laval, 2300 rue de la Terrasse, 418/656-7377, www.rougeetor.ulaval.ca

Remparts de Québec

Ever since they won the Memorial Cup (the Canadian Junior Championships) in 2006, the Remparts, Québec's Major Junior Hockey team, have become the hottest show in town. And things will probably stay that way so long as this crazy-about-hockey city doesn't have an NHL team. Their home rink is the Colisée Pepsi, the former home of les Nordiques (RIP), which moved to Colorado in 1995.

They're coached by former goalie Patrick Roy, considered one of the best goalies in the history of the game. Roy, who ranks with Celine Dion as far as Québec hero hierarchy goes, brings a colorful edge to the team. Famous Remparts alumni include legendary player Guy Lafleur, ex-Nordiques Michel Goulet, left-winger Simon Gagné, center Mike Ribeiro, and right-winger Alexander Radulov.

MAP 5: Colisée Pepsi, 250 blvd. Wilfrid-Hamel, 418/525-1212, www.remparts. qc.ca

WATER SPORTS

Baie de Beauport

A world of boating fun is only a five-minute drive from downtown Québec City. Though swimming in the river is forbidden, a ton of boating and beach activities make you feel like you're on the coast. Canoe, kayak, sailboard, dinghy, and catamaran rentals are offered at various rates and lengths, and those looking to learn how to sail can sign up for classes. Beach soccer and volleyball courts are free for all to use and the large children's park keeps the kids busy.

MAP 5: Eastern end of blvd. Henri-Bourassa, 418/266-0722, www. baiedebeauport.com; mid-June-mid-Aug. daily 10am-9pm

Québec has a long history with commerce. As the site of the first settlement in New France, its entire founding was based on trade with the Amerindians, and as the colony grew, trade became vital to its survival. Its genetic makeup as a commercial city is still apparent, and over the centuries it has created some of Canada's most recognized stores and brands.

Many of those same stores exist today. Holt Renfrew, La Maison Simons, and J. A. Moisan (the oldest grocery store in North America) are businesses that first bloomed in Québec and whose rich past can still be seen when you enter their establishments.

With all that history, however, it's important to have something new, and the revival of rue St-Joseph in Saint-Roch has been one of the most important developments of the past few years. The area was abandoned by businesses that opted for the malls of the late 1950s, but new customers and retailers are now emerging in the area. Filled with young, modern stores and independent boutiques, it has given the city a much-needed boost of cool. Rue St-Jean, outside of the walls, is experiencing a similar rejuvenation, with youthful stores popping up, many with an eye on local products and design.

Unlike most major Canadian cities, when it comes to the downtown core, Québec sticks to its roots. Here, stores like H&M, Gap, and Zara are relegated to the malls, about a 15-minute drive away. Though some chains can be found (mostly in Upper Town), they are few and far between. Instead, the historic houses and beautiful Beaux-Arts buildings are small independent boutiques or established businesses.

Highlights

★ **Best Hat Store: Bibi et Compagnie** has approximately 3,000 men's and women's hats for all kinds of weather and in all kinds of styles (page 135).

★ **Unique Gifts:** Connoisseur of kitsch, Mr. Blouin carries everything from old milk jugs to vintage magazines at the cabinesque **Magasin Général P.L. Blouin** (page 138).

★ **Best Store for Romantic Gifts: Pont Briand Joallier** has a number of beautiful, handcrafted pieces perfect for that special someone (page 139).

★ **Best Artisanal Crafts:** Carrying the work of over 125 local artisans, **Boutique des Métiers d'Art** is a perfect one-stop shop for everything from jewelry to salad bowls (page 140).

★ **Best Place to Rock:** If you're a fan of rock, specifically garage, punk, hardcore, and indie, and specifically on vinyl, then **Le Knock-Out** has got you covered (page 149).

★ **Best Toy Store:** Parents can let kids run wild and kids can let parents do the same at toy emporium **Benjo** (page 150).

★ **Most Accommodating:** Located in a former bank, women's boutique **Esther P** not only carries a number of stylish lines, but has a couch on hand for weary shoppers (page 150).

★ **Best Selection of Local Designers:** Dedicated to local designers, **Jupon Pressé** exclusively carries lines from some of the province's most exciting emerging designers and does it with some fun in a bright, eclectic boutique (page 151).

★ **Best Design:** Known for its cutting-edge, sartorial choices, menswear boutique **Philippe Dubuc,** with its mirrored walls, high ceiling, and austere displays, is the last word in cool (page 152).

★ **Best Outdoor Gear:** If you're headed for an outdoor adventure, **Mountain Equipment Co-op** has everything from bike gear to arctic sleeping bags to get you ready (page 156).

There are independent jewelry stores throughout Québec City. Rue Petit-Champlain has a good mix of high-end and more artsy offerings. In fact, these are the two main kinds of jewelry stores found all over the city: super kitsch costume jewelry and high-end designer pieces. One thing that remains the same in upscale or costume jewelry is that it's all handcrafted.

If you're on the hunt for antiques, look no further than the narrow cobblestone rue St-Paul, where just about every other store is dedicated to antiques. If you're looking for something specific, it's best to pop into them all. Just about every single store is stocked full of everything from antique bedposts to silverware.

Though Québec doesn't have crafts in the traditional sense, there is a certain aesthetic found in the various artisanal works. A mix of materials is one element, as is an unexpected juxtaposition of colors and shapes. Inuit art, though not exclusive to the province, can also be found in a number of arts and craft shops, since northern Québec is home to many native and Inuit tribes.

If you're looking for a relaxing massage or facial, look no further than your hotel: Most have exquisite facilities. For those that don't, there are a few spas within the city that offer everything from quick therapeutic massages to daylong adventures in pampering.

English books are hard to come by in Québec City. Although most hotels carry a few national and international English-language papers, finding anything more than a bestseller can be tough. Magazines, however, are much easier to find, and both European and North American versions are readily available.

If you want to pick up some vintage Félix Leclerc after an inspiring night at a *boîte à chansons,* head along rue St-Jean, where you'll find both new and used vinyl and CDs. The implosion of the record industry has been tough on Québec's independent music stores, but a few gems remain.

Many of the stores that line the streets of Vieux-Québec's Upper and Lower Town cater to tourists. Though many of them strive to have their own personality, a lot blend into one another. The stores included in this chapter, however, all offer something a bit different and less well known.

It's not surprising that in a city so defined by its food, its best markets revolve around farmers and fresh produce. And though winters can be harsh, the farmers markets keep going all year long.

Québec City spends at least six months out of the year under snow, so that may explain why there are two stores dedicated entirely to Christmas decorations. Situated kitty-corner to each other, snowy landscape or not, these places are packed even in the summer.

In high tourist season during the summer, boutiques in Upper and Lower Town stay open late, some even as late as midnight, if the crowds are still out. In winter, stores often close early, or for months at a time, depending on the nature of their business. If there's a store you particularly want to visit, it's always best to call ahead, especially in the off-season.

SHOPS

Vieux-Québec's
Upper Town

Map 1

ACCESSORIES AND JEWELRY

Zimmermann

Having studied jewelry design and gemology in Paris, Michel Zimmermann returned to Québec in the late 1970s to open his very own jewelery shop. Zimmermann's has since become one of the most respected jewelers in the business, known for unique handcrafted gems. The pieces are all meticulously handcrafted without the use of any cast, working exclusively with 925/1000 silver and 18-carat gold or platinum. Styles vary from simple, leaf-shaped earrings to detailed wedding bands and teardrop birthstone pendants.

MAP 1: 46 Côte de la Fabrique, 418/692-2672, www.zimmermann-quebec.com; Mon.-Wed. and Sat. 9:30am-5:30pm, Thurs.-Fri. 9:30am-9pm

ARTS AND CRAFTS

Boutique Canadeau

Situated in the heart of Vieux-Québec's Upper Town, this small boutique located in a historic building offers high-end pieces from artists in the region. Stone and ivory carvings, both Inuit and local, are some of the more sought-after pieces, as are intricately carved chess pieces. It's a popular tourist shop, and handmade hunting knives are among the less conventional items, as are woven and knitted goods like the handmade sweaters reminiscent of the kind Bill Cosby made famous in the 1980s.

MAP 1: 1124 rue St-Jean, 418/692-4850, www.canadeau.com; summer daily 10am-7pm, winter daily 10am-6pm

Galerie d'Art les Trois Colombes

Situated in a beautiful historic house complete with a red-peaked roof and white-washed facade, Galerie d'Art les Trois Colombes is one of the most picturesque of arts and craft stores. Filled with selections from both Québécois and Canadian arts and crafts, it also carries works by Inuits and Amerindians, including thick-wool parkas trimmed with fur and moccasins and mukluks in both child and adult sizes. Authentic snowshoes, soapstone sculptures, and weavings occupy the downstairs, while, upstairs, visitors will find handmade hats, rag dolls, and sweaters.

MAP 1: 46 rue St-Louis, 418/694-1114; Mon.-Wed. 9:30am-7pm, Thurs.-Sun. 9:30am-9pm

Lambert & Co.

This teeny-tiny store, approximately two meters wide, in the interior courtyard of Château Frontenac is a splendid gem. The emphasis here is on quality not quantity, and their finely made, striped wool socks, black-and-red checkered blankets, and fur-trimmed hats have become a recognized brand in this region. Alongside the cozy woolen goods (and pillows that make great souvenirs), they also sell a few natural beauty products, like moisturizer, body wash, and shampoo, for both people and their pets.

MAP 1: 1 rue des Carrières, 418/694-2151, www.lambertco.ca; Mon.-Fri. 10am-7pm, Sat.-Sun. 9:30am-6:30pm

BATH, BEAUTY, AND SPAS
Boutiuqe & Spa Signé Prevonia

Located inside the Hôtel Manoir Victoria, this full-service spa offers manicures ($52), pedicures ($73), and signature treatments like Cocoon facials ($100), Jin Shin Do massage ($100), and maple body scrubs ($85). A 30-minute Swedish massage will set you back $65. It's frequented by hotel guests, but nonguests may also make a reservation here. Many of the treatments use products made with local, organic maple sugar, and a day-package to the spa also gives visitors access to the hotel's gym, sauna, and indoor pool, all of which have an early-20th-century, Turkish-bath feel with mosaic tiles and arched columns around the pool.

MAP 1: 44 Côte du Palais, 800/463-6283, www.manoir-victoria.com; daily 9am-9pm

Payot Institute

Opened in 2010, the Payot Institute is located in the Château Frontenac, but you don't have to be a hotel guest to benefit from the treatments offered by this renowned institution. Started by Dr. Nadia Payot, the first woman to graduate from the Lausanne School of Medicine in France in 1913, the spa offers treatments that go beyond the regular massages and facials to include an entire beauty philosophy. Facial acupuncture, a face and body scrub with caviar, myrrh and amyris, and Dr. Payot's signature facial, which includes 42 specialized movements designed to halt aging, hair elixir, and precious oils are all available. They also offer a number of treatments designed specifically for men, including foot, hand, and nail care. The decor is soft gray with hints of purple, which complements the institute's calm atmosphere. The prices are at the high-end of the scale.

MAP 1: 1 rue des Carrières, 418/977-7790, www.fairmont.com; Mon.-Thurs. 8:30am-8pm, Fri.-Sat. 8:30am-9pm, Sun. 9am-5pm

BOOKS AND MUSIC
Archambault

One of the biggest music stores in the province, Archambault has 15 stores throughout Québec and sells everything from CDs and DVDs to books, magazines, newspapers, video games, and musical instruments. Deep red walls are the backdrop for this location's selection of small instruments and musical accessories. It was founded in 1896 by Edmond Archambault, who wanted to open a sheet music store; he teamed up with piano man and musical instrument specialist J.A. Hurteau to create the first Archambault retail outlet. Locals pop in here to pick up a new release or get strings for their guitar.

MAP 1: 1095 rue St-Jean, 418/694-2088, www.archambault.ca; Jan.-May Sun.-Wed. 9:30am-6pm, Thurs.-Sat. 9:30am-9:30pm; June-Dec. daily 9:30am-9:30pm

Librairie Pantoute

Founded in 1972 by a bunch of counterculture kids, Librairie Pantoute (its name means "not at all" in Québécois lingo) is one of the most important independent bookstores in the province. Situated in the heart of Upper Town, this location has high ceilings and walls full of bookshelves. They carry popular English titles, mostly best-sellers like John Grisham and Ken Follett, although they usually have a title or two by still popular but slightly lesser-known authors. No matter what you're looking for, the well-informed, usually bilingual staff will be able to help.

MAP 1: 1100 rue St-Jean, 418/694-9748, www.librairiepantoute.com; Mon.-Sat. 10am-10pm, Sun. noon-10pm

Maison de la Presse Internationale

If it is published on a daily, weekly, or monthly basis, they likely have it here. From periodicals to newspapers to magazines and specialized reviews in a number of languages—English, Spanish, Russian, German, Arabic—this is your best bet for finding your favorite daily. *Le Monde, le Figaro,* the *New York Times,* the *Wall Street Journal,* and the *International Herald Tribune* can all be found here. If you want something with a bit more meat, they also have books, including paperbacks, usually bestsellers, in English. Also set up partially as a gift shop, it sells postcards and trinkets and offers money exchange.

MAP 1: 1050 rue St-Jean, 418/694-1511; Mon.-Sat. 7am-11pm, Sun. 8am-11pm

Première Issue

Die-hard comic fans will want to make Première Issue a definite stop on their map. Sitting at a 45-degree angle in Vieux-Québec's Upper Town directly across from Les Fortifications, this comic book paradise is filled with back issues of DC and Marvel comics, as well as cult classics like *The Watchman.* Local fans can be found browsing and reading or having an intense discussion about *Tintin* with staff. The atmosphere is laid-back with a bit of whimsy. Though they also carry comics from Québec and France, known as *bande dessinée,* the focus here is on classic English-language comics.

MAP 1: 27A rue d'Auteuil, 418/692-3985, www.librairiepremiereissue.com; Mon.-Fri. 10am-7pm, Sat. 10am-5pm, Sun. 11am-5pm

CHILDREN'S STORES
Boutique l'Échelle

Established in 1966, this chaotic boutique just inside of the old walls carries old-time toys. Marionettes, matryoshka dolls, model cars, trains, and stuffed animals line the walls, alongside traditional Québécois wood toys like spoons for playing traditional songs and the *gigueux,* a wooden doll that is made to dance the jig on a platform. Board games for all ages and in both English and French are available, as are party favors and balloons.

MAP 1: 1039 rue St-Jean, 418/694-9133, www.boutiqueechelle.com; summer daily 10am-11pm, winter Mon.-Wed. 10:30am-5pm, Thurs.-Fri. 10:30am-9pm, Sat. 10am-5pm, Sun. noon-5pm

CLOTHING AND SHOES

★ Bibi et Compagnie

If you ask the owner of this headwear wonderland tucked down a quiet side street how she would describe her store, she will tell you, "I sell hats. That's it. Point final." And she's right. Men's hats, women's hats, they are all available here from panamas to fedoras, caps to cloches, and in an array of colors and sizes, stacked up along the shelves or modeled by body-less mannequins. The service is hands-off, unless customers show real interest, and the atmosphere quite sober, depending on the mood of the staff, who are mostly mature women who look lovely in hats.

MAP 1: 42 rue Garneau, 418/649-0045, www.bibietcie.com; Feb.-Oct. Mon.-Sat. 9am-7pm, Sun. 10am-6pm; Nov.-Jan. Thurs.-Sun. noon-7pm

La Maison Darlington

One of the oldest boutiques in Québec, it's named after an English tailor who took over a business that sold military garments and turned it into a wool and cashmere boutique. The antique till and specialized wooden sweater shelves are reminders of times past and though the styles may have changed since he opened in 1872, the ethos remains the same and you'll find a range of accessories, toques, berets, mittens, and scarves of only the highest-quality from brands such as Ballantyne, Johnston of Elgin, and Tilley Endurables. Dapper gentlemen who still wear caps are fans, as are well-heeled older women who come for their cozy knits.

MAP 1: 7 rue de Buade, 418/692-2268; Mon.-Wed. 9:30am-6pm, Thurs.-Fri. 9:30am-7pm, Sat. 9:30am-5pm, Sun. 10am-5pm

DEPARTMENT STORES

La Maison Simons

One of the city's most important businesses, La Maison Simons was started in 1840 by 17-year-old John Simons, who opened a dry goods store near Porte St-Jean. Thirty years later, in 1870, the store moved to a new location close to the basilica, and here it has remained. Though opened in the late 19th century, it has a definite art deco feel, with a beautiful, concave ceiling made of pearl glass. A large section of the building has recently been remodeled and features high-ceilings, sleek, white modern stairs, and a live DJ on weekends. They carry a number of labels, both mid-range (Canada Goose) and luxury (Kenzo, Chloe) as well as their private label collection. Locations can be found at Place Ste-Foy (2450 blvd. Laurier, 418/692-3630) and Galeries de la Capitale (5401 blvd. des Galeries, 418/692-3630).

MAP 1: 20 Côte de la Fabrique, 418/692-3630, www.simons.ca; winter Mon.-Wed. 9:30am-5:30pm, Thurs.-Fri. 9:30am-9pm, Sat. 9:30am-5pm, Sun. noon-5pm; summer Mon.-Sat. 9:30am-9pm, Sun. noon-5pm

Clockwise from top left: Laliberté, Saint-Jean-Baptiste and Saint-Roch; menswear boutique Philippe Dubuc, Saint-Roch; toy wonderland Benjo, Saint-Jean-Baptiste and Saint-Roch.

GIFTS AND HOME
Boutique Artisans Canada

Open since World War II, this large, open boutique in Vieux-Québec's Upper Town has subsequently been run by three generations of the Théberge family. It stocks jewelry, leather goods, fur hats, plush toys, sweaters, T-shirts, and outerwear. The majority of the lines are made and designed in Québec. It's recommended by the *New York Times* as a store to visit, and staff will remind you of this designation. The back of the store is dedicated to toy soldiers, and they have a huge collection of figurines, including the French battling the English at Waterloo and on the Plains of Abraham.

MAP 1: 30 Côte de la Fabrique, 418/692-2109, www.artisanscanada.com; summer daily 9am-10pm, winter daily 10am-6pm

Boutique Claude Berry

Open since 1981, Boutique Claude Berry specializes in European earthenware. Situated just in front of the basilica, this is the only store in the city dedicated to this particular kind of ceramics. Walking in here can be a bit of a visual overload; patterned platters, teapots, cups and saucers, and tableware are set out before you, each item perfectly displayed so as to give visitors the optimal view of the pattern. At this family-run business, service is hands-off unless you get too close to the products. This is the only store in North America to carry Faience d'Art de Gien earthenware.

MAP 1: 6 Côte de la Fabrique, 418/692-2628, www.claudeberry.com; mid-Sept.-mid-May Mon.-Wed. 9:30am-6pm, Thurs.-Fri. 9:30am-9pm, Sat.-Sun. 10am-7pm; mid-May-mid.-Sept. daily 9am-9pm

La Boutique de Noël

No matter the time of year, it's always Christmas at La Boutique de Noël. In a three-story building whose facade is permanently decorated with fairy lights, the interior is painted a deep hunter green with red trim and high-flying angels. Fully decorated Christmas trees line the aisles, while the walls are hung with an almost inconceivable number of ornaments, from Disney characters to sophisticated icicles and everything in between. They also carry Nativity scenes, stockings, tinsel, and anything else you want to hang on your tree. If you're unsure of the number of days left until the big event, this place has a running countdown.

MAP 1: 47 rue de Buade, 418/692-2457, www.boutiquedenoel.ca; Jan.-Apr. daily 10am-5pm, May-June and Oct. daily 9am-10pm, July-Aug. daily 8am-midnight, Sept. daily 9am-11pm, Nov.-Dec. daily 9am-9pm

Boutique Le Sachem

A silent statue of a native chief greets you at the entrance of this boutique, setting the tone for what's inside. This entire store is filled with Amerindian-inspired pieces, from moccasins to hunting knives, traditional woven blankets, and fur hats, even some à la Davy Crockett. One of the most serious gifts on display, however, has to be the stuffed wolf retailing for a cool $4,000. If you can get past the overwhelming kitsch of the place, there are some nice traditional crafts to be found.

MAP 1: 17 rue des Jardins, 418/692-3056; summer daily 9am-9pm, winter daily 10am-6pm

★ Magasin Général P.L. Blouin

Without a doubt one of the best stores in the city, Magasin Général P.L. Blouin is filled with novelty items and pieces of historic kitsch. Old Québec license plates line the walls, along with models of old cars. They stock everything here, from brand-new checkered hunters' caps to vintage magazines, old Coca-Cola paraphernalia, and magnetic Elvises. Owner Mr. Blouin is a connoisseur of kitsch, and people wanting to get rid of 40 years' worth of junk in the attic come to him first.

MAP 1: 1196 rue St-Jean, 418/694-9345, www.magasingeneralplblouin. com; Nov.-Apr. Sun.-Wed. 9am-6pm, Thurs.-Sat. 9am-9:30pm; May-Oct. daily 9am-10pm

GOURMET TREATS

Confiserie C'est si Bon

This picturesque shop has the feel of an old-time *confiserie*, or candy shop. The shelves are lined with containers full of candy, old-fashioned treats, novelty cups and saucers, magnets, and bowls, making it a great place to pick up a gift. Homemade chocolate, fudge, and hot chocolate are made on the premises and there's also an emphasis on local products like spices, teas, candies, and maple goodies. It's been open for over 20 years, and just about everything here is for sale, from the antique display case to the squares of maple sugar candy sitting temptingly at the cash register.

MAP 1: 1111 rue St-Jean, 418/692-5022; summer daily 9am-9pm; winter Mon.-Wed. 9am-5pm, Thurs.-Fri. 9am-9pm, Sat.-Sun. 9am-5:30pm

Les Délices de l'Érable

Everything here is drizzled with maple, from the blueberry gelato to the fleur du sel. Part store, part café, one side of this large, open store is dedicated to pastries, coffees, desserts, and gelatos, while the other is filled with rows of gourmet maple syrup, maple cookies, maple pork rub, coffees, teas—you get the idea. A small seating area at the back is a pleasant place to try a taste of their hot maple-flavor milk, but the real draws here are the gourmet products.

MAP 1: 1044 rue St-Jean, 418/692-3245, www.mapledelights.com; fall and spring Mon.-Thurs. 7am-9pm, Fri. 7am-10pm, Sat. 9am-10pm, Sun. 10am-10pm; winter Mon.-Thurs. 7am-8pm, Fri. 7am-9pm, Sat. 9am-9pm, Sun. 10am-9pm; summer Mon.-Fri. 7am-midnight, Sat. 9am-midnight, Sun. 10am-midnight

MARKETS

Artisans de la Cathédrale

This outdoor market runs throughout the summer on the grounds of the Holy Trinity Anglican Cathedral, in the shadow of Château Frontenac. The cozy, makeshift stalls erected here put you in direct contact with the artist

The Oldest Grocery Store in North America

If you're tired of museums but still want a trip back in time, head to **J. A. Moisan** (699 rue St-Jean, 418/522-0685, www.jamoisan.com, daily 9am-10pm), the oldest grocery store in North America, established in 1871. The Victorian-era look of the store has been meticulously recreated. Every little detail has been accounted for, from the crisp white shirts of the serving staff to the large wooden framed display cases, to the tin roof, wooden shelves lined with goods, and the French music from the 1930s and '40s piping in over the speakers.

When it first opened, Moisan's aim was to offer the area's well-to-do clients gourmet foods, and that tradition continues today with items like charcuterie, imported foie gras, biscuits, chocolates, and even soaps, filling the walls of the two-room grocery store. What has changed, however, is the addition of a small café near the entrance, where locals come to grab a quick lunch or indulge in a fresh pastry and coffee. Built in the early 1800s, it is one of the oldest buildings in St-Jean and was one of the few structures that wasn't destroyed by the great fire of 1881, which decimated the area. Though it retains a Victorian aesthetic, it is still a functioning grocery store, with locals popping in to get their morning bread and fresh produce. It may look and feel like the oldest grocery store in North America but it is also very modern.

or crafter who made the goods, making the shopping and browsing experience all the more memorable. The products are completely unique and different than what you'll find in other artisan and gift shops. Vendors sell everything from jewelry to sweaters to glass and woodwork.

MAP 1: 31 rue des Jardins, www.artisansdelacathedrale.com; mid-June-early Sept. daily 10:30am-10pm

Vieux-Québec's Lower Town
Map 2

ACCESSORIES AND JEWELRY
★ **Pont Briand Joallier**

Open for over 40 years, this high-end jeweler located in a historic stone house in Petit-Champlain is one of the city's best. The super-sleek interior with white display cases built into the walls gives it an added bit of glamour. The pieces here, many of which are made by Québec artisans, are exquisitely crafted with a wide range of styles and materials available, from rough-hued gold rings set with brilliant turquoise from the exclusive Louis Perrier collection to refined platinum engagement rings with a simple butterfly setting.

MAP 2: 48 rue du Petit-Champlain, 418/977-5800, www.pontbriand.net; winter daily 10am-5:30pm, summer Mon.-Sat. 10am-9pm, Sun. 10am-6pm

SHOPS VIEUX-QUÉBEC'S LOWER TOWN

ANTIQUES

Antiquités Bolduc

Owned and staffed by a young helpful and friendly couple, Stéphanie and Frédéric Bolduc, this small antique store situated in an old stone house is bright, uncluttered and artfully laid out with furniture, chandeliers, and just about anything else. Clocks and sconces line the walls, while tables, cabinets, and dressers are topped with children's toys, rotary telephones, firefighters' helmets, china tableware, steak knives, and vanity sets.

MAP 2: 89 rue St-Paul, 418/694-9558, www.lesantiquitesbolduc.com; Mon.-Fri. 9:30am-5pm, Sat. 10:30am-5pm, Sun. 11am-5pm

Boutique aux Mémoires Antiquités

A staple on the strip since the 1970s, Boutique aux Mémoires Antiquités is filled with treasures like Victorian furniture, oil lamps, old office desks, glittery chandeliers, and other curiosities. The low tin ceilings add even more charm to the crowded space in this historic building. The owner has a keen eye for finery, so fans of Tiffany lamps, fine silverware, and dinner china should keep their eyes peeled here. Though most of the stuff will look like it could come from anywhere, just about all of the finds here are directly from Québec's past.

MAP 2: 105 rue St-Paul, 418/692-218; Mon.-Sat. 9:30am-5pm

Maison Dambourgès

Named after a French shopkeeper who was also the head colonel of the militia in 1790, Maison Dambourgès is one of the larger stores on the street. Specializing in 19th-century pine country furniture from Québec and folk art, the store is perfectly curated. The large store is spacious compared to others on the strip and has a country feel. Just about everything here looks like it was fished out of an abandoned farmhouse in the country, and the owners have an impeccable eye for everything from stoneware jugs and weather vanes to old pine hutches with peeling paint and armoires built for the sole purpose of cooling pies.

MAP 2: 155 rue St-Paul, 418/692-1115; Mon. and Thurs.-Fri. 11am-5pm, Sat.-Sun. 11am-4pm

ARTS AND CRAFTS

★ Boutique des Métiers d'Art

Devoted to the work of Québécois artisans, the Boutique des Métiers d'Art showcases the work of over 125 craftspeople, all members of the Québec Craft Council. Situated on the famous Place Royale, it couldn't be better located, with huge, floor-to-ceiling windows and shelves and display cases lining the stone walls. Everything is well plotted out. Goods here are divided by materials and include wood, ceramic, metals, and glass, though other materials can be found in the work throughout the shop. Whether it is simple wood kitchen utensils you're looking for, a tin candelabra, or a unique silver pendant, you'll find it here.

MAP 2: 29 Place Royale, 418/694-0267, www.metiers-d-art.qc.ca; June 24-late-Aug. daily 9:30am-9:30pm; Sept.-Dec. Sat.-Wed. 9am-6pm, Thurs.-Fri. 9:30am-9pm; Jan.-late-Apr. daily 9:30am-6pm; May-June 24 Sat.-Wed. 9:30am-6pm, Thurs.-Fri. 9:30am-9pm

Pauline Pelletier

Pauline Pelletier's ceramic and porcelain artwork is both unconventional yet modern. Using unusual shapes as a base, a square teapot for example, the ceramic is then smoke-fired to create the final effect, giving it a marbled finish. The unusual pieces of art, popular with tourists and locals alike, include vases, tea sets, and serving platters. The colors are unconventional—navy blue, red, and jade, many with a touch of rich gold adorning the edges. The boutique, open since 1983, also carries the work of other Québec artisans and jewelers, giving it a more dynamic atmosphere and added quirkiness.

MAP 2: 38 rue du Petit-Champlain, 418/692-4871, www.paulinepelletier. com; Oct.-May Mon.-Wed. 9:30am-5:30pm, Thurs.-Fri. 9:30am-9pm, Sat.-Sun. 9am-5pm; June-Sept. daily 9am-9pm

Soierie Huo

This unique shop is run by artist Dominique Huot, who has been creating her one-of-a-kind silk products since the late 1970s. A descendant of Québécois artist Charles Huot, Dominique uses natural silk and wool fibers to create her scarves and men's ties. The designs on many of the scarves are spontaneous, though she continually recreates certain themes, including abstracts, florals, and maple leaves. The shop itself is quite small with the scarves predominantly displayed throughout.

MAP 2: 91 rue du Petit-Champlain, 418/692-5920, www.soieriehuo.com; summer daily 9:30am-8pm, winter daily 9:30am-5pm

CLOTHING AND SHOES
Atelier La Pomme

This store, located in the quaint Petit-Champlain district, carries lines by Québécois designers, from young, lesser-known labels like Véronique Miljkovitch (whose bias-cut dresses and asymmetrical shapes have won her the adoration of fashion insiders) to the mixed-textile playfulness of Myco Anna. Situated in a historic building, the interior is plain, featuring white walls with red trim. Carrying both men's and women's wear, it's a popular tourist shop for watches, jewelry, leather bags, and seasonal products like fur coats and hats, all made in Québec.

MAP 2: 47 rue Sous-le-Fort, 418/692-2875; Sept.-June Sat.-Wed. 10am-5pm, Thurs.-Fri. 10am-9pm; July-Aug. daily 9am-9pm

Le Capitaine d'Abord

If you need a pea coat or a striped Breton sweater this is a good place to start, whether you're a man or a woman. The goods here all have a nautical flair and evoke Cape Cod even when it's mid-January outside. The bright blue walls, low ceilings, and high-gloss wood floors give the vague impression you're on a ship, but the thick, knitted sweaters and heavy down jackets will remind you of the weather outside. They are exclusive carriers of yachting brands like Paul & Shark, Armor-Lux, and Meyer, and if you're sailing the St-Lawrence, this is the only store you need.

MAP 2: 59 and 63 rue du Petit-Champlain, 418/694-0694, www.capitainedabord. com; Sun.-Tues. 9am-6pm, Wed.-Sat. 9am-9pm

Fourrures Richard Robitaille

Established in 1894, Richard Robitaille is a family business passed down through four different generations. While visitors are invited to browse the luxurious fur coats and hats (worn just as much by men and women in this province), the real draw here is to see how the coats get made. Serge Richard repairs and makes fur coats from scratch and invites you to see the process, from the skins to the final product, at the store's Eco Musée. Richard will tell you about different hunting methods and species, and the evolution of fur in fashion, all while creating a brand-new look.

MAP 2: 329 rue St-Paul, 418/692-9699, www.economusees.com; Mon.-Sat. 9:30am-4pm

Oclan

This two-floor store on the tiny rue de-Petit-Champlain carries contemporary designer brands, including Martinique for men and Michael Kors for women. Entering the menswear section, you'll find a fairly small floor space tastefully packed with the latest from GStar, J Lindeberg, and Energie, among others. Down a camouflaged staircase you'll reach the women's floor (which you can also enter or exit from the larger rue Champlain), similar in size but much more stocked, with pieces from Velvet, In Wear, and Nougat, among others.

MAP 2: 67½ rue du Petit-Champlain, 418/692-1214, www.oclan.net; Sat.-Wed. 10am-6pm, Thurs.-Fri. 10am-9pm

GIFTS AND HOME
Machin Chouette

This place takes things you love but seemingly have no real use for, like that first pressing of the Grateful Dead's "Anthem to the Sun," and turns them into something useful like a CD rack. The brainchild of Lise Maheu, this large, open boutique in the Vieux-Port has some great pieces, from the aforementioned vinyls-turned-CD racks. They also turn old butter boxes into ottomans and teapots into lights and carry various kinds of furniture, from old country pine tables to contemporary pieces that would look just as good in a loft as in a 19th-century townhouse.

MAP 2: 225 rue St-Paul, 418/525-9898, www.machinchouette.com; Mon.-Wed. and Sat. 10am-5pm, Thurs.-Fri. and Sun. 10am-6pm

Pot en Ciel

This split-level store in Petit-Champlain carries ceramics and kitchenware. On the lower floor they carry an array of charming things for the home, including mugs with mustaches, checkered canisters, and artisanal pieces like carved owls and polar bears, as well as a few gourmet products like dried pasta imported from Italy and loose-leaf teas from France. On the upper level, it's all serious kitchen stuff like baking sheets, cookie cutters, and French brands like Emile Henry, as well as a range of Bodum presses.

MAP 2: 27 rue du Petit-Champlain, 418/692-1743; July-Aug. daily 9am-10pm, Sept.-June Sun.-Wed. 9am-6:30pm, Thurs.-Sat. 9am-9:30pm

GOURMET TREATS

La Fudgerie

As the name suggests, this place is a fudge fanatic's fantasy. Well established outside of the city, this cozy, old-timey store is the company's first in downtown Québec. The low ceilings, old wood floors, and exposed ceiling beams make you feel as though you're stepping into the past, a feeling added to by the workers in pristine white coats who circle the store with a platter offering tastes of their divine homemade fudge. Nougat, gourmet hot chocolate, and candied pecans are also made here.

MAP 2: 16 rue du Cul-de-Sac, 418/692-3834, www.lafudgerie.com; Mon.-Wed. 9:30am-5:30pm, Thurs.-Fri. 9:30am-9pm, Sat.-Sun. 9:30am-5pm

Madame Gigi Confiserie

This sweets shop in Petit-Champlain boasts one of the most dangerous sounding treats—chocolate pizza. With floor-to-ceiling windows and display cases prettily decorated with the day's chocolate special, this place will easily break your resolve and lure you in to try their various goodies, including fudge, chocolate-dipped fruit kebabs, and Belgian chocolate. In summer, they also have homemade ice cream, and their homemade jam is available year-round.

MAP 2: 84 rue du Petit-Champlain, 418/694-2269; winter Mon.-Wed. 9am-5:30pm, Thurs.-Fri. 9am-9pm, Sat.-Sun. 9am-6pm; summer daily 9am-11pm

O Petites Douceurs du Quartier

Less exciting than some of the other gourmet stores, this bright, feminine shop—it's all creams and soft pinks—in Petit-Champlain carries old-fashioned sweets and local products. Creamy nougats, flavored oils, spices, fair-trade chocolate, sweets, teas, and spreads (such as Verger du Sureau's organic jams and jellies) are some of the goods available. They also carry non-foodie gifts like beauty products from Blue Lavender and small ceramics for the home.

MAP 2: 51 rue du Petit-Champlain, 418/692-4870; Apr.-Aug. Mon.-Sat. 9:30am-9pm, Sun. 9:30am-5pm; Sept.-Oct. Mon.-Wed. 9:30am-5:30pm, Thurs.-Fri. 9:30am-9pm, Sat.-Sun. 9:30am-5pm; Nov.-Mar. Sat.-Wed. 10am-5pm, Thurs.-Fri. 10am-9pm

La Petite Cabane à Sucre de Québec

This little shop at the end of the rue du Petit-Champlain is all kitted out in wood paneling, both inside and out. Exclusively selling maple goods, it is the downtown extension of a sugar shack outside of the city. "The little

Clockwise from top left: Jupon Pressé, Saint-Jean-Baptiste and Saint-Roch; Le Capitaine d'Abord, Vieux-Québec's Lower Town; Quartier du Petit-Champlain, Lower Town.

sugar shack" sells maple syrup, maple candy, ice cream, maple lollipops, nougat, butter and spreads, and a ton of other maple products.

MAP 2: 94 rue du Petit-Champlain, 418/692-5875, www.petitecabaneasucre. com; winter Sat.-Wed. 10am-5pm, Thurs.-Fri. 10am-9pm, summer daily 9am-9pm

MARKETS
Le Marché du Vieux Port

Located right on the marina, this is the city's largest farmers market. A tradition that's been going on since 1841, the Marché du Vieux Port continues the practice of country farmers bringing their goods to city dwellers. Everything available here is locally grown and produced, and many of the products are organic. You'll find everything from fruits and vegetables to cheese, meats, and seafood to wine and beer. If seeing all that food makes you hungry there are a number of places to grab a sandwich or a light lunch. There's also a section dedicated to gifts and artisanal goods, including handmade jewelry, knitted scarves and socks, artwork, and leather goods.

MAP 2: 160 Quai St-André, 418/692-2517, www.marchevieuxport.com; Jan.-mid-Mar. Thurs.-Sun. 9:30am-5pm; mid-Mar.-Sept. Mon.-Fri. 9am-6pm, Sat.-Sun. 9am-5pm; Oct.-late Nov. daily 9am-5pm; late Nov.-Dec. Sat.-Wed. 9am-5pm, Thurs.-Fri. 9am-9pm

SHOPPING DISTRICTS AND CENTERS
Quartier du Petit-Champlain

Full of artisanal shops, many of which double as artists' workshops, Quartier du Petit-Champlain is the perfect place to support the local arts and pick up some unique gifts. It's run as a co-op, and there is a real neighborhood spirit and camaraderie here due in part to the fact that many of these stores have been here since its inception in the late-1980s. Expect to find silk scarves, leather goods, gourmet fudge, maple syrup, expensive handmade jewelry, and more.

MAP 2: Between Place Royale and rue Petit-Champlain

Rue Saint-Paul

This narrow cobblestone street in the Vieux-Port is Québec City's antiques row. With the exception of a few cafés, bars, and restaurants, almost all of the stores here are filled with antiques. There is a real emphasis on classic antiques—that is to say, don't expect to walk in and find a midcentury modern gem (though it could happen). The pieces aren't often dated later than the 1940s, and even objects from that period can be hard to find. Instead, the focus in many stores is on traditional Québécois antiques.

MAP 2: Between rue St-Pierre and rue Rioux

Parliament Hill and the Plains

Map 3

ARTS AND CRAFTS
Ketto

Located in a skinny corner house decorated with deep blue trim, lots of flower pots, and their unmistakable yellow sign, Ketto has an aesthetic all its own. In the late 1990s, Onge was working at a ceramic store when the pieces with her cutesy, big-headed, stick-limbed characters painted on them started flying off the shelves. Today, Ketto carries hand-painted ceramics, jewelry, clothing, glassware, and stationery all with Onge's signature style. The interior can be a bit chaotic, but everything is perfectly laid out, with a simple wood cabinet full of cups and saucers taking up almost an entire wall.

MAP 3: 951 ave. Cartier, 418/522-3337, www.kettodesign.com; Mon.-Wed. and Sat.-Sun. 10am-5pm, Thurs.-Fri. 10am-9pm

BATH, BEAUTY, AND SPAS
Izba Spa

This spa mixes traditional Russian Banya treatments (steam baths) with therapeutic massage. Banya treatments here involve a humid environment in which the person starts to perspire; soaked oak leaves are then warmed and used to stroke, brush, and tap the body before a honey rub is used to draw out toxins and soften the skin. Trained and certified staff will give you a 60-minute Izba massage that starts at $90, or a deluxe Izba with facial and seawater wrap for $175. The stone walls, low lighting, and vaulted ceilings give it an especially luxurious feel.

MAP 3: 36 blvd. René-Lévesque E., 418/522-4922, www.izbaspa.qc.ca; Mon.-Tues. 9am-7pm, Wed.-Fri. 9am-10pm, Sat.-Sun. 9am-5pm

BOOKS AND MUSIC
Sillons Le Disquaire

This is one of the best independent music stores in the province, open since 1984; what they lack in floor space they make up for in the huge choice. It's close to the Plains of Abraham. The staff here are highly knowledgeable and can advise you on everything from Ye-Ye pop to the latest Québec rock sensation. The selection is contemporary with 15,000 to 20,000 CDs available in-store. Listening booths are set up around the store.

MAP 3: 1149 ave. Cartier, 800/287-7455, www.sillons.com; Mon.-Fri. 10am-9pm, Sat. 10am-5pm, Sun. 11am-5pm

CLOTHING AND SHOES
Urbain Prêt-à-Porter

This corner boutique in a well-heeled part of town carries fashion-forward brands aimed at women of various ages. The decor changes throughout, from the deep gray walls and designs that cater to more mature women, to an adjoining white space that features younger brands like Miss Sixty and Nolita. The store also has its own shoe section, with seasonal footwear from the likes of Diesel and Ilse Jacobsen, among others, as well as a wall dedicated to denim.

MAP 3: 996 ave. Cartier, 418/521-1571; Mon.-Wed. 10am-6pm, Thurs.-Fri. 10am-9pm, Sat. 10am-5pm, Sun. 11am-5pm

GIFTS AND HOME
Zone
This modern living and design store carries an array of products, all chic, sleek, and sophisticated for your home. The all-white store is artfully decorated with stock arranged as you might arrange it in your own home. Recently expanded, the store now takes up not only the corner lot but the one next to it, with mirrors, chandeliers, table lamps, drinking glasses, tableware, shower curtains, jewelry boxes, cool wall clocks, and furniture from kitchen tables to small couches and chairs.

MAP 3: 999 ave. Cartier, 418/522-7373, www.zonemaison.com; Mon.-Wed. 9:30am-6pm, Thurs.-Fri. 9:30am-9pm, Sat. 9:30am-5:30pm, Sun. 10am-5pm

MARKETS
Les Halles du Petit Quartier
Less like a market than a mini-gourmet shopping center, Les Halles du petit Quartier is a brick and mortar building filled with great shops. It's popular with locals. An organic fruit and produce stand, a fishmonger, butcher, cheese shop, fresh pasta shop, a pastry, and a bakery shop all offer top-quality products. It also boasts not one, but two coffee shops where you can take a break with a cappuccino; get one to go as you carry on with your browsing.

MAP 3: 1191 ave. Cartier, 418/688-1635, www.hallesdupetitquartier.com; Mon.-Wed. and Sat. 7am-7pm, Thurs.-Fri. 7am-9pm, Sun. 7:30am-7pm

Saint-Jean-Baptiste and Saint-Roch

Map 4

ACCESSORIES AND JEWELRY
Mademoiselle B
This narrow storefront would be easy to miss if it weren't for the floor-to-ceiling windows and old-fashioned sign that pops out over the door. Situated in a newer building in the Saint-Roch neighborhood, Mademoiselle B has an Old-World charm with dark chocolate parquet floors, soft pink walls, and plush velvet display shelves. In keeping with the romantic interior, the costume jewelry here is very girly, with collections coming from France, the south of Italy, and, of course, Québec.

MAP 4: 541 rue St-Joseph E., 418/522-0455; Mon.-Wed. 10am-5:30pm, Thurs.-Fri. 10am-9pm, Sat. 10am-5pm, Sun. 11am-5pm

Rose Bouton

A lot of time could be spent in this kitschy store filled with overwhelming amounts of jewelry and accessories and vibrantly decorated with bubble-gum pink walls, bright florals, pink fun fur, and circle motif wallpaper. Expect to find fabric-covered earrings, hand-drawn pins, long-fringe pendants and earrings, and bracelets and necklaces made with buttons, the store's namesake *bouton*. A fun and vibrant store, it also carries seasonal accessories like bags, scarves, and hats.

MAP 4: 387 rue St-Jean, 418/614-9507, www.boutiquerose.blogspot.com; Tues.-Wed. 11am-5pm, Thurs.-Fri. 11am-9pm, Sat.-Sun. 11am-5pm

ANTIQUES
Déjà Vu

Specializing in furniture and objects from the 1930s to the 1970s, the selection at Déjà Vu is much more mid-century modern than what you'll find in most antique stores in the city. Full of Formica tables, colored glass cocktail sets, and electric blue sectionals from the late 1950s, it's a fun place to stop in if only because the act is akin to a 20th-century flashback. Unlike flea market finds, the treasures here have been lovingly and expertly restored by owners Marie-Claude and François Gagnon. Prices can be higher than anticipated, but knickknacks and anything to do with cocktail hour—ice buckets, martini shakers—are well-priced and the perfect unique souvenir.

MAP 4: 834 rue St-Joseph E., 418/914-2483, www.dejavumeubles.com; Tues.-Wed. 10am-5pm, Thurs.-Fri. 10am-8pm, Sat. 10am-5pm, Sun. noon-5pm

ARTS AND CRAFTS
Point d'Exclamation

Founded by Diane Bergeron of Euphory Design in 2004, Point d'Exclamation was at the forefront of the movement to champion Québec-based designers. Nowadays, the entire neighborhood is full of shops dedicated to locally produced and designed goods (Jupon Pressé, Code Vert, Rose Bouton), but it was Bergeron and her eye for local artisanal work that got the ball rolling. The boutique carries the work of 30-40 local designers at any one time, and the goods range from jewelry to accessories and clothes. The all-white interior is a bit too bright at times but puts the focus on the work, while their constantly-changing storefront window is always a feast for the eyes.

MAP 4: 762 rue St-Jean, 418/525-8053; Sat.-Wed. 10am-6pm, Thurs.-Fri. 10am-9pm

BATH, BEAUTY, AND SPAS
Cosmétiques Bloomi

This sleek and modern cosmetics store is reminiscent of the international chain Sephora. Products are beautifully arranged on white high-gloss lacquered shelves and the whole interior is given an added bit of warmth thanks to the exposed brick walls. It carries high-end makeup lines, a large range of perfumes, and just about any color of polish you could want. Pop in to get a manicure or pedicure, your makeup done for a special occasion, or just to get some tips from the beauticians, who are always ready to give **149** you some pointers and a bit of a touchup.

MAP 4: 507 rue St-Joseph E., 418/529-7470, www.bloomi.ca; Mon.-Wed. 9:30am-5:30pm, Thurs.-Fri. 9:30am-9pm, Sat. 9:30am-5pm, Sun. 11am-5pm

La Quintessens

This urban spa in Saint-Roch is great for a massage or a quick bit of pampering. The decor is relatively simple, with the rooms filled with massage tables and not much else. Though they offer treatments, the focus is on massage, and five different kinds are available: Swedish, Californian, Amma (also known as Japanese massage), Thai-yoga massage, and massage with hot stones. Hour-long massages cost $65 and body wraps, including chocolate, algae, and sea salt, are $75. They also offer half-hour lunchtime massages (11:30am-1:30pm, $25) and 15-minute chair massages ($15).

MAP 4: 656 rue St-Joseph E., 418/525-7270, www.quintessens.ca; Mon. noon-5pm, Tues.-Fri. 10am-7pm, Sat. 10am-5pm

BOOKS AND MUSIC
CD Mélomane

Established in 1996, this is the best record store in the city. Totally unpretentious, the staff here simply know their stuff, with certain clerks knowing the store's entire stock almost by heart. New and used CDs are available, as are racks upon racks of vinyl, which take up the majority of the space. Brick arches divide the store. They'll happily transfer your cherished 33s, 45s, and 78s onto CD.

MAP 4: 248 rue St-Jean, 418/525-1020, www.cdmelomaneinc.supersites.ca; Mon.-Wed. and Sat. 10am-5pm, Thurs.-Fri. 10am-9pm, Sun. noon-5pm

★ Le Knock-Out

Vinyl is king at this Saint-Roch record store. Tired of having to buy vinyl on the Internet, owners Jean-Philippe Tremblay and Roxann Arcand decided to open a store dedicated to genres and media they most wanted to hear played. Specializing in rock (indie, math, pop), garage, punk, and local, the shop has an impressive collection of both new and used records. The space is open concept and airy: There's even a foosball table near the large floor-to-ceiling window and a makeshift stage where shows are played at the back. The walls are lined not only with music but also books, zines, DVDs, and magazines about the bands and genres they love. The walls are fairly sparse, but the work of Mathieu Plasse, illustrating the history of rock through outfits, is pretty much all you need.

MAP 4: 832 St-Joseph E., 581/742-7625; Tues.-Wed. 11am-6pm, Thurs.-Fri. 11am-9pm, Sat. 11am-5pm, Sun. noon-5pm

Librairie Phylactère

Comics and graphic novels are a huge part of Francophone culture. Just think of Tin Tin. Librairie Phylactère (the name means "speech bubble" in English) is here to cater to that love and is the go-to stop in the city for all of your graphic novel needs. Whether you're looking for the latest Manga

SHOPS

SAINT-JEAN-BAPTISTE AND SAINT-ROCH

or Adrian Tomine, chances are you'll find it in this Saint-Roch boutique. Comic book artwork adorns the walls and there are a few comfy seats for reading but otherwise they let the books be the focus.

MAP 4: 685 rue St-Joseph E., 418/614-2443; Tues.-Wed. 10:30am-6pm, Thurs.-Fri. 10:30am-9pm, Sat.-Sun. 10:30am-5pm

CHILDREN'S STORES
★ Benjo

You could spend all day at this 25,000-square-foot store, and that's exactly the point. It's filled with educational toys, accessories for infants, model trains, planes, automobiles, party favors, candy, books, and a whole lot of costumes; if it's meant for children you'll likely find it here. Take the kids to lunch at the Benjo restaurant, or sign them up for a ceramic painting, jewelry, or paper-making workshop. The staff is always helpful and delightfully off-kilter, as is mascot Benjo, a frog, whom the kids can meet on weekends (Sat.-Sun. 11:15am-3:15pm).

MAP 4: 550 blvd. Charest E., 418/640-0001, www.benjo.ca; Mon.-Wed. 10am-5:30pm, Thurs.-Fri. 10am-9pm, Sat.-Sun. 9:30am-5pm

CLOTHING AND SHOES
Boutique Lucia F.

Tucked down a quiet side street in Saint-Roch, Boutique Lucia F. is a vintage store carrying everything from old 45s to women's pumps. Owned by a young graduate of design, there is an easy feel to how the whole place has been put together; bags line the windowsills, hats are pegged on the exposed brick wall, and old mismatched sitting room chairs are placed throughout the store. Styles for men and women are carried, and the majority of prices are $10-20. And if you like that magazine rack currently holding scarves, well, you can likely buy that too.

MAP 4: 422 rue Caron, 418/648-9785; Wed.-Fri. 11am-6pm, Sat. 11am-5pm

★ Esther P

Located in a former bank, women's boutique Esther P is one of the most stunningly designed stores on St-Jean. The store carries labels that are typically hard to find in Québec City—James Perse, French Connection, Ella Moss, Graham & Spencer. Owner Esther Pichette's aim is to dress women of all ages. The boutique has an open-concept feel with high ceilings that show off the original moldings, blonde-wood floors, punches of red, and lots of windows and glass to keep things modern.

MAP 4: 873 rue St-Jean, 418/704-7774, www.estherp.com; Mon.-Wed. and Sat. 10am-6pm, Thurs.-Fri. 10am-9pm, Sun. 11am-5pm

Fanamanga

Fans of manga and cosplay congregate at this store turned hangout that brings a touch of Tokyo to Québec. It's filled with Gothic Lolita outfits, cosplay accessories, manga, magazines, Japanese treats like Okonomiyaki chips, curry-flavored sweets, and any number of trinkets, dolls, and ephemera associated with the culture. The stools at the bar are usually filled with fans in cosplay, sipping their bubble-tea and bobbing their heads to the Visual Kei videos playing on the TVs above. They also have a karaoke box you can rent by the hour that has songs in Japanese, English, Korean, Chinese, and Vietnamese.

MAP 4: 383 rue du Pont, 418/614-5052, www.fanamanga.com; Tues.-Wed. 10:30am-5:30pm, Thurs. 10:30am-10pm, Fri. 10:30am-11:30pm, Sat. 11am-11:30pm

Flirt

As the name suggests, this brightly colored boutique is all about clothes that bring out your inner flirt, specializing in lingerie for both men and women. The walls are lined with intimate apparel hanging tantalizingly in rows. The store prides itself not only on the many hard-to-find European brands they import, like Eva Racheline and Parah, but also on the fact that they carry hard-to-find sizes, including the line Empreinte, for the fuller-busted woman. Those looking for swimwear can pick from lines here like Cristina and Canadian company Shan. They also offer made-to-measure, but you must make an appointment first.

MAP 4: 525 rue St-Joseph E., 418/529-5221, www.lingerieflirt.com; Mon.-Wed. 9:30am-5:30pm, Thurs.-Fri. 9:30am-9pm, Sat.-Sun. 10am-5pm

★ Jupon Pressé

This inviting women's boutique on St-Jean is dedicated to emerging designers from Québec City, Montréal, and beyond. Brightly decorated with purple walls, flashes of yellow, bright floral wallpaper, and an inflatable moose head, the shop has an especially clean layout with pieces from designers like Eve Gravel, Supayana, and Valérie Dumaine. Nicely hung and spaced, nothing looks too crowded. T-shirts are perfectly piled on Formica tables, while accessories are laid out deliciously on cake plates; jewelry is displayed like art, framed and hung on the wall, though always easily accessible. Along with things for you to wear, they also carry cute, kitschy finds for the home.

MAP 4: 790 rue St-Jean, 418/704-7114; Mon.-Wed. 10am-6pm, Thurs.-Fri. 10am-9pm, Sat.-Sun. 10am-6pm

Kitsch

Hit this boutique up if you're a young woman who is always on trend, faithfully follows Queen Bey, and wishes Nasty Gal was your own personal closet. Carrying everything from Cheap Monday jeans to silky, floral bomber jackets and Ain't Laurent (without Yves) T-shirts, this store caters to the coolest looks and latest pieces. Owned by two super stylish and savvy mavens, this is their second location (the first Kitsch is located in Sherbrooke) and can be found on the über-hip St-Joseph, just a few doors down from that dictator of cool, Urban Outfitters. Curved, white furniture, like the kind you'd find in an 8-year-old's bedroom is used as display cases, while the rest of the space is open and airy. The shop's staff is eternally youthful, but also extremely helpful and competent, so don't be shy.

MAP 4: 425 rue St-Joseph, 418/528-2222, www.boutiquekitsch.com; Mon.-Wed. 10am-5:30pm, Thurs.-Fri. 10am-9pm, Sat. 10am-5pm, Sun. 11am-5pm

Lobo Lavida

Fans of vintage will get a kick out of this high-ceilinged store, filled to the gills with vintage and consignment pieces. From a pair of barely worn knee-high boots to hats from the 1930s and authentic RayBan aviators, this store has it all. Situated in what was once an old house, the entire first floor has been taken over with display cases full of costume jewelry and purses, with clothes lining the walls and on carousels in the center of the room. The prices are reasonable, and those usually put off by secondhand goods should know that everything here has been cleaned, ironed, and hung according to color.

MAP 4: 511 rue St-Jean, 418/521-3397; summer Mon.-Wed. and Sat. 11am-7pm, Thurs.-Fri. 11am-9pm, Sun. noon-6pm; winter Mon.-Wed. noon-5:30pm, Thurs.-Fri. 11am-8pm, Sat. 11am-5:30pm

★ Philippe Dubuc

This Québec City boutique of Montréal-based designer Philippe Dubuc couldn't be sleeker. The long, narrow store is like a mirrored corridor with all-white floors, ceilings, and walls giving it an extra modern kick. Distinctly masculine clothes are represented in the store, made all the more cool by its location in the Saint-Roch neighborhood. Though Dubuc is primarily a menswear designer, fashion-forward women shouldn't think twice about trying on a piece or two in this fabulous hall of mirrors.

MAP 4: 537 rue St-Joseph E., 418/614-5761, www.dubucstyle.com; Tues.-Wed. 10:30am-5:30pm, Thurs.-Fri. 10:30am-9pm, Sat. 10:30am-5pm, Sun. noon-5pm

Schüz

Casual shoes for men and women can be found at this relaxed boutique on St-Jean. Steve Madden, Tsubo, and Chinese Laundry are available for women, while men's brands include Asics, Onitsuka Tiger, and Camper for both sexes. Though there is definitely more of a choice for women, men looking for something unfussy, masculine, and modern, or just a new pair of everyday sneakers, are sure to find it here. The decor is minimal with the shoes displayed on the wall and the center of the room taken up with seating and seasonal displays. Winter boots are one of their specialties, so they always have a range of styles for both sexes come autumn.

MAP 4: 748 rue St-Jean, 418/523-4560, www.schuz.ca; mid-June-mid-Oct. Mon.-Sat. 10am-9pm, Sun. 11am-7pm; mid-Oct.-mid-June Mon.-Wed. and Sat. 10am-6pm, Thurs.-Fri. 10am-9pm, Sun. 11am-5:30pm

Signatures Québécoises

This relatively new shop in Saint-Roch is dedicated to local designers. If you're interested in a snapshot of Québécois fashion as it's made here, then this shop is a must. Taking over the semi-basement of a church, the space has been completely refurbished and modernized, so much so that you'd never realize you were in a church basement. Open and sprawling, the space features the work of a number of different designers and different styles and price ranges. Expect everything from street-wear brands like Lady Dutch and Kärv to specialty brands Yoga Jeans and Blank and higher-end

Top: Librarie St-Jean-Baptiste. **Bottom:** Déjà Vu, Saint-Jean-Baptiste and Saint-Roch.

designers like Stacey Zhang, Harricana, and Tavan & Mitto. The clothes and accessories suit just about any age and style, though there's much less choice for men.

MAP 4: 560 rue St-Joseph E., 418/648-9976, www.signaturesquebecoises.com; Mon.-Wed. 10am-5:30pm, Thurs.-Fri. 10am-9pm, Sat.-Sun. 10am-5pm

Swell & Ginger

Proof that Saint-Roch is indeed the fastest (and coolest) growing neighborhood in the city, style savvy womenswear boutique Swell & Ginger put down roots here in mid-2013. Modern, open, and sparsely decorated with heavy wood tables and steel fixtures, the boutique would fit right in in New York's East Village or London's Portobello Road. Labels include Rich and Skinny Jeans, Tiger of Sweden, and House of Harlow. Don't let the label love mislead you, however. Prices are surprisingly reasonable.

MAP 4: 765A rue St-Joseph E., 581/742-7080, www.swellandginger.com; Mon.-Wed. 10am-6pm, Thurs.-Fri. 10am-9pm, Sat. 10am-5pm, Sun. 11am-5pm

Tohu Bohu

Though this store specializes in upscale footwear and carries lines like Emilio Pucci, Kate Spade, and Marc by Marc Jacobs, it's not just a shoe store—they also do pedicures. With a name that means "confusion" and "hubbub," Tohu Bohu may surprise you. The store's dynamic streamlined design—plush gray banquettes mixed with high-gloss, red-and-black shelving and illuminated cubbies—puts the emphasis on the shoes and bags. Come to browse or come just for a pedicure or manicure, which you can enjoy while you eat; their pedi-sushi deal allows you to chow down on dinner from Yuzu while you get your toes prepped for those new peep-toes.

MAP 4: 775 rue St-Joseph E., 418/522-1118, www.tohubohu.ca; Mon.-Wed. 10am-5:30pm, Thurs.-Fri. 10am-9pm, Sat.-Sun. 10am-5pm

DEPARTMENT STORES

Laliberté

In May 1867, 24-year-old Jean-Baptiste Laliberté founded a modest fur shop that by the beginning of the 20th century was one of the best fur stores in North America. From its humble beginnings, the store eventually grew to become an arresting five-floor department store with huge arched windows and a corner clock tower looking over St-Joseph. When many stores upped and moved to the new malls outside of town, Laliberté was one of the few that stayed. Though the store has since been scaled back (the unused floors are now lofts), Laliberté continues to be a leader in furs. Bring your old furs to be remodeled here or browse their seasonal collections.

MAP 4: 595 rue St-Joseph E., 418/525-4851, www.lalibertemode.com; Mon.-Wed. 9:30am-5:30pm, Thurs.-Fri. 9:30am-9pm, Sat. 9:30am-5pm, Sun. noon-5pm

GIFTS AND HOME

Balthazar

This two-floor home and design store in Saint-Roch brings together modern furniture, trendy kitchen utensils, and various objets d'art to place around your home. Super sleek in design, the over-100-year-old building **155** has been meticulously redesigned so that the black slate staircase to the second floor blends in seamlessly with the ground floor walls lined with products like vases, espresso cups, and kitschy alarm clocks. Filled with brands that come from all over the world that are typically hard to find in the city, the store also carries collections from Québécois design firms.

MAP 4: 461 rue St-Joseph E., 418/524-1991, www.baltazar.ca; Mon.-Wed. 10am-5:30pm, Thurs.-Fri. 10am-9pm, Sat. 10am-5pm, Sun. 11am-5pm

GOURMET TREATS
Champagne Le Maître Confiseur
This chocolate and sweets shop has a few unique specialties. With only a few marble-topped tables to sit at, this fairly small store serves up some of the best marzipan treats in the city and also offers a range of fine sugar-free chocolate made in the European tradition in flavors that range from saffron to goat cheese with honey. Port glasses made of chocolate are the ultimate companion to the aged wine, as are their buttery French biscuits. The most unusual treat, though, is the cherry blossom—cherries soaked with champagne and cherry kirsch, covered in dark chocolate, and topped with a chocolate-dipped marshmallow. Totally decadent.

MAP 4: 783 rue St-Joseph E., 418/652-0708; Mon.-Fri. 8am-9pm, Sat.-Sun. 10am-6pm

Choco-Musée Erico
Established in 1987, this artisanal chocolatier is one of the most decadent stops in the city. Chocolate lines the walls in this quaint kitchen and boutique, with an array of seasonal treats (like nachos dipped in chocolate) on one side, and displays of freshly made chocolates (with flavors like chestnut cream, rum, and allspice) on the other. Line up to get your gourmet hot chocolate, ice cream, or one of their many desserts—the brownies and chocolate cake here are said to be among the best in the province. The adjoining room is the Chocolate Museum, which gives you a history of the treat, lets you taste some wares, and allows you to watch the magic being made in the kitchen.

MAP 4: 634 rue St-Jean, 418/524-2122, www.chocomusee.com; Mon.-Wed. and Sat. 10am-5:30pm, Thurs.-Fri. 10am-9pm, Sun. 11am-5:30pm

Epicerie Européenne
This shop was founded in 1959 by two Italians, nostalgic for their homeland. The massive wooden shelves are stocked with imported products. Italian coffees, olive oils, pestos, and balsamic vinegars take center stage, while at the back you'll find a cheese and meat counter, where you can order a great panini—but hurry up, they go fast. Along with the groceries, they also sell imported kitchen accessories, coffee makers, crockery, and the famous French Laguiole knives. Stop in and try one of their specialties, an authentic *espresso ristretto*—the shortest coffee around.

MAP 4: 560 rue St-Jean, 418/529-4847, www.epicerie-europeenne.com; Mon.-Wed. 9am-6pm, Thurs.-Fri. 9am-9pm, Sat. 9am-5pm

OUTDOOR GEAR
★ Mountain Equipment Co-op

Better known as MEC, this co-op was started by a couple of Canadian climbers in the 1970s and now has almost three million people as registered members. You must sign up to become a member in order to make a purchase, but the five bucks good-for-life membership pays for itself by the time you get to the checkout. The open-concept store design give you lots of room to roam the goods, which include everything from cycling gear to hiking boots, tents to sleeping bags. Even rental equipment is available; there really isn't a better store dedicated to the outdoors (unless you want to hunt). Eco-friendly and pro-sustainability, the store hires clerks that are friendly, patient, and know their stuff.

MAP 4: 405 rue St-Joseph E., 418/522-8884, www.mec.ca; Mon.-Wed. 10am-7pm, Thurs.-Fri. 10am-9pm, Sat. 9am-5pm, Sun. 10am-5pm

SHOPPING DISTRICTS AND CENTERS
Rue Saint-Jean

Whether inside or outside the walls, rue Saint-Jean is Québec City's main shopping street. In Vieux-Québec's Upper Town you'll find a string of well-known stores, including Québec chains, women's stores Jacob, San Francisco, Le Château, and internationally recognized brands like Crocs, American Apparel, and Foot Locker. It's also along this strip that you'll find magazines and bookstores selling English-language material. If you want to shop like the locals, check out the independent clothing boutiques and record stores in Faubourg Saint-Jean-Baptiste, a continuation of the same street; you'll find interesting shops just beyond the fortifications.

MAP 4: Between rue Couillard and ave. Salaberry

Rue Saint-Joseph

The main shopping strip in the Saint-Roch neighborhood, this street has an illustrious past that has recently been revived. Once the Fifth Avenue of Québec City, it is now the city's coolest shopping district. You won't find many well-known chains here except for the recently opened Urban Outfitters, the only store of its kind in the city. Independent lingerie boutiques can be found as well as some great shoe stores, home stores, and other fashion-forward boutiques. The best children's store in the province, Benjo, is also located here, with a VIP entrance especially for the little ones.

MAP 4: Between rue St-Dominique and rue Caron

Greater Québec City   Map 5

BOOKS AND MUSIC
La Maison Anglaise
The only bookstore dedicated to English books in Québec City is in Place de la Cité, one of the mega malls on the outskirts of town. The staff knows their English-language stuff and is always ready to help. The selection is, unsurprisingly, unbeatable, from *New York Times* best-sellers to literary fiction, humor, philosophy, travel, and kids books. It might not be as big as your local Barnes & Noble but it does have the most comprehensive collection of English books in the city and the atmosphere is quiet and calm—like it should be.

MAP 5: Place de la Cité, 164-2600 blvd. Laurier, 418/654-9523, www.lamaisonanglaise.com; Mon.-Wed. 9:30am-5:30pm, Thurs.-Fri. 9:30am-9pm, Sat. 9:30am-5pm, Sun. 11:30am-5pm

CHILDREN'S STORES
Univers Toutou
A special treat for kids of all ages, this store is located in one of the malls outside of the city. Over 20 different kinds of plush toys are available, from teddy bears to rabbits, moose, and pigs. Once the selection has been made, the plush is then stuffed and given a passport with its date and place of birth printed inside. The staff is kid-friendly and excited about helping kids pick a companion. Choices hang at kid-level all around the brightly decorated store. Clothing like bathrobes and boxers and accessories like sunglasses and jewelry can added to give the new plush toy a bit of its own personal style.

MAP 5: Galeries de la Capitale, 5401 blvd. des Galeries, 418/623-5557, www.plushfactory.com; Mon.-Wed. 9:30am-5:30pm, Thurs.-Fri. 9:30am-9pm, Sat. 9am-5pm, Sun. 10am-5pm

DEPARTMENT STORES
Holt Renfrew
Originating on rue Buade in Vieux-Québec's Upper Town, this high-end department store is now the only branch of Holt Renfrew in Québec City. Opened at this location in 1965, it retains its elegance, with high ceilings, simple design, and the designer brands customers have come to expect. This location also offers fur services, which include everything from proper storing and cleaning to alterations and remodeling. Made-to-measure tailoring is available here as well.

MAP 5: Place Ste-Foy, 2452 blvd. Laurier, 418/656-6783, www.holtrenfrew.com; Mon.-Wed. 9:30am-5:30pm, Thurs.-Fri. 9:30am-9pm, Sat. 9:30am-5pm, Sun. 11am-5pm

OUTDOOR GEAR
Latulippe
With over 70 years of history, Latulippe is one of the highly regarded stores in the region when it comes to gear for hunting and fishing. What used to be just a tiny, family-run store was recently renovated and is now a large, modern, two-floor store with everything you need for an outdoor adventure—boots, bags, tents, waterproof outerwear, and accessories. They even have gear for snowmobiling and ammunition, guns, and knives for hunting. And the staff is always full of advice and helpful tips, so just ask.

MAP 5: 637 rue St-Vallier W., 418/529-0024, www.latulippe.com; Mon.-Tues. 8:30am-5:30pm, Wed.-Fri. 8:30am-9pm, Sat. 9am-5pm, Sun. 11am-5pm

SHOPPING DISTRICTS AND CENTERS
Galeries de la Capitale
About a 20-minute drive from downtown Québec City, Galeries de La Capitale is one of the most fascinating malls in the province (especially for kids). Opened in 1981, it was the brainchild of businessman Marcel Adams and was filled with Canadian department store heavyweights Eaton's, The Bay, Simons, and Woolco. Today, it has 280 stores, 35 restaurants, the biggest IMAX theater in Canada, and an indoor amusement park. Called Le Mega-Parc, it has 20 rides, including a Ferris wheel, roller coasters, a skating rink, and smaller rides and games that will make kids go wild.

MAP 5: 5401 blvd. des Galeries, 418/627-5800, www.galeriesdelacapitale.com; Mon.-Wed. 9:30am-5:30pm, Thurs.-Fri. 9:30am-9pm, Sat. 9:30am-5pm, Sun. 10am-5pm

Laurier Québec
The biggest of the three malls, Laurier Québec, formerly called Place Laurier, is three levels high and boasts 350 stores. Opened in 1961, it is the largest mall in eastern Canada and one of the city's top tourist attractions. Well-known stores like Old Navy, H&M, The Bay, Nike, Aldo, and American Apparel are all situated here, as are specialized boutiques including Laine, which carries wool and other knitting materials, and Vision Rock, where you can get a tattoo while you pick up a KISS wall-clock and T-shirt from your favorite hard-rock band. Laurier Québec offers free shuttle service between Vieux-Québec and the mall as well as to the nearby Aquarium du Québec.

MAP 5: 2700 blvd. Laurier, 418/651-5000, www.laurierquebec.com; Mon.-Wed. 10am-5:30pm, Thurs.-Fri. 10am-9pm, Sat. 9am-5pm, Sun. 10am-5pm

Place de la Cité
Part of the large shopping complex on boulevard Laurier in Sainte-Foy, Place de la Cité stands out thanks to the 17-story office building that's attached to the mall's concourse. It's the home of 150 stores and restaurants, and you'll find independent boutiques including Simone Paris, which caters to sizes 6-18; Québécois label Myco Anna; and Corset Corsaire, carrying exclusive prêt-à-porter labels from Europe. La Maison Anglaise, the only bookstore dedicated to English books in the region, is located here,

as are sports stores including O'Neill, Sport Select, and Québec brand Chlorophylle.

MAP 5: 2600 blvd. Laurier, Sainte-Foy, 418/657-6920, www.placedelacite. com; Mon.-Wed. 9:30am-5:30pm, Thurs.-Fri. 9:30am-9pm, Sat. 9am-5pm, Sun. noon-5pm

Place Ste-Foy

One of the three shopping malls that make up the impressively large complex in the region close to Université Laval just outside of the city, Place Ste-Foy is also one of the oldest. Built in 1958, it is considered the best shopping center in Québec City for upscale boutiques and labels. Canada's preeminent luxury department store, Holt Renfrew, has been located here since 1965, and among the mall's 135 stores you'll find other top-of-the line brands like Birks, Swarovski, Lacoste, and BCBG Maxazria.

MAP 5: 2452 blvd. Laurier, 418/653-4184, www.placestefoy.ca; Mon.-Wed. 9:30am-5:30pm, Thurs.-Fri. 9:30am-9pm, Sat. 9am-5pm, Sun. 10am-5pm

Hotels

PRICE KEY

$ Less than $100 per night

$$ $100–200 per night

$$$ More than $200 per night

S taying in Québec City can be expensive. There is a lack of choice when it comes to affordable accommodations, and it can sometimes feel as though hotels are taking advantage of a lucrative situation. However, service, at both moderately priced and more expensive hotels,

couldn't be better. Like restaurants, hotels don't lack in numbers, and the highest concentration of hotels can be found in Vieux-Québec's Upper Town, where on about every little street you'll find a couple of smaller inns. It's here as well that the Château Frontenac is located, standing sentinel on the cliff and casting a shadow on some lesser-known but equally good hotels. Because of its proximity to sights such as the Château and the Citadelle, as well as a number of restaurants, Upper Town is the most sought-after area, but by extension it's also the most touristy.

If you're a fan of sleek, minimal boutique hotels, opt for something in Vieux-Québec's Lower Town or Vieux-Port, once the center of the city's financial district. Old banks, office buildings, and warehouses have been converted into some of the most exciting new hotels. Though it's just as much a tourist attraction as Upper Town, the area has a more relaxed vibe. And although you step out of your hotel into one of the oldest places in North America, it maintains a neighborhood feel that gives it a unique touch of authenticity.

One thing that stands out in Québec City's hotel landscape is the lack of major chains. The Delta and Hilton can be found in Upper Town on René-Lévesque just outside of the city walls, but they are just about the

Previous: Fairmont Le Château Frontenac, Upper Town; Auberge Le Vincent, Saint-Roch. **Next:** a room in the Fairmont Le Château Frontenac.

Highlights

★ **Best Hostel:** One of the few hostels in the city center, **Auberge Internationale de Québec** is friendly, affordable, and couldn't be closer to the action (page 164).

★ **Most Romantic Hotel:** Situated in two of the most beautiful buildings in Vieux-Québec's Upper Town, **Auberge Place d'Armes** has a 17th-century meets 21st-century decor that makes it perfect for a getaway for two (page 164).

★ **Most Luxurious Hotel:** The **Fairmont Le Château Frontenac** is one of the most recognized hotels in the world. A stay here is nothing short of a fantasy (page 165).

★ **Best Location:** Tucked away on an unassuming side street near the old walls, **Hôtel Manoir Victoria** makes for an easy walk to just about anywhere in the city (page 167).

★ **Best Budget Hotel:** A charming bed-and-breakfast in Vieux-Québec's Upper Town, **La Marquise de Bassano** is both affordable, well located, and, above all, welcoming (page 168).

★ **Most Distinctive Building:** A former marine warehouse, **Auberge Saint-Antoine** has high ceilings, exposed beams, and stone floors that match perfectly with the minimal but opulent decor (page 168).

★ **Best Place to Bring the Gang:** Situated in the Old-Port and with modern suites at reasonable prices, **Hôtel Port-Royal** is ideal if you're traveling with the kids (page 169).

★ **Best Boutique Hotel:** With an accommodating staff and awesome views of the St-Lawrence River and Lower Town, chic **Hôtel 71** is a great home-away-from-home (page 171).

★ **Best Guesthouse:** Situated above the oldest grocery store in North America, **Auberge J.A. Moisan** is authentically Victorian without being stuffy (page 171).

★ **Hippest Hotel:** The modern, sleek interior, stunning views, and location in the heart of Saint-Roch make **Hôtel Pur** the ultimate hip hotel (page 173).

only ones. Most chain hotels are located outside of the city center, close to a collection of shopping malls in Sainte-Foy on the aptly named Avenue des Hôtels. Most of these hotels offer competitive rates and daily shuttles to downtown in the summer. In winter, this service doesn't necessarily apply, and though city buses are available they take much longer but aren't complicated. If you're traveling without a car, it might be more practical to spring for something closer to downtown.

If you want to be close to the action but also want to experience a bit of the city's hipper, younger side, check out hotels in the Saint-Roch and St-Jean Baptiste areas. Since they are not traditional tourist areas, the rates can be more competitive, and though you might not find yourself looking out onto the oldest square in North America, the history here is just as rich.

CHOOSING A HOTEL

When choosing a hotel in Québec City, one of the first things to consider is mobility and how you travel. Charles Dickens famously called it the "Gibraltar of America," and that's still a fitting description. Though it's possible to spend your entire trip in either Upper Town (on the hill) or Lower Town (below the hill), it is unlikely, and even then you'll encounter inclines and hills no matter where you go. Québec isn't a large city by any stretch, but, if you're limited in mobility or by the length of your stay, getting a hotel near the sights you most want to see makes sense. Upper and Lower Town are easily accessible by the funicular and Ecobuses, but if you like boutique hotels, for example, and only have a night, plan it all in the Vieux-Port and spend the next morning doing the rounds in Upper Town. Driving to the sights, especially in summer and unless they are far way, will be much more hassle than it's worth.

The competitive prices of Sainte-Foy hotels might be tempting, but if you're arriving by train or bus at the main station, you'll end up crossing the entire city just to get there. Instead, pick something more modest in the Vieux-Port or Saint-Roch neighborhoods that can be easily accessible when you arrive. Or make sure you get a ticket to the Sainte-Foy station instead.

The majority of hotels have standard North American-style rooms and amenities like air-conditioning and coffee in the room. But since many of the hotels are also in historic buildings, the rooms in Québec City are usually more European in size. If you book a room in a quaint-looking Victorian house, avoid disappointment and expect it to be smaller than usual. Since they are old homes, it means some of them might not have elevators; it's worth inquiring before you book, though most will have a bellhop for those purposes.

Breakfasts also come in European sizes or not at all. Many hotels don't include breakfast as part of the room, or if they do, they are continental with fresh pastries, breads, cheeses, and fruit. In some cases it's wisest to skip the hotel breakfast altogether and head to one of the city's many bistros for a filling first meal instead.

Packages offer different options for guests when they book and can include breakfast as part of the deal as well as things like tours, museum entrances, and bottles of champagne. Parking, even at bigger hotels, can be hard to come by, but most paid parking lots are safe and relatively affordable. If you're staying near the Plains you might be lucky enough to find free street parking amid the upscale homes. Even if they don't provide parking themselves, the hotels are usually more than willing to help you find a spot or at the very least give you various options.

Vieux-Québec's Upper Town

Map 1

★ Auberge Internationale de Québec §

This hostel is a member of Hostelling International, and you won't find a more affordable place to stay in Vieux-Québec. Situated in what used to be a convent, this comfortable youth hostel has been providing sparse but spacious and spotless rooms for over 40 years. Along with dormitories—male, female, or mixed—they also offer private rooms available for 1-5 people, perfect if you're traveling with a group. Communal areas include a self-serve kitchen and a café bistro, a great place to relax and chat with fellow travelers. In summertime, you can enjoy breakfast in their charming little interior courtyard. The bilingual staff is warm and welcoming and offers a number of different activities, from tours outside the city to organized pub crawls.

MAP 1: 19 rue Ste-Ursule, 418/694-0755, www.aubergeinternationaledequebec.com

★ Auberge Place d'Armes §§

Spread throughout two buildings, one an old hotel and the other an old wax museum, Auberge Place d'Armes is one of the most beautiful hotels in the city, situated in the shadow of Fairmont Le Château Frontenac. Although walls date back to the 17th century, there is nothing old about this hotel; it's just charming. The rooms are all decorated in a mix of modern meets antiques, the most lavish of which is, appropriately, The Marie Antoinette Suite. With its eggshell-blue walls, ornate gold moldings, and rich fabrics, the room is kept light by the addition of pieces like a Plexiglas take on an baroque lamp and Philippe Stark-inspired Louis XIV chairs. Complimentary breakfast is served at Le Pain Béni, their on-site restaurant and one of the best in the city. Those traveling with pets can bring them here (for a small extra fee) but must request a specific room at time of booking.

MAP 1: 24 rue Ste-Anne, 418/694-9485, www.aubergeplacedarmes.com

Le Capitole de Québec §§

Blink and you might miss the sliver of a sign marking this discreet hotel. Tucked into an old building near the St-Jean Gate that includes restaurant Il Teatro and Le Capitole theater—special packages for all three are available—this small four-floor hotel with 45 rooms is in a great location. The interior is distinctly contemporary with bright colors and modern takes on classic furniture shapes. Rooms, however, can be quite small, and though they all boast ensuite bathrooms, some tubs are located next to the bed. It may be romantic, but it's not necessarily practical.

MAP 1: 972 rue St-Jean, 800/363-4040, www.lecapitole.com

Chez Hubert ❸

Tucked away on a quiet side street, this small three-room bed-and-breakfast is a good option for those looking for the Upper Town experience without the cost. This grand old Victorian townhouse has chandeliers in every room, stained-glass windows, and a beautiful curved staircase at the entrance. Owner Hubert is warm and amiable and offers guests a hearty buffet breakfast. Each of the rooms is decorated in soft hues, and one room looks out on the Château while another has a balcony. All three rooms, however, share bathroom facilities.

MAP 1: 66 rue Ste-Ursule, 418/692-0958, www.chezhubert.com

★ Fairmont Le Château Frontenac ❸❸❸

This is luxury at its finest. And having just undergone major renovations and refurbishing, this historic hotel and landmark is one of the chicest and most sought-after temporary addresses in the city. Just entering the sumptuously decorated lobby you feel as though you've stepped into a Victorian salon, with its rich wood paneled walls and ceilings, wall sconces in the shape of candelabras, and antique chandelier hung above the grand staircase. The decor of the 618 rooms and suites follows suit with high ceilings, classic fabrics, and Victorian-style wood furnishings. Like most fine hotels, it has all the amenities you'd expect: pool, spa, gym, and ballroom.

MAP 1: 1 rue des Carrières, 418/692-3861, www.fairmont.com

Hôtel Cap Diamant ❸❸

Located in a historic building on a small and quiet street not far from the walls of the Citadelle, Hôtel Cap Diamant is a charming bed-and-breakfast. Each of the 12 rooms is furnished with rich antiques, giving it a European charm. It's run by Mme. Guillot and her daughter, and the staff is warm, welcoming, and helpful. Guests are treated to a complimentary continental breakfast, which they're welcome to eat in the hidden backyard, full of flowers in the summer. Though there's an elevator for luggage, guests will have to climb the stairs to their rooms, some of which are on the fourth floor.

MAP 1: 39 ave. Ste-Geneviève, 418/694-0313, www.hotelcapdiamant.com

Hôtel Château Bellevue ❸❸

Located in front of the Jardin des Gouverneurs just behind the Château Frontenac, this 48-room hotel offers great views of the St-Lawrence River and access to all the major sites on foot. Taking over four stately homes that were built at the turn of the 20th century, the rooms here are smaller than what you might be hoping for but are comfortably appointed with homey touches like throw pillows and antiques. The hotel offers a complimentary breakfast as well as free Internet and access to a fitness facility. Those up

Chill Out at the Ice Hotel

Come winter, the **Hôtel de Glace** (www.hoteldeglace-canada.com) is one of the most magical places to lay your head. Started in 2001, it was the first ice hotel in North America and has since become one of the most extraordinary hotel experiences in the city. Open from January to March, and situated just outside of the city, the hotel takes roughly a month and a half and 60 workers to construct, with the ice built around a metal base that forms its foundations. Entirely redesigned and rebuilt every year, each incarnation is built around a different theme.

Though the design, theme, and architecture change, the materials don't. The interior is always decked out with ice furniture, sculptures, and touches of fur and animal hide to soften and warm up the space. Everything here, except for the heated bathrooms in a separate building, is made of ice, from the glasses at the bar, to the bar itself, the lobby chairs, the serving plates, and of course, the beds. Made of blocks of ice, the base of the bed is then layered with solid wood as well as a mattress, which is topped with an insulating bed sheet and pillow that are brought to your room just as you're getting ready for bed, along with an arctic sleeping bag. Though temperatures outside might dip to -25°C (13°F), the four-foot thick walls keep the room between -3°C and -5°C (27°F and 23°F) no matter the temperature outside.

A typical night at the Ice Hotel starts at three in the afternoon with a check in at the Four Points by Sheraton, the base for the ice hotel; this is also where guests eat a hot breakfast the following morning. A free shuttle takes guests out to the hotel, where they can spend the afternoon and evening drinking in the ice bar, trying out the gigantic ice slide, or warming up in the outdoor hot tubs before heading to their rooms later in the night. Some rooms and suites even come with an optional fireplace or both a fireplace and private spa, perfect for a romantic getaway. The hotel even has its very own ice chapel for midwinter marriages. A night at the hotel will typically cost $400-500 per person, which includes a hotel room at the Four Points Sheraton as well as breakfast at Le Dijon, among other perks. Early-bird specials are available starting in the fall with prices hovering around $225 per person.

If you're not convinced sleeping in -3° weather is for you but feel oddly compelled to try out the **Nordic slide** (and who could blame you), tours are available daily between 10:30am and 4:30pm.

for the walk also have access to the saltwater pool and urban spa at the Château Laurier, the hotel's sister site, located about a 15-minute walk away. **MAP 1:** 16 rue de la Porte, 418/692-2573 www.hotelchateaubellevue.com

Hôtel Clarendon $$

Built in 1858 and designed by Charles Baillairgé, this historic hotel is the oldest in Vieux-Québec. First a home, then offices, it became a hotel in 1870 and has remained one since. Originally a four-story building, it underwent two additions in the 20th century, one to include two floors and the mansard roof and the other a six-floor art deco extension, making it particularly striking. It's across the street from City Hall and next door to Édifice Price. Upon entering the Clarendon you're immediately hit with the art deco feel—wood beams feature on the ceiling and large mirrors are placed throughout. The rooms themselves are rather modest with simple decor, though some feature gorgeous circular windows.

MAP 1: 57 rue Ste-Anne, 418/692-2480, www.hotelclarendon.com

Hôtel Le Champlain ⑤⑤

Eclectically decorated with bright modern furniture and subtly bold wallpaper, Hôtel Le Champlain is a welcoming boutique hotel. Surrounded by historic buildings, the hotel is distinctly modern, though the hardwood floors and exposed brick walls add a bit of European charm to the 49 rooms. Ideally located on a quiet street, it is close to everything but avoids the noise and bustle of streets like St-Jean and St-Louis. Guests are treated to a complimentary breakfast, as well as cappuccinos and espressos that are available throughout the day in the lobby.

MAP 1: 115 rue Ste-Anne, 418/694-0106, www.champlainhotel.com

Hôtel Le Clos Saint-Louis ⑤⑤

If you're an old-fashioned romantic, you will swoon at Hôtel Le Clos St-Louis. Calling itself the "most romantic Victorian hotel in the city," it's fastidiously decorated with period antiques, including wardrobes, four-poster beds, and fainting couches. Its location close to the St-Louis gate makes sights both inside and outside the walls walkable. Catering to couples, this isn't a place for kids. They offer a variety of packages, including Engagement, Newlywed, and the Babymoon package, for expectant mothers.

MAP 1: 69 rue St-Louis, 418/694-1311, www.clossaintlouis.com

★ Hôtel Manoir Victoria ⑤⑤

Though the building that now houses the Hôtel Manoir Victoria was built in 1904, the hotel's history dates back to the 1830s when Thomas Payne opened the city's most exclusive hotel across the street from its current location. Situated just off of St-Jean in Upper Town on a street that connects to Lower Town and the Saint-Roch area, Hôtel Manoir Victoria is sumptuously decorated with rich, embellished fabrics and classically comfortable furnishings. The rooms are modern but still traditional, and there's a homeyness to both the superior rooms and more luxurious suites. Though still beautiful, the hotel enjoyed its heyday in the 1920s, and no place is this more evident than with the pool. With its Grecian columns and small black-and-white tiles, it's like something out of The Great Gatsby. It's also connected to the Bistro Boréal, so you don't have to leave the premises to eat well.

MAP 1: 44 Côte du Palais, 418/692-1030, www.manoir-victoria.com

Hôtel Ste-Anne ⑤⑤

Chic and sophisticated is the best way to describe the feel of this 20-room hotel just across the square from Château Frontenac. Located on a busy cobblestone street, this historic building has been perfectly transformed into a sleek, boutique-style hotel. The stone walls, exposed ceiling beams, and Norman-style windows are the prefect complement to the simple, clean lines of the furnishings and the ultramodern bathrooms—black slate tiles, glass shower doors. The rooms can be quite small, however, so keep size in mind if you're choosing between a superior room and a junior suite.

MAP 1: 32 rue Ste-Anne, 418/694-1455, www.hotelste-anne.com

★ La Marquise de Bassano ⑤

Located on a quiet street lined with historic homes in Vieux-Québec's Upper Town, this charming bed-and-breakfast is steps away from Château Frontenac and Les Fortifications. It's run by a young, outgoing couple, and the five rooms of this gray-stone townhouse are uniquely decorated, and priced, with touches like a full bookshelf, writing desk, and vintage type-writer in the "library room," a claw-footed bathtub, or antique pieces. Only two rooms have their own bathrooms, however; the other three must share. Breakfast is served in the cold European style with meats, hardboiled eggs, and various breads and pastries.

MAP 1: 12 rue des Grisons, 418/692-0316, www.marquisedebassano.com

Vieux-Québec's Lower Town
Map 2

★ Auberge Saint-Antoine ⑤⑤⑤

Once a port-side warehouse, Auberge St-Antoine retained its high ceilings, exposed beams, and stone floors, all the things that make it one of the most inviting hotels in the city today. It was built on the archaeological site of Îlot Hunt, an area full of wharfs and warehouses at the peak of Québec's port history, and artifacts that were found on this site have been incorporated into the hotel design. The rooms are sleek and modern with a touch of luxury: plush headboards with unique motifs and heated bathroom floors. Many also have balconies, terraces, or fireplaces, so request one when you book. Unique services include an archaeological tour, on-site cinema, and Wednesday drinks with the family of owners. One of the city's top restaurants, Panache, is also located here, in what was once the warehouse lobby.

MAP 2: 8 rue St-Antoine, 418/692-2211, www.saint-antoine.com

Auberge Saint-Pierre ⑤⑤

The first of the boutique hotels to open in Québec City, Auberge Saint-Pierre has a charm all its own. Though it's been recently been remodeled with slightly sleeker furniture and a more minimalist decor, the Saint-Pierre still makes you feel as though you're staying with a close friend or family (but without the bickering). Brick walls and classic black and white photos are the backdrop for cozy white wooden furniture and pops of bright color. Each room comes with its own coffee maker, iron, and umbrella—now that's thinking ahead. The feeling of home continues in the main

area with a complimentary gourmet breakfast in the relaxed dining room and a library with a roaring fireplace, perfect for relaxing with a nightcap.
MAP 2: 79 rue St-Pierre, 418/694-7981, www.auberge.qc.ca

Hôtel Belley ⚫

Looking out over the marina and farmers market, Hôtel Belley is just a close walk to sights in both Upper and Lower Town and is a stone's throw from the cool Saint-Roch area. This tiny eight-room hotel has a definite laid-back atmosphere, perhaps helped in part by the historic tavern on the ground floor, which provides an excellent place to socialize and relax all year long. The rooms here are small and simply furnished, but the views, especially at night, are lovely. Come summer, *terrasses* are open in both the front and back of the building, attracting locals and tourists alike.
MAP 2: 249 rue St-Paul, 418/692-1694, www.quebecweb.com/hotelbelley

Hôtel Le Germain-Dominion ⚫⚫⚫

With its grandiose neoclassical facade and modern, understated interior, you'd never guess that this chic boutique hotel started off as a fish ware-house. Located in the former financial district, this nine-floor hotel, the first of Le Germain's to open in North America, offers great views over both the St-Lawrence and Lower Town. The large, open lobby with big windows, comfy couches, and a laid-back atmosphere is immediately inviting. You'll want to spend all morning in the adjoining dining room, sinking back into your plush seat with a paper while you finish off breakfast. The rooms themselves are equally inviting, with big windows, simple, uncomplicated design, and a Nespresso machine making it the ultimate getaway.
MAP 2: 126 rue St-Pierre, 418/692-2222, www.germaindominion.com

Hôtel Le Priori ⚫⚫

At the base of Cap Diamant in the Vieux-Port on one of the oldest streets in North America, Hôtel Le Priori occupies the space that was once the home of architect Jean Baillairgé. In summer, its white-washed facade is punctuated with color from hanging flowers and vines that crown the entrance and its surrounding windows. Inside, a modern interior contrasts with the stone walls that date as far back as 1734. The hotel features 21 bedrooms and five suites. The emphasis is on minimalist chic but with a touch of art deco at this boutique hotel. Furniture in asymmetrical shapes and unusual colors like deep purple or bright red can be found in most rooms. Each suite, however, is uniquely decorated. Make sure to take advantage of the secluded outdoor *terrasse* or make reservations at the in-house restaurant Toast!
MAP 2: 15 rue du Sault-au-Matelot, 418/692-3992, www.hotellepriori.com

★ Hôtel Port-Royal ⚫⚫

This old storehouse with gray stone exterior in the center of the Vieux-Port has since been converted exclusively into suites. Offering three different types of suites (deluxe, superior, and executive), Hôtel Port-Royal provides a home away from home with each suite equipped with living room and kitchenette, a great option if you want to save costs by eating in. The decor

---

Top: Fairmont Le Château Frontenac from the interior courtyard, Vieux-Québec's Upper Town; **Below:** inside the Hôtel de Glace.

© Renaud Ph

throughout is simple and modern with wood floors, sandy-colored walls, and each suite decorated just so, whether with dramatic striped wallpaper or a colorful, floral couch. It's perfect if you're traveling with the family.

MAP 2: 144 rue St-Pierre, 418/692-2777, www.leportroyal.com

★ Hôtel 71 $$$

Located on a cobblestone street in what was once the city's financial district, Hôtel 71 is in a building that was once the National Bank's head office. The neoclassical facade of this boutique hotel is juxtaposed against the sleek, modern interior. Rooms are uncluttered, with earth-toned furniture with clean lines giving them an especially Zen feeling. The bathrooms, too, are relaxing, with gray slate tiles and geometric lines. Large windows in almost every room allow not only for natural light but also great views of the city and surrounding area. It's the choice of design lovers with a larger budget. Breakfast is served in the adjoining restaurant and offers a delicious cappuccino to wash down your hearty continental breakfast.

MAP 2: 71 rue St-Pierre, 418/692-1171, www.hotel71.ca

Parliament Hill and the Plains
Map 3

Hôtel Château Laurier $$

Set back from the Plains of Abraham and a two-minute walk to Vieux-Québec's Upper Town, Hôtel Château Laurier is ideally located. The newly renovated lobby is open and inviting with a blazing fire in the winter. Rooms here run the gamut from European-style rooms that are smaller than usual North American rooms and simply decorated to big, bright, newly renovated rooms with updated modern furniture and more of a Zen quality. No matter your room type, all guests are welcome to try the indoor saltwater pool.

MAP 3: 1220 Place Georges-V W., 418/-522-8108, www.oldquebec.com/en/laurier

Saint-Jean-Baptiste and Saint-Roch
Map 4

★ Auberge J.A. Moisan $$

This four-bedroom guesthouse invites you to be a part of history by sleeping above the oldest grocery store in North America. Charmingly decorated with impeccable moldings, antique furniture, homemade quilts, and Laura Ashley prints, it gives just a taste of what it was like to be a successful businessman in the 19th century. The beautifully restored Victorian house

also boasts a living room, library, solarium, and *terrasse,* all of which guests have access to. Just to take things a little bit further, 4 o'clock tea is served.
MAP 4: 699 rue St-Jean, 418/529-9764, www.jamoisan.com/auberge

Auberge L'Autre Jardin $$

If traveling gives you eco-anxiety, then staying at Auberge L'Autre Jardin will give you a clear conscience. This 28-room hotel is dedicated to sustainable and responsible tourism, with organic breakfasts made with fair-trade products and furnishings that come from sustainable sources. Owned by Carrefour Tiers-Monde, a Québec-based charity that raises awareness on issues in developing countries, the hotel is the money-making side of the business. The rooms are tastefully decorated and feel more like a friend's place, with classic but not swank bedding. They're decorated with art from Africa, Asia, and India. The hotel also has a fair-trade store selling coffee, jewelry, and different international art crafts and accessories.
MAP 4: 365 blvd. Charest E., 418/523-1790, www.autrejardin.com

Auberge Le Vincent $$

The keyword here is "concierge." Every effort is put into making your stay nothing less than fantastic and tailor made. From the made-to-order breakfasts to in-house movie rentals (there are over 100 to choose from at the front desk), the staff evinces old-school charm, taking care of dinner reservations, walking tours, and more—you name it and they're on it. Of course they can handle it all because this is a small, 10-room hotel located in the trendy Saint-Roch area. It is impeccably designed. Each room is uniquely decorated, but all feature exposed brick walls, 400-thread-count sheets, and the most modern bathrooms, often separated by a crystal-clear glass window—with optional blind.
MAP 4: 295 rue St-Vallier E., 418/523-5000, www.aubergelevincent.com

Château des Tourelles $$

Just across the street from Château du Faubourg is this light and airy bed-and-breakfast, marked by a turret that stands out on this strip of St-Jean, which is lined with neighborhood bistros and small boutiques. Climb a flight of stairs into this warm and welcoming place. Wood floors and exposed brick give the rooms a cozy and a little bit country feel, without being kitschy. A filling breakfast is served in the sunny dining room, and a roaring fire in the sitting room is great for guests in the winter, while the rooftop terrace offers views of (nearly) all of the sights in the city.
MAP 4: 212 rue St-Jean, 418/346-9136, www.chateaudestourelles.qc.ca

Le Château du Faubourg $

Set back from the road on busy rue St-Jean is a huge Second Empire-style chateau. Built by the rich Imperial Tobacco family in the 1800s, it retains its original grandeur and is one of the city's most impressive bed-and-breakfasts. A gilded staircase and chandelier greet you as you enter and set the tone for the rooms, which give off the air of an old manor house with rich antique furnishings, sumptuous fabrics, and, in the case of one room, an

entire library as headboard. Each room has its own individual bathroom.
Breakfast is served in a grand library, and though the owners are lovely and
charming, their 12 pet birds get on the nerves of some.

MAP 4: 429 rue St-Jean, 418/524-2902, www.lechateaudufaubourg.com

★ Hôtel Pur $$

This chic, boutique-style hotel in the heart of Saint-Roch, one of the city's
up-and-coming neighborhoods, couldn't be cooler. Standing 18 floors
tall, it's the highest building in the area, so just about every room has a
view from the floor-to-ceiling windows, looking out on to the city, the
Laurentian mountains, or the newly refurbished Saint-Roch church. The
sleek design and minimal color palette—gray, black, and white with bursts
of orange—give it an uncluttered but still relaxed vibe. The slate-gray bathrooms give it an added touch of Zen, as do the Japanese-style baths and
glass-door showers. Visitors can dine in the adjoining restaurant Table,
which is equally as chic with long communal tables, comfy couches, and a
menu that goes all day long.

MAP 4: 395 rue de la Couronne, 418/647-2611, www.hotelpur.com

Greater Québec City $\qquad$ Map 5

Château Bonne Entente $$

This large, sprawling hotel outside of the city offers an alternative to those
who want the feel of a country getaway with a close proximity to the downtown. Just about every room in this cottage-style hotel with mansard roofs
and soft-yellow clapboard is distinctly decorated, from the hardwood floors
and country fabrics of the "Cocooning" room to the carpeted, sleek but
comfortable decor of the "Business" room. With an on-site spa, large outdoor pool and hot tub, and golf course, relaxation is never far away.

MAP 5: 3400 chemin Ste-Foy, 418/653-5221, www.chateaubonneentente.com

Hôtel Sépia $$

Located outside of the city center and close to other hotels, the city's largest shopping malls, and the aquarium, Hôtel Sépia is a bit of urbania in
suburbia. With its sleek modern design—rain shower heads, Barcelona
chairs, and refinished wood floors—this boutique-style hotel will make
you feel like you're in the middle of downtown even when you're not. It's
approximately a 15-minute drive to downtown, and the hotel offers free
shuttle services during the summer months; those traveling without a car,
however, might find it impractical come winter. This hotel might not give
you a great view of the Vieux-Port but it will give you a great view of the
famous Québec Bridge.

MAP 5: 3135 chemin St-Louis, 418/653-4941, www.hotelsepia.ca

Excursions from Québec City

Visiting Québec City might give you a clear picture of the province's urban population, but if you really want to get to know the province and see the culture and nature that have shaped it, you have to go north.

Referred to as the *régions* (regions), the forests and the jagged cliffs of the St-Lawrence provide a real sense of the province and its rugged beauty. Barely a half-hour-drive from Québec you'll find yourself in the picturesque Côte-de-Beaupré, lined with quaint ancestral homes—most continue to be residential homes. Not every historical event took place in and around the city; in fact, this area was where General Wolfe and his men camped before they laid siege to the city.

Once mostly farmland the area is now a large tourist destination thanks to the pilgrimages to the Basilique Sainte-Anne-de-Beaupré and Chute Montmorency. Across the water on the Île d'Orléans, however, things have stayed much the same as they have for hundreds of years. Île d'Orléans is full of vineyards and farms, and agri-tourism is a big part of the island; visitors should take full advantage by picking their own fruits and vegetables to take home.

Navigating the Côte-Nord (North Coast) couldn't be easier; two highways take you to the same destination, and it all depends on whether you want the scenic route, Route 362, or the faster route, Route 138. Truth be told, even the faster route could be described as scenic; the high cliffs, rolling hills, and patches of tundra landscape as you head farther north are hard to ignore. Baie-Saint-Paul seems to emerge like a mirage, its church steeple sparkling on the shores of a low valley flanked by stone cliffs and

Previous: vineyard, Côte-de-Beaupré; Le Massif ski resort, Charlevoix.

Highlights

★ **Best Historic Road:** One of the oldest roads in North America, **Route de la Nouvelle France** is lined with ancestral homes dating back hundreds of years (page 179).

★ **Best Waterfall:** Taller than Niagara Falls, **Chute Montmorency** is an impressive sight, especially when you're on the suspension bridge over the falls with 360-degree breathtaking views (page 179).

★ **Oldest Pilgrimage Site:** Built in honor of Sainte-Anne, the patron saint of shipwrecked sailors, the **Basilique Sainte-Anne-de-Beaupré** is one of the oldest pilgrimage sites in the world. The interior is lined with crutches as a testament to its healing powers (page 179).

★ **Best Place to Pick Your Own Fruits and Vegetables: Île d'Orléans** is an island in the middle of the St-Lawrence River. It has some of the oldest homes in the region and some of the best agriculture. Head to the island to pick your own fresh fruit and vegetables (page 180).

★ **Most Artistic Town:** The birthplace of Cirque du Soleil, **Baie-Saint-Paul** is full of galleries and folk art boutiques (page 184).

★ **Best Skiing:** Overlooking the St-Lawrence River and cutting through the boreal forest, the hills at **Le Massif** offer views just as stunning as the slopes themselves (page 188).

★ **Best Bike Excursion:** Only 11 kilometers long and 3 kilometers wide, the **Isle-aux-Coudres,** near Tadoussac, is filled with old churches, windmills, and other rarities, to be discovered by bike (page 189).

★ **Best Place to Play Blackjack:** Located in a long-established holiday town, the **Casino de Charlevoix** is the one place you should place your bets (page 193).

★ **Best Hiking:** The gorges and fjords of **Parc National des Hautes-Gorges-de-la-Rivière-Malbaie,** along with its unique mix of tundra and taiga, make it one of the most breathtaking sites to hike in the region (page 193).

★ **Best Whale-Watching:** At the confluence of the Saguenay and St-Lawrence Rivers, the shores surrounding the historic town of **Tadoussac** have one of the most diverse ecosystems in the world. This is the annual meeting place for 10 species of whales, from humpbacks to belugas (page 195).

North again, La Malbaie sneaks up on you from the corners of the twisting turning road, and though the sites aren't much, the landscape is lovely. Once you're this far north you might as well continue to the jewel of Charlevoix and cross the majestic Saguenay by ferry to Tadoussac. The massive cliffs that plunge into the river make for breathtaking scenery, and if you're lucky enough to catch a view of the diverse whale life that thrives in these waters, you'll understand the atypical beauty that defines the region and the province.

PLANNING YOUR TIME

Some of these excursions can be done by day or even an afternoon by car. However, some places, including Tadoussac and the Saguenay Fjord are three hours (or sometimes more) away, so plan to spend at least a night in these locations. Of course, no matter how far afield you're willing to travel, if you have the time, it's always fun to stay a bit longer in order to really get to know a place. Though Québec is a big province and you could drive for hours without hitting on any sights, all the excursions in this section are easily reached, the longest taking at most three hours from the city.

Most of the sights are accessible by national highways, though in some places these highways slim down to two lanes. If you're driving in winter, the journey could take longer, especially if there are bad driving conditions. Snow tires are required by law December-March; if you don't have them on your car, avoid trips into the rocky and hilly Charlevoix, or rent a car with the right tires.

High season is May-October; those traveling north to Charlevoix later in the year should make sure to plan well ahead, or opt for a package deal at places like La Massif. Getting a hotel, dinner, and recreation in one deal will allow you to see the beauty of the area without worrying about whether there'll be restaurants open or not.

Côte-de-Beaupré and Île d'Orléans

Minutes outside of Québec on Route 138, you'll reach the Côte-de-Beaupré. Located on the banks of the St-Lawrence River, this historical area boasts ancient ancestral homes and open farmland running along the Route de la Nouvelle France, one of the oldest roads in North America. As you pass along the 50 kilometers of roadways, you'll pass through a number of small towns, all of which are between the high cliffs of the Laurentians and the shores of the river.

From the Côte-de-Beaupré you can see the Île d'Orléans, an island in the stream of the St-Lawrence. Linking the two historical areas is the Île d'Orléans Bridge, which can be used by car, bike, or foot. The island itself has one main road, Chemin Royal, which circles the entire island. It's dotted

EXCURSIONS FROM QUEBEC CITY

Lac Kénogami
Laterrière
Saint-Bruno
170
Parc National du Saguenay
170
Saint-Félix-d'Otis
Lac Brébeuf
Lac Ha! Ha!
Le Trou-de-la-Vieille
381
Parc National des Hautes-Gorges-de-la-Rivière-Malbaie
175
Lac-Pikauba
Lac des Martres
10 mi
10 km
Parc national des Grands-Jardins
Lac-Fronsac
138
Lac Beauséjour
Lac Jacques-Cartier
L-Étape
Lac-Malbaie
To Saint-Siméon and Tadoussac
Saint-Joseph-de-la-Rive
Lac-des-Neiges
362
Baie-Saint-Paul
Mare-du-Sault
Parc National de la Jacques-Cartier
Isle-aux-Coudres
La Barrière-du-Maurice
Grande-Pointe
175
St. Lawrence River
Parc du Mont Sainte-Anne
138
Île-aux-Oies
Cape-Tourmente National Wildlife Area
Île-aux-Grues
Lamartine
Beaupré
Saint-Gabriel-de-Valcartier
ROUTE DE LA NOUVELLE FRANCE ★
Île d'Orléans
Montmagny
Lac Saint-Joseph
CHUTE MONTMORENCY ★
Beauport
20
Val-Bélair
Charlesbourg
Sainte-Pétronille
L'Acienne-Lorette
QUÉBEC CITY
To Montreal
40
Saint-Romuald
Neuville
Charny
Saint-Jean Chrisostome
Saint-Nicolas
20
216
73
Sainte-Claire
© AVALON TRAVEL

with towns, but much of the island is devoted to local agriculture and can be visited year-round.

SIGHTS
★ Route de la Nouvelle France

Leave Québec City heading northeast and you'll soon be on the **Route de la Nouvelle France** (www.routenouvelle-france.com), one of the oldest roads in North America. In 1626 Samuel de Champlain established a livestock farm on Cap Tourmente farther along the river, but it was Bishop Monsignor de Laval who originally traced the road, which brought provisions from the Côte-de-Beaupré to the city.

All along the 50-kilometer road are heritage homes, some dating as far back as the 1600s. Each is designed in its own particular style, indicative of early New France architecture. Though many of the homes are private residences, the public can visit **Maison Vézina** (171 rue des Grenadiers, 418/822-3183, www.maisonvezina.ca, May-late-Aug. Tues.-Sat. 10am-4pm, Sept.-Apr. Tues.-Sat. noon-4pm, free). Built in 1720, it's now an interpretation center and exhibition space. If you're looking to get in touch with your roots, **Centre de Généalogie** (277 rue du Couvent, 418/824-3079, www3. telebecinternet.com/archives.chateau-richer, summer daily 9am-4pm, free) can help you with genealogical research, a popular Québécois pastime.

If you want a little history of the area, the **Centre d'Interprétation de la Côte-de-Beaupré** (7976 ave. Royale, 418/824-3677, www.histoire-cotedebeaupre.org, May-Oct. daily 9:30am-4pm, Oct.-May Mon.-Fri. 9:30am-4:30pm, $6) has lots of documentation and exhibits and is housed in an old seminary.

As you travel along the road, you'll notice cavern-like structures built directly into the hillsides; these are root cellars, some of which date back more than 300 years. Also along the route is the **Moulin du Petit Pré** (7007 ave. Royale, 418/824-7007, www.moulin-petitpre.com, mid-Apr.-mid-Oct. daily 9am-5pm, $5 adult, $3 child). Founded in 1695, it's the oldest operating flour mill in North America. Take a guided tour, then have lunch at the on-site café or get some bread for the road.

★ Chute Montmorency

Carry on along the Route de la Nouvelle France and you'll soon reach **Chute Montmorency** (4300 blvd. Ste-Anne, 800/665-6527, www.sepaq. com/ct/pcm) an 83-meter-high waterfall (even taller than Niagara Falls, as everyone will point out) that dominates the landscape between the cliffs of the Laurentians and the St-Lawrence. It's a stunning natural wonder in the middle of lush greenery, and visitors can discover the falls by foot or take a cable car ($12 adult, $6 child round-trip). There's access at either side of the falls year-round and a suspension bridge that allows you to cross along the top; it offers great views of Île d'Orleans and even looks onto Québec City.

★ Basilique Sainte-Anne-de-Beaupré

This is the oldest pilgrimage site in North America, and people have been coming to **Basilique Sainte-Anne-de-Beaupré** (10018 ave. Royale,

418/827-3781, www.shrinesaintanne.org, May daily 6am-7pm, June-late-Sept. daily 6am-9pm, Oct.-Apr. Mon.-Sat. 6am-6pm, Sun. 6am-5pm) since the 1660s. The first chapel was constructed on the site in 1658 as a place of worship for the area's new settlers and to house a statue of Sainte-Anne, Québec's patron saint. She's also the patron saint of shipwrecked sailors, and it was a group of Breton sailors caught in a storm that vowed to erect a chapel in Sainte-Anne's honor if they got safely back to land. While the chapel was being constructed, a man with rheumatism was said to have been cured after laying just three bricks, and a pilgrimage was born.

The first basilica was built in 1876 to accommodate the legions of pilgrims who visited the shrine. The structure that exists today, built in the shape of a Latin cross and featuring 214 stained-glass windows, was constructed in 1926 after the first church was destroyed by fire in 1922. One image that strikes you as you enter the church is the multitude of crutches, club shoes, and other pieces of ephemera that hang on the pillars from those who have been cured. A small museum in the church's parking lot exhibits some of the church's treasures as well as donations made by pilgrims.

★ Île d'Orléans

Located five kilometers from downtown Québec City, Île d'Orléans is an island in the middle of the St-Lawrence and one of the oldest parts of New France to be colonized. It measures 34 kilometers long and 8 kilometers wide. Explorer Jacques Cartier first called it Île de Bacchus, because of the amount of wild grapes found growing on the island. Today, it's home to a number of small villages, but agriculture is still a large part of life on the island.

The first parish was founded here in 1661, and a visit to **Maison Drouin** (4700 chemin Royal, 418/829-0330, www.fondationfrancoislamy.org, mid-June-Aug. daily 10am-6pm, Sept. Sat.-Sun. 1pm-5pm, Oct.-May dates vary, $4) will give you an idea of what the early houses looked like. Built in 1730, it has been preserved in its original state.

Manoir Mauvide-Genest (1451 chemin Royal, 418/829-2630, www.manoirmauvidegenest.com, June-Aug. daily 10am-5pm, Sept.-Oct. Tues.-Sun. 10am-5pm, $6 adult, $5 senior and student, $4 child, children 5 and under free) offers a view of the seignorial home of the 18th century, with furniture, objects, and reenactments of daily life on view.

Agri-tourism is a big draw to the island; you can visit **Cassis Monna & Filles** (721 chemin Royal, 418/828-2525, www.cassismonna.com, May-Nov. daily 10am-6pm, free) and learn about how they make their black currant liqueur, or go for a tasting at **Vignoble de Sainte-Pétronille** (1A chemin du Bout-de-l'Île, 418/828-4554, www.vignobleorleans.com, May-Dec. daily 10am-5pm, free) and try their reds and whites as you look at the Chute Montmorency. Visitors are also welcome to pick their own fruits and vegetables at local farms, including **Ferme la Rosacée** (165 chemin Royal, 418/828-9662, June-mid-Oct. daily 8:30am-6:30pm, free), where you can pick everything from raspberries to seasonal vegetables and buy homemade products like jam, pickles, and ketchup.

RESTAURANTS

If you left Québec City early in the morning, stop in at **Patisserie Praline et Chocolat** (7874 ave. Royale, 418/978-0528, www.pralinechocolat.ca, mid-June-early Sept. daily 8am-6pm, early Sept-mid-June Thurs.-Sun. 8am-6pm, $10) for some mouthwatering pastries. They offer 10 different kinds of *viennoiseries* (baked goods) made fresh daily, as well as artisanal bread, jams, and other treats.

Whether you're looking for breakfast or dinner, **L'Aventure** (355 rue Dupont, 418/827-5748, www.laventure.ca, daily 11am-11pm, $30) in Beaupré has you covered with everything from grilled trout and filet mignon to eggs Benedict, all in a relaxed atmosphere. If you're in the mood for something less refined, **Casse Croute Chez Chantale** (17 rue de l'Église, 418/827-7005, daily 8:30am-7:30pm, $10) has over 100 different kinds of poutine on the menu, including the house specialty, poutine with goose.

On Île d'Orléans, tuck into some traditional cuisine or take part in the *cabane à sucre* experience at **Le Relais des Pins** (3029 chemin Royal, 418/829-3455, www.lerelaisdespins.com, June-Sept. daily 11am-9pm, winter by reservation only, $15). Open year-round, this delightful log cabin has lots of natural light and a modern take on decor.

If you've got a sweet tooth, **Chocolaterie de Île d'Orléans** (150 chemin du Bout de Île, 418/828-2250, www.chocolaterieorleans.com, $10) will satisfy with rich chocolate desserts, homemade ice cream, and delicious coffees.

Treat yourself to fine dining overlooking the St-Lawrence at **La Goéliche** (22 chemin de Quai, 418/828-2248, www.goeliche.ca, daily 8am-8:30pm, $40), where breakfast includes dishes like French toast with custard, and dinner has choices like rack of lamb and boneless rib eye with shallots.

RECREATION
Bird-Watching and Hiking
Cap-Tourmente

The site of a livestock farm established by Samuel de Champlain in the early 1600s, **Cap-Tourmente** (570 chemin du Cap-Tourmente, 418/827-4591, www.captourmente.com, mid-Apr.-Nov. daily 8:30am-5pm, Jan.-Mar. daily 9am-5pm, $6) became a farm headed by Monsignor de Laval in 1664. It was an active farm well into the 20th century, and some of the early buildings still remain. Today the area is mostly a nature reserve; it's a great place to bird-watch and learn about the greater snow goose and American bulrush marshes. Interpretive guides and 20 kilometers of hiking trails are available.

Golf
Le Grand Vallon

One of the best courses in eastern Canada, **Le Grand Vallon** (100 rue Beau-Mont, Beaupré, 418/827-4561, www.legrandvallon.com, May-Nov. daily dawn-10pm, $45-95 for 18 holes), designed by Howard Watson, was once nicknamed the "minister's club" because of the number of high-level politicians that frequented the links. Along the 6,583-yard course there are four

Clockwise from top left: Hôtel Le Ferme, Baie-Saint-Paul; Chute Montmorency, Cote-de-Beaupré and Île d'Orleans; the sand dunes in Tadoussac, Charlevoix.

lakes and 42 white-sand bunkers, and the changing scenery moves from rolling tree-lined fairways to a large open plan at mid-course. Equipment rentals, driving range, and lessons are also available here and an electric cart and use of the practice range are included in the green fee.

Skiing, Snowboarding, and Snowshoeing
Mont-Sainte-Anne

The most popular ski station in the Québec City region, **Mont-Saint-Anne** (2000 blvd. Beau Pré, Beaupré, 888/827-4579 www.mont-sainte-anne. com, mid-Nov.-mid-Apr. Mon.-Fri. 9am-9pm, Sat.-Sun. 8:30am-9pm, $64 adult, $68 senior, $53 youth, $36 child 7-12) offers both day and night skiing, with the highest elevation of night skiing in the country. Officially opened in 1966, the history here goes back to 1947, when the Canadian Championships where held on these slopes. About an hour's drive north of the city, 66 trails cover both the north and south face of the mountain. It also has popular cross-country and snowshoeing trails.

HOTELS

Cozy but modern, the 31 rooms at **Auberge la Camarine** (10947 blvd. Ste-Anne, 800/567-3939, www.camarine.com, $100-250) in the Côte-de-Beaupré are often fitted with a warming gas fire, perfect after a long day outdoors.

On Île d'Orléans, grab a room with a view at **Auberge La Goéliche** (22 chemin de Quai, 418/828-2248, www.goeliche.ca, $104-144). Named after a small schooner, the white clapboard house has charm in spades; the views of the river and well-appointed rooms with country touches like handmade quilts make it an ideal choice.

Total country charm is the best way to describe **Auberge Le Canard Huppé** (2198 chemin Royal, 800/838-2292, www.canard-huppe.com, $150-250). The oversized wood furniture, pine paneling, and wood floors are welcoming, and the beautiful garden and seasonal regional cuisine on offer in the restaurant are the icing on the cake.

INFORMATION AND SERVICES

Before you go to the area, read up on the Côte-de-Beaupré area at **www. cotedebeaupre.com,** which offers the useful information on restaurants, hotels, grocery stores, and events. Once you're on the ground, the **Côte-de-Beaupré Tourist Office** (3 rue de la Seigneurie, Château-Richer, 866/932-9082, Mon.-Sat. 9am-5pm, Sun. 10am-4pm) can provide you with hands-on information.

The year-round **Île d'Orléans Tourist Office** (490 Côte du Pont, St-Pierre, 418/828-9411 or 866/941-9411, www.iledorleans.com, July-Aug. daily 8:30am-7:30pm, Sept.-June. daily 10am-5pm) has a wealth of information and tips on hand.

GETTING THERE AND AROUND
By Bus

Old Québec Tours, also known as **Tours Dupont** (800/267-8687, www.

tourdupont.com, June-Oct. daily 9am and 1pm, Nov.-May daily 1pm, $50), offers different tours that essentially drop you off at the highlights along the Côte-de-Beaupré and pick you up later. They leave from three points throughout Québec City for your convenience, so check before you book.

Sainte-Anne-de-Beaupré can be reached by **Intercar** (320 Abraham Martin, 888/861-4592, www.intercar.qc.ca) coach, which leaves from Québec City's Gare du Palais bus terminal heading toward Baie Comeau three times a day Monday-Saturday and once on Sunday. A return ticket costs $16 and the journey takes 25 minutes.

By Bike

Bike path **Corridor du Littoral** will take you right from Québec's Vieux-Port all the way to Chute Montmorency and even along the **Route de la Nouvelle France.** Once you've made it onto the Île d'Orléans, bikes are available to rent from **Écolocyclo** (517 Chemin Royal, 418/828-0370, www.ecolocyclo.net, May-mid-June Sat.-Sun. 9am-6pm, mid-June-Sept. daily 9am-6pm). The Chemin Royal encircles the island and is a great way to sightsee by bike.

By Car

The simplest and quickest way to get around is to take Autoroute 440 east out of Québec City and watch for the signs; all of the sights are well marked out with the exits that accompany them. To get to Île d'Orléans, take the Pont Île d'Orléans to the island.

Charlevoix

Some of the most stunning views of the province can be found here. People come here to camp, hike, and to catch a glimpse of the whales.

Follow Route 138 north out of Québec City and you'll come across some of the most spectacular scenery you've ever seen. The impact of a meteorite 350 million years ago has shaped the face of the Charlevoix region and could be the cause of its mysterious seismic activity (rest assured—most temblors hit little more than 2.0 on the Richter scale).

One of the first vacation destinations in Canada thanks to a couple of enterprising Scottish soldiers, Charlevoix's landscape is distinct in its variety. At times pastoral and hilly, the region's high cliffs and breathtaking fjords are adorned with tundra, while nearby, steep sand dunes rise unexpectedly along the coastline. These manifold landscapes translate into an area rich in biodiversity, where moose and caribou thrive alongside an astounding range of sea life. Where else can you sit on a sandy beach waiting to catch a glimpse of a pod of white beluga whales?

★ BAIE-SAINT-PAUL

One of the biggest towns in Charlevoix, Baie-Saint-Paul is known for its unique artist community, galleries, off-beat boutiques, and as the birth place of Cirque du Soleil. The home of roughly 7,000 full-time inhabitants,

Tradition Meets Contemporary: Wendake Reserve

Drive northwest out of Québec City and you'll soon come across Wendake, a First Nations reserve that is home to over 3,000 residents. The home of the Huron-Wendat tribe since 1697, this unique reserve offers both a historical and modern perspective on the tribe and its people. It's an active town, and many of the 19th-century buildings resemble those found back in the city—white-washed houses and clapboard churches—but look a little closer and you'll see something entirely different.

Shaped like an old Algonquin smokehouse, the **Huron-Wendat Museum** (15 Place de la Rencontre, 418/847-2260, www.museehuron-wendat.com, mid-June-Oct. daily 9am-4pm, Nov.-mid-June Wed.-Sun. 9am-4pm, $14 adult, $7 child) conserves and promotes the tribe's heritage. The permanent exhibit—Territories, Memories, Knowledge—takes visitors from the creation myth to the forming of the Huron-Wendat people and events that shaped the tribe right up until today. The museum also offers tours of the numerous heritage sites throughout the town, including Notre-Dame-de-Lorette Church, the Kabir Kouba waterfall, and Tsawenhohi House.

Those who want to experience the past firsthand can head over to **Onhoüa Chetek8e** (575 Chef Stan-islas-Koska St., 418/842-4308, www.huron-wendat.qc.ca), a traditional Huron site, where a tour guide will take you through typical buildings and rituals of the Huron First Nations people. Visitors will get to meet the Clan Mother, enter a traditional long house, learn about meat preservation at the smokehouse and the drying tent, and also how to make canoes. Native games, traditional cooking, and dances are part of the visit.

One of the latest additions to Wendake is the **Hôtel-Musée Premières Nations** (5 Place de la Rencontre, 866/551-9222, www.hotelpremieresnations.ca, $180-400), a beautiful hotel connected to the museum. Its 55 rooms seamlessly blend minimal contemporary design with natural accents, including tree trunks and stone. While you're here, have dinner at **La Traite Restaurant,** which takes inspiration from traditional Huron cooking to create dishes like grilled bison and pan-seared seal.

To orient yourself when you get here, head to the **Wendake Tourism Center** (100 blvd. Bastien, Wendake, 418/847-1835, www.tourismewendake.ca, mid-June-mid. Oct. Mon.-Fri. 8:30am-4:30pm, Sat.-Sun. 9am-5pm; mid-Oct.-mid-June Mon.-Fri. 8:30am-4:30pm) for useful maps and other information.

the downtown core is quaint, full of shops and cafés, and is a lovely place to spend the afternoon strolling the streets no matter the season.

Sights

Musée d'Art Contemporain Baie-Saint-Paul (23 rue Ambroise-Fafard, 418/435-3681, www.macbsp.com, summer Tues.-Sun. 11am-5pm, winter Tues.-Sun. noon-5pm, $6 adult) honors the area's artistic heritage with a collection and temporary exhibits dedicated to contemporary works. Founded in 1992, the museum is located in what was once an old cinema and is a definite must on any itinerary.

Born in Switzerland in 1895, artist René Richard moved to Canada with his family as a child and was working as a fur trapper in northern Alberta by the time he was 18. By the 1940s he'd settled in Baie-Saint-Paul, where he painted some of his best-known landscapes and hosted a number of revered Canadian artists, including members of the Group of Seven. His century-old house, **Maison René-Richard** (104 rue St-Jean-Baptiste, 418/435-5571, daily 10am-6pm, free), has remained unchanged and is located on the main street. Visitors get the chance to see both his home and his work in the adjoining gallery.

On the outskirts of town you'll find **Le Moulin de la Rémy** (235 Terrasse de la Rémy, 418/435-6579, www.moulindelaremy.com, summer Tues.-Sun. 10am-4pm, $5). Built in 1827, this is one of the few flour mills still active in Québec; tours and tastings are available throughout the summer and visitors are invited to explore the surrounding paths and countryside. Pick up a fresh loaf at the bakery, traditionally made with wheat grown in Charlevoix and ground on-site.

Sustainability is the focus of **Habitat 07** (212 rue Ste-Anne, 418/435-5514, www.habitat07.org, May-Aug. daily 10am-6pm, Sept.-mid-Oct. Sat.-Sun. 10am-6pm, $5 adult, $2 student), an ecofriendly house built to showcase the latest developments in new energy and recycling. Opened in 2007, the construction methods used were inspired by ancient practices and used local, sustainable materials. The best part of the house, though, is the amazing view of the St-Lawrence River.

Restaurants

Baie-Saint-Paul has the best range of restaurants in the region. Fans of a good microbrew shouldn't miss **Le Saint-Pub** (2 rue Racine, 418/240-2332, www.saint-pub.com, late May-Oct. daily 11:30am-10pm, Nov.-late May daily 11:30am-8pm, $25). This pub and bistro keeps things local and serves seasonal mussels, fresh fish, Charlevoix sausage, and deer steaks. They also offer more regular pub-style dishes like nachos and fries.

Relaxed dining can be found at **Vice-Café** (1 rue Ste-Anne, 418/435-0006, daily 11:30am-onward, $20), situated directly in front of the church. Their specialties include grilled salmon and crêpes. Head there for dinner on Friday night and stay for the local musical entertainment.

A French-born and trained chef puts his skills to work on local ingredients at the **Mouton Noir** (43 rue Ste-Anne, 418/240-3030, www.mouton-noirresto.com, daily 11:30am-3pm and 5pm-10pm, $35). The emphasis here is on modern French cuisine and the menu includes everything from organic pork tongue to quail and beet ravioli. Book ahead, and expect a crowd and lively atmosphere.

When Hotel La Ferme opened its doors in 2012, it brought a new level of culinary excellence to its surroundings. Their in-house restaurant, **Les Labours** (50 rue de la Ferme, 418/240-4123, www.lemassif.com, Sun.-Wed. 11:30am-2pm and 6pm-9pm, Thurs.-Sat. 11:30am-2pm and 5pm-10pm, $25), serves up tasty, modern cuisine—wild mushroom salad, roasted arctic char, pan-seared veal liver—in a chic yet cozy atmosphere. Get a seat at the

Le Train Le Massif du Charlevoix

Take a leisurely trip up the St-Lawrence on Le Train le Massif du Charlevoix.

If you want to travel through Charlevoix region in luxury forgo the convertible and grab a seat on Le Train Le Massif du Charlevoix. Inaugurated in 2012, the train chugs along a long-dormant track of railroad that follows the shore of the great St-Lawrence River all the way from Québec City to La Malbaie. The 140-kilometer-long train trip is an awe-inspiring journey and it's all thanks to Daniel Gauthier, co-founder and former president of the Cirque du Soleil, and his project to entice tourists to explore the region and the town of Baie-Saint-Paul, in particular.

Gauthier first started his project with Le Massif, a ski station just minutes away from the town that's quickly become one of the best in the country. For his second act, he's created a gourmet train journey that disposes travelers in front of one of the most modern and welcoming hotels ever built in the province. Hôtel Le Ferme is a vision of what accommodations in this region should be like and it's a response to the stuffy guesthouses and humdrum highway motels that have long ruled the area. Called a hotel "terroir," Le Ferme is integrated with the environment. A flock of 50 sheep graze near the grounds, vegetable gardens greet you as you come off the train, and the hotel is heated by geothermal heating.

Despite the hotel's charms, however, it's the train that's the real star of the show. With its high, arched ceilings, picture windows, and interactive displays, it immerses you in the surroundings. Trains for Baie-Saint-Paul ($175 per person) and La Malbaie ($275 per person) depart from the base of Chutes Montmorency, about a 20-minute drive outside of Québec City, 11 months out of the year (May-Oct. and Dec.-Apr.). Once on board, guests are treated to a gourmet breakfast and tapas, or an elaborate four-course meal on the return journey.

It's definitely not the most affordable way to get to your destination, but it is perhaps the most memorable.

bar and watch as the chefs do their magic. This is a great way to experience the hotel, even if you're not staying here.

Hiking
Parc National des Grands-Jardins

Once you're in the area you might as well take advantage of the nature that's available to you. West of Baie-Saint-Paul is the **Parc National des Grands-Jardins** (800/665-6527, www.sepaq.com/pq/grj), open year-round. This gorgeous national park has some of the most interesting vegetation, with a mix of both taiga and tundra. The landscape is vaguely arctic, with thick layers of lichen and black spruce forest. Home to a large caribou population, it has many activities available, including 34 kilometers of hiking trails in the summer, as well as kayaking and canoeing. In winter, visitors can use the 55 kilometers of cross-country ski trails and try their hand at ice fishing.

Skiing
★ Le Massif

One of the best hills in the province, **Le Massif** (877/536-2774, www.lemassif.com, mid-Dec.-mid-Apr. daily 8:30am-4pm, $64 adult day pass) is the area's largest ski mountain. Many high-ranking skiers come to train here, but even if you're more comfortable on the bunny runs, the views alone are worth the fees. It's on a cliff that looks out over the St-Lawrence, and there are times on these runs when you're sure the bottom is going to be on the shores. With 49 different trails of varying levels, it has something for everyone.

Hotels

Daniel Gauthier, one of the founding members of Cirque de Soleil, opened **Hôtel La Ferme** (50 rue de la Ferme, 418/240-4100, www.lemassif.com, $150-400) as a way of giving back to the community, and as such, the hotel is more than just a place to rest your head. Located on a tract of landed facing the St-Lawrence and between two rolling hills, it has a concert hall, two restaurants, a café, a spa, a gym, and a mini-farm, as the name suggests. It also happens to be the final destination on the whistle-stop train, La Massif, which brings visitors to the region by way of a riverside journey. The hotel itself is well-appointed, with a modern rustic design—exposed ceiling beams, heavy gray felt blankets, all-white decor—and is made up of a cluster of four buildings. With 145 rooms on offer (including a few dorm options), they can accommodate just about any budget.

The stone-clad, 30-room inn **Maison Otis** (23 rue St-Jean-Baptiste, 418/435-2255, www.maisonotis.com, $120-260) in Baie-Saint-Paul has its own sort of cozy charm with wood furniture, floral bedding, and stone walls. Slightly more modern but still with that floral country vibe, **Auberge La Muse** (39 rue St-Jean-Baptiste, 800/841-6839, www.lamuse.com, $120-400) is ideally located on a tree-lined street in the center of town, and the rooms are tastefully decorated.

Information and Services

Baie-Saint-Paul Tourist Office (6 rue St-Jean-Baptiste, 800/677-2276, winter daily 9am-4pm, summer daily 9am-7pm) is just off the highway on a hill overlooking the city below; it's a great view, but the turnoff is sharp. The website **www.tourisme-charlevoix.com** is also a great online resource.

Getting There and Around
By Bus

Intercar (320 Abraham Martin, 888/861-4592, www.intercar.qc.ca) coaches leave from Québec City's Gare du Palais bus terminal heading toward Baie Comeau three times a day Monday-Saturday and once on Sunday. The same bus runs all along the Charlevoix coast. A round-trip ticket to Baie-Saint-Paul costs $39 and the ride takes one hour and 15 minutes and drop off is at the Baie-Saint-Paul Library (9 rue Forget) in the middle of the town. When heading out of town, the bus departs from a gas station at 909 boulevard Monseigneur-de-Laval, which can be reached by either a local bus system or a taxi (418/435-5000). Check with the bus company at the time of departure to be sure.

By Car

Take Autoroute 440 out of Québec City and continue past Côte-de-Beaupré on Route 138 all the way to Baie-Saint-Paul. Depending on traffic and weather conditions, the drive should take approximately an hour and 20 minutes.

By Train

The exclusive **Train Le Massif de Charlevoix** (877/536-2774, www.lemassif.com, Mar.-mid-Oct., $110-275) offers stunning views, great food, and a totally unique way to get from Québec City to Baie-Saint-Paul. The train departs Québec City twice daily from the base of the Chute Montmorency, once early in the morning and once at noon. The train pulls into the station at La Ferme, about a five-minute walk from Baie-Saint-Paul's downtown core.

★ ISLE-AUX-COUDRES

Off the shores of Baie-Saint-Paul is Isle-aux-Coudres, one of the most picturesque islands in the St-Lawrence. Hop on the free ferry from St-Joseph-de-la-Rive just south of Baie-Saint-Paul and take the 15-minute ride out to the island.

Sights

Once on the island, it's easy to be transported to an earlier time. **Les Moulins de Isle aux Coudres** (36 chemin du Moulin, 418/760-1065, www.lesmoulinsdelisleauxcoudres.com, mid-May-mid-Oct. daily 10am-5:30pm, $9 adult, $5 child), a watermill and windmill that were built in 1825 and 1838, respectively, are a visceral link to the past. Still in operation today, you can tour these working mills and learn how the buckwheat and wheat were

EXCURSIONS FROM QUÉBEC CITY

Top: the majestic Fairmont Le Manoir Richelieu in La Malbaie, Charlevoix. **Bottom:** skiing at Le Massif, Charlevoix.

once ground all over the region. Guided tours are available, but you're also welcome to explore all buildings and surroundings on your own.

With a parish that dates back to 1741, **Église Saint-Louis de Isle-aux-Coudres** is one of the oldest religious sites on the island, built in 1885. It boasts hand-painted frescoes and impressive stone work.

No matter the season, stop in at **Cidrerie et Verger Pedneault** (3384 chemin des Coudriers, 418/438-2365, www.vergerspedneault.com). Opened in 1918, this family-run apple orchard also creates their own apple cider (alcoholic and non), jams, syrups, and honey. They offer tours of their premises year-round and apple-picking come the fall.

Restaurants

On Isle-aux-Coudres, many restaurants are located in hotels. **La Marinière** (1933 chemin des Coudriers, 418/438-2208, daily 5pm-10pm, $25) is located in the interestingly named Hôtel Motel Les Voitures d'Eau (Hotel Motel for Water Vehicles) but offers a menu pre pared exclusively with local products, including Charlevoix meats and seafood. The food is so fresh here that the menu changes daily.

If you like a little entertainment with your meal, **Le Cabaretier** (1064 chemin des Coudriers, 418/438-1070, daily 10am-5pm, $25) does double duty as both a bistro and wine bar as well as a typical *boîte à chansons,* the perfect end to a day cycling around the island. Another great option for the hungry traveler is a stop at **Casse-Croûte Le Mouillage** (922 chemin des Coudriers, 418/438-2208), where specialties include hot dogs, poutine, club sandwiches, BLTs, and anything else that's greasy yet delicious.

The menu at **Hôtel du Captitane** (3031 chemin des Coudriers, 418/438-2242, daily 5pm-9pm, $25) meanwhile focuses on healthier local recipes and also has an extensive menu of crepes.

Recreation

Named Isle-aux-Coudres after the hazelnuts that Jacques Cartier found here, the 11-kilometer-long and 3-kilometer-wide island is easily explored by bike. **Vélo-Coudres** (2926 chemin des Coudriers, 418/432-2118, www. charlevoix.qc.ca/velocoudres, May-June and Sept. daily 9am-5pm, July-Aug. daily 8am-sunset, $7/hour) has different models available, including tandem, kids' bikes, and even quadricycles with room for a family of four.

Hotels

Located on the northern tip of the island, **L'Hôtel Cap-aux-Pierres** (444 chemin la Baleine, 888/222-3308, www.dufour.ca, $84-250) has 46 rooms, tastefully decorated with wood floors, antique-style furniture, and a coun-try feel. Each room has classic views of both the river and the garden. The hotel also has an outdoor pool.

Hôtel du Capitaine (3031 chemin des Coudriers, 418/438-2242, www. hotelducapitaine.com, $90-150) is also located on the northern tip, but closer to where the mainland ferry docks. The rooms have a country feel with their floral bedspreads and wooden furniture; the views of the river,

Parc National de la Jacques-Cartier

Less than a half-hour drive from downtown Québec City is **Parc National de la Jacques-Cartier** (700 blvd. Lebourgneuf, Stoneham, 418/848-3169 summer, 418/528-8787 winter, www.sepaq.com/pq/jac). Situated in a valley with the same name, this park boasts both calm waters and rapids. Home of a 26-kilometer-long river, this is the perfect place to learn basic maneuvers. Those who haven't had the opportunity to learn how to canoe or kayak can do so here. They also have a number of mini-rafts, inflatable canoes, and inner tubes to rent for more relaxed water fun. Though the park is open year-round, equipment rental (canoe $14 per hour, kayak $13 per hour, dinghy $11 per hour) is only available mid-May-mid-October. There are also a number of bike trails for those who want to do some off-roading.

however, are stunning and you can opt to have a gourmet dinner included in the price. The breakfasts are complimentary.

Boating fans might want to opt for the **Hôtel Motel Les Voitures d'Eau** (1933 chemin des Coudriers, 418/438-2208, $90-200), since a stay here means you can check out their boating museum. The accommodations have a rustic feel reminiscent of a cottage getaway, though the exterior looks like just about any highway-side motel. In addition to the mini museum, they also offer bike rentals and have a saltwater pool.

Information and Services

Isle Aux Coudres Tourist Office (1024 chemin des Coudriers, 800/667-2276, mid-May-mid-Oct. daily 8am-noon and 1pm-4pm) can be found on the main road, just a short walk from the quay. Though it's open daily during the peak-months, it closes during the off-season (typically after Canadian Thanksgiving). Read up on the island at **www.tourismeisleauxcoudres.com** before packing your bags.

Getting There and Around
By Boat

The only way to get to the island is by ferry. The ferry departs from Saint-Joseph-de-la-Rive and arrives at Saint-Bernard-sur-Mer on the west coast of the island. The trip takes about 15 minutes. It can take approximately 367 passengers and 55 vehicles. The boats are run by a government agency **Traversiers** (877/787-7483, www.traversiers.com) and as such the service is free. Boats leave the mainland and the island about once an hour during peak-season, but travelers should contact the company directly before making concrete plans. Once on the island, visitors are welcome to drive or ride a bike.

LA MALBAIE

If you want to continue exploring the region of Charlevoix, stay on the mainland and continue north from Baie-Saint-Paul on Route 362 until you arrive at La Malbaie, one of the oldest tourist spots in the region. Originally called Murray Bay, the area was first made popular by two Scottish officers who saw the potential in the area's beauty and made it the top resort choice from the 19th century right up until the 1950s.

Sights
Musée de Charlevoix

Learn all you need to know about the region at **Musée de Charlevoix** (10 chemin du Havre, 418/665-4411, www.museedecharlevoix.qc.ca, June-mid-Oct. daily 9am-5pm, mid-Oct.-May Mon.-Fri. 10am-5pm, Sat.-Sun. 1pm-5pm, $7 adult, $5 senior). This charming museum offers exhibitions about the region's culture and history, including photographs of beluga whale-hunting, artifacts from Manoir Richelieu, and folk art from the 1930s and '40s.

★ Casino de Charlevoix

In more recent times, one of the biggest draws to the region has been the **Casino de Charlevoix** (183 ave. Richelieu, 800/665-2274, www.casino-de-charlevoix.com, Mon.-Thurs. and Sun. 11am-midnight, Fri.-Sat. 11am-3am, free). Opened in 1994, it has cherrywood paneling, granite floors, and is a step up from most casinos. Visitors must be 18 years old or over to enter.

Restaurants

Run by two head chefs, **Vices Versa** (216 St-Etienne, 418/665-6869, www.vicesversa.com, Tues.-Sat. 6pm-10pm, $65 for a table d'h ôte) is a unique take on fine dining. Customers are presented with two menus (one created by each chef) and must decide between the two. Choices include sautéed scallops vs. scallop cerviche, or duck breast with potatoes and fennel or duck confit with quinoa cake and goat cheese cream. At the restaurant, it's all about pleasing the diner and the chefs' friendly rivalry. Situated on a busier street, it has a relaxed elegance that perfectly suits the flavors flowing from the kitchen.

Sometimes a little comfort food is the only way to go. **Pizzaria Du Poste** (448 rue St-Étiennem, 418/665-4884, www.pizzariaduposte.ca, June-Aug. daily 11am-midnight, Sept.-May Sun.-Tues. 11am-10pm, Wed.-Sat. 11am-midnight, $20) serves up Italian favorites like spaghetti, lasagna, and pizza in a convivial and sometimes raucous atmosphere. The pizza is thin-crusted and topped with the usual suspects and some that are more unexpected (shrimp and crab, anyone?). What's best about this place is the low-key atmosphere and the outdoor patio in the summer.

Hiking
★ Parc National des Hautes-Gorges-de-la-Rivière-Malbaie

Named after a series of valleys, **Parc National des Hautes-Gorges-de-la-Rivière-Malbaie** (800/665-6527, www.sepaq.com/pq/hgo, late May-Oct.

daily 24 hours) has steep sloping mountains that fall to meet Rivière Malbaie. With its unique mix of fauna, Hautes-Gorges is one of the most beautiful spots in eastern Canada. Not far west from La Malbaie, it offers a huge amount of outdoor activities, like boat cruises, rock climbing, cycling, and 33 kilometers of hiking. Swimming, canoeing, and kayaking can also be done here.

Golf

Murray Bay Golf Club (1013 chemin du Golf, 877/665-2494, www.golfmurraybay.com, $44) is one of the oldest courses in the country and the third oldest in North America. It first opened its links in 1876. Built high above the cliffs that look out over the St-Lawrence, it's a spectacular place to tee-up and a must for any golfer visiting the area.

Hotels

In La Malbaie, one of the area's biggest draws is the romantic **Fairmont Le Manoir Richelieu** (181 rue Richelieu, 866/540-4464, www.fairmont.com, $140-350). Built in 1899, in a similar style as the Château Frontenac, it sits atop the Pointe-au-Pic overlooking the St-Lawrence River. Destroyed by fire and rebuilt in 1929, the hotel today is a luxury resort with an adjoining 18-hole golf course and an on-site spa, as well as five different restaurants. The rooms are elegant and tastefully decorated and aim for a comfortable instead of sleek luxury.

If you're looking for a more intimate luxury, head to **La Pisonniere** (124 rue St-Raphaël, 800/387-4431, www.lapinsonniere.com, $240-450), a family-run inn with incredible views and the stamp of approval from the Relais Château. Modern yet cozy, the rooms feature fireplaces, sumptuous linens, classic wingback chairs for reading, and private balconies. If you want to leave your abode, you have the option of heading to the indoor pool, their private beach, the in-house spa, or the wine cellar for a tasting.

Auberge des Peupliers (381 rue St-Raphael, 418/665-4423, www.aubergedespeupliers.com, $140-250) keeps things luxurious but at a more affordable price point. There's a contemporary edge to this hotel that others in the region lack, making it ideal for urbanites or those looking for a modern hotel in rustic settings.

Information and Services

La Malbaie Tourist Office (495 blvd. de Comporté, Route 362, 800/667-2276, daily 8:30am-4:30pm) is right on the water looking out over the river and has a nice park in front in which to take a break.

Getting There and Around
By Bus

If traveling by public transport, hop on the **Intercar** (320 Abraham Martin, 888/861-4592, www.intercar.qc.ca) coach which leaves from Québec City's Gare du Palais bus terminal heading toward Baie Comeau three times a day Monday-Saturday and once on Sunday. The trip will take about two hours from Québec City and you'll be dropped off and picked up at Dépanneur

Saguenay Fjord

Before you arrive in Tadoussac, a charming town three hours north of Québec City, you come to a dead stop. It's here that the cliffs widen to reveal the banks of the Saguenay River and the majestic fjord beyond. It's a rare natural wonder, the fjord is one of the most southerly in the world and was created by the weight of a glacier turning a crevice into a wide, calm river approximately 200 million years ago.

Once a hotbed of activity for the logging industry, the region's forests were critically depleted by the 1920s. In order to preserve the fjord, the government began buying up land, eventually turning it into a national park in the 1980s. The Parc national du Fjord-du-Saguenay has since become one of the most popular in the province with close to a million visitors in 2010. Activities in the park include everything from skiing to hiking and camping, but it's the kayaking adventures offered by the park, which allow you to explore the fjord firsthand, that are the most exciting.

In addition to the awesome cliffs that rise out of the water, the fjord is also home to a number of species, including four species of whales: the blue whale, the fin whale, the minke, and the beluga.

J. E. Otis (46 rue Ste-Catherine) in the middle of the town. A round-trip ticket costs $60.

By Car
Follow Autoroute 440 out of Québec City and continue north on Route 138 all the way to La Malbaie. Depending on traffic and weather conditions, the drive should take approximately two hours.

★ TADOUSSAC
Tadoussac is the meeting point of the Saguenay and St-Lawrence Rivers. Before you can get to Tadoussac, however, you have to take a ferry across the convergence of these two mighty waterways. A free ferry will take you the short trip across the water to the historic town, one of the oldest places in Québec. It was France's first trading post and was established in 1600. Today the area's main draw is the rich marine life that thrives here, thanks to the warm St-Lawrence saltwater and the freshwater of the Saguenay.

Sights
Though the town itself is quite small, it's completely charming, the perfect place to stroll around. Visit **Chauvin Trading Post** (157 rue Bord De L'Eau, 418/235-4433, June 1-June 21 daily 10am-6pm, June 22-Sept. 20 daily 9:30am-7pm, Sept. 21-Oct. 13 daily 10am-noon and 3pm-6pm, $4 adult, $3 senior, $2.50 student and child). This may just be a reconstruction, but it's still cool to visit a reasonable facsimile of the first trading post in Québec, and the exhibitions, though brief, are informative.

About five kilometers northeast of the town are sand dunes, an incongruous natural phenomenon in the region. **La Maison des Dunes** (chemin du Moulin-à-Baude, 418/235-4238, free) is a restored house that's been turned into an interpretation center that explains exactly how the sand dunes came about.

After the French arrived in 1600, the Jesuit monks quickly followed. **La Petite Chapelle de Tadoussac** (rue Bord de L'Eau, 418/235-4324, June-Oct. daily, free) was constructed in 1747, and is the oldest wooden church still in existence in North America. In addition to offering great views of the river, it's also home to a number of religious artifacts. It's a bit of untouched history in the region.

Restaurants

In Tadoussac most of the restaurants are only open May-October, something to keep in mind if you're traveling north in winter. If you're visiting in summer, there's a lot more choice but it isn't always varied. One of your best bets for a light breakfast, lunch, or dinner is **Café Bohême** (239 rue des Pionniers, 418/235-1180, daily 8am-10pm, $15). Serving different types of fair-trade coffee, they also have a selection of desserts (try the brownie) and other treats as well as a range of soups, sandwiches, and salads. On the second floor, they also have a small book exchange library and you can pick up some gourmet Charlevoix products.

For something more upscale, there is the **Restaurant le William** (165 rue Bord-de-l'Eau, 418/235-4421, www.hoteltadoussac.com, daily 5pm-10pm, $70 tasting menu) in the Hotel Tadoussac, which offers a four-course tasting menu and views over the Bay of Tadoussac and the St-Lawrence.

Recreation

Between mid-May and mid-October tourists come from all over the world to see the whales that flock to the region; approximately 10 different species can be found every year, including humpback, finback, blue whales, and white belugas. The best places to catch a glimpse of these majestic creatures are the **Parc Marin du Saguenay-Saint-Laurent** (182 rue de l'Église, 888/773-8888, www.parcmarin.qc.ca) and **Parc du Saguenay** (91 rue Notre-Dame, Rivière-Éternité, 800/665-6527, www.sepaq.com/pq/sag). Both of these national parks offer a number of different ways to see the whales, including boat excursions and sea kayaking. Interpretation centers are open along the trails and they both offer stunning views of the fjords and the rivers.

Independent companies offer up-close and personal whale tours, including **Croisières AML** (Baie du Tadoussac, 866/856-6668, www.croisieresaml.com, May-Sept., $70) and **Group Dufour** (329 Hwy. 138, Baie-Sainte-Catherine, 800/463-5250, www.dufour.ca, May-Sept., $70), both of which offer tours of varying lengths. Most of the tours take place on larger boats with food facilities and naturalists who'll walk you through the action; tours on Zodiacs (sleek, low boats) let you get even closer to the animals. Passengers are given life jackets and waterproof overalls but will likely get wet anyhow as you bump along the waves. Departure times vary depending on the day of the week, the month, and the type of tour you'd like to take. However, there is typically only one tour of a certain type per day, so book and plan ahead.

For the brave and experienced, kayak trips are also available through **Mer et Monde Ecotours** (866/637-6663, www.meretmonde.qc.ca, May-Sept., $50), whose three-hour-long tours start at the bay of Tadoussac, just past the lawn of the Hotel Tadoussac.

Hotels

Sitting on the Baie de Tadoussac, **Hôtel Tadoussac** (165 rue Bord-de-l'Eau, 800/561-0718, www.hoteltadoussac.com, $150-250) stands out on the horizon with its red copper roof and white clapboard siding. Opened in 1864, it's one of the oldest hotels in the region and maintains its historic feel (it has no air-conditioning in summer, but then again you don't really need it). The rooms have recently been modernized and have a nice, airy quality about them. Tadoussac chapel is also on the property. Built by Jesuit missionaries, it is the oldest wooden church in North America and still has some of its original artifacts.

Information and Services

Before you go, check out the website **www.tourisme-charlevoix.com** for all the necessary tips and information.

The **Tadoussac Tourist Office** (197 rue des Pionniers, 866/235-4744, www.tadoussac.com, May-late Oct. Mon.-Sat. 9am-5pm and Sun. 10am-4pm) is in the center of town and hard to miss. It has loads of information on the region as well as a few historical exhibits to give you more of an idea about the place, its culture, and history.

Getting There and Around
By Bus

Intercar (320 Abraham Martin, 888/861-4592, www.intercar.qc.ca) coaches leave from Québec City's Gare du Palais bus terminal heading north three times a day Monday-Saturday and once on Sunday. The same bus runs all along the Charlevoix coast. A round-trip ticket to Tadoussac costs $90 and the ride takes 3.5 hours, depending on traffic and weather. The bus pick-up and drop-off is located at Accommodation JB (443 Bateau-Passeir) in the center of the town.

By Car

From Québec City take Autoroute 440 and then Route 138 all along the coast to Tadoussac. The drive should take a little over 3 hours depending on the weather and traffic conditions.

Background

The Land

GEOGRAPHY

Québec is Canada's largest province and covers an area of 1,540,681 square kilometers, basically the size of France, Germany, Belgium, Spain, Portugal, and a couple Switzerlands put together, all in all an enormous territory. For the most part, it is filled with boundless forests and innumerable lakes (some say more than 400,000), vestiges of the huge Sea of Champlain that flooded the area 10,000 years ago.

Québec's geography can be divided into three main regions. The Canadian Shield goes from the extreme north down to the plain of St-Lawrence River and includes the Laurentian mountains, said to be the oldest mountain range in the world. The Appalachians, at the south of that plain, turn the landscape into a green and hilly area characteristic of the Eastern Townships region and extend down to the United States. A rift valley between these two antediluvian geological formations, the St-Lawrence is a 1,200-kilometer-long river that takes its source from the Great Lakes and ends up in the world's largest estuary. Most of Québec's residents live along the banks of the river, and it's also the center of Québec's development. Looking out over the landscape from the window of a plane, along with the sprawling cities of Montréal and Québec City, you can see the rural landscape divided into narrow rectangular tracts of land extending from the river: These patterns denote the seigneurial land system and date back to the settlement of 17th-century Nouvelle France (New France).

Québec City, with a population of half a million, thrives on the north bank of the St-Lawrence near its meeting point with the St-Charles River and not far from the foothills of the Laurentian mountains. Built on top and around the 98-meter-high Cap-Diamant, it overlooks the dramatic narrowing of the river that takes place in the St-Lawrence after Île d'Orléans. It's from this narrowing that the city gets its name, taken from the Algonquin word *kebec,* which means "where the river narrows."

It's this particular position that made it, in the mind of the colonizers, a logical commercial port as well as a strategic military point. The ramparts surrounding Vieux-Québec's Upper Town, the only fortified city left in North America, have made it an architectural jewel and helped the city earn the name the "Gibraltar of North America." Near the southern edge of Cap-Diamant, the Plains of Abraham (Québec's version of Central Park) extend along the cliffs. It was on these rolling hills that North America's fate was sealed in the haze of a battle between the British and the French in 1759.

One of the main physical features of the city is its two-level construction. Cap-Diamant and its cliffs break the urban landscape in two, prompting significant opposition between Haute-ville (Upper Town) and Basse-ville (Lower Town). This opposition is as significant sociologically as it is topographically. Thus, Upper Town (with the exception of Faubourg

---

Previous: First Nations canoe; Tour Martello.

Saint-Jean-Baptiste) is historically the home of the ruling bourgeoisie, while Lower Town (Limoilou, Saint-Roch, Saint-Sauveur), which developed along the shores of the St-Lawrence and St-Charles Rivers, was the home of sea-men, dock workers, and factory workers. This antagonism is in flux now-adays as exemplified by Nouvo Saint-Roch's gentrification. Motivated by the 400th anniversary's celebrations, much urban redevelopment has been done, particularly along the banks of the rivers, making Québec City one of the most likable cities in the world.

CLIMATE

"Mon pays ce n'est pas un pays, c'est l'hiver" (My country is not a country, it's winter) sang Québec's premier *chansonnier,* Gilles Vigneault. Truer words have never been spoken, especially regarding the six months during which winter takes over, changing the landscape and affecting the mood of its re-signed inhabitants. Yes, wintertime temperatures have an average of -10°C and can drop down to -30°C. However, the winters aren't as harsh, cold, and snowy as they used to be, thanks to global warming. But the freezing wind, blowing *poudreuse* (drifting snow) everywhere like a tempest in the desert, is probably the toughest thing about being here in the winter. When the temperatures dip to bone-chilling proportions, make sure to cover up everything from your nose to your toes or you could end up with frostbite.

Approximately three meters of snow fall every winter, but sometimes there's more. Snowstorms are frequent and can last up to a day if not more. Snow removal can be interesting to watch if you're a tourist and have never seen it before. The sidewalk and road snowplows can also be deadly, so be careful, especially when walking at night.

Despite being harsh and long, winters in Québec are also sunny, with a bright luminosity that can sometimes be blinding. Because of the length of the season, stoical locals have adopted a "if you can't beat 'em join 'em" attitude in order to survive, and you'll be surprised to see just how active Quebeckers can be in winter, putting on their skates and snowshoes after every snowstorm, sometimes going to work on cross-country skis and pull-ing their kids in toboggans along the sidewalks.

Of course, Québec isn't just about winter, and people are often surprised to see just how hot and humid the summers are, with temperatures often reaching 35°C. After having complained about the cold all winter, locals curse the heat and turn their air-conditioning on full blast.

Autumn and spring are shorter in Québec, but in many ways they are the most impressive seasons. In spring, the snow melts away, revealing new blossoms, while autumn has a particular beauty as the trees change to a rainbow of colors before shedding their leaves.

Flora and Fauna

The best place to explore Québec's rich and diverse fauna and flora is in the national parks. National parks offer interpretive materials and guides to help you understand just exactly what it is you're surrounded by.

There's not much chance to run into a moose or a black bear while getting a pint of milk at the *dép* (corner store). But, the city has Parc des Plaines d'Abraham, with protected fauna and flora, where you might see animals that can be exotic for some: red and gray squirrels, chipmunks, and raccoons.

Québec City is remarkably green for its size, with trees lining just about every side street. Originally part of the Laurentian forest ecosystem, the vegetation has changed over time due to urbanization.

History

EARLY INHABITANTS

Long before its European takeover, the North American continent was home to the indigenous people for thousands of years. Historians date the population back to 12,000 years ago, when hunting tribes crossed the Bering Strait in pursuit of game from Siberia. Those tribes then scattered all over the land, developing diverse ways of life as they adapted to different environments. At the time explorers arrived, the area that would eventually become known as the St-Lawrence valley was populated by the nomadic Algonquin and sedentary Iroquoian tribes who lived off game, fish, and crops, and were particularly well adapted to their environment.

EUROPEAN ARRIVAL

When it comes to the "discovery" of Canada, it's French explorer Jacques Cartier's name that usually pops up. But what's less known is that by the time he finally made it to Québec in 1534, Newfoundland's coastline was being periodically cruised by explorers and fishermen from different nations and that Vikings had sailed its coast and even put down a few roots 500 years before.

What Jacques Cartier did first, though, before other Europeans, was explore the interior of the river, a river that he named in honor of the saint on the calendar the day he reached it: St-Lawrence. Sent by the king of France, Francis I, with the mandate of finding gold and—the typical request of the day—a passage to Asia, the sailor explored the region thoroughly, visiting Iroquoian villages Stadacona (Québec) and, farther upstream, Hochelaga, which he rechristened Mont-Royal, in honor of the king. After many voyages, he found neither gold nor Asia, bringing home instead a bunch of made-up stories told by fabulist natives and a handful of rocks he thought were diamonds (a popular French saying of the time was "*faux comme un diamant du Canada*" (fake as a Canadian diamond). Deemed inhospitable and dull, the land of Canada would remain unvisited and almost forgotten by the French for half a century.

NOUVELLE FRANCE (NEW FRANCE)

Two things rekindled the French interest in this part of the world: the fur trade and an appetite for colonial expansion. In addition to these two motives, the Catholic Church saw an opportunity to spread the gospel to the Amerindian population and sent missionaries along on the expedition. Seeing promise in the new European fashion of fur hats and coats, trading companies quickly formed, including the Compagnie des Cent-Associés, which set up outposts around Québec where the Amerindians and French could trade.

In 1608, Samuel de Champlain set up the first permanent European trading post in an abandoned Iroquoian village that Jacques Cartier had visited 80 years before, building a wooden fort he called l'Abitation de Québec (*kebec* in Algonquin means "where the river narrows"). That first winter, most of the settlers died of scurvy and harsh weather, but the colony continued even though it faced numerous difficulties and was slow to grow. In 1635 (the year Samuel de Champlain, the Father of New France, died), the population was slightly more than 300 settlers, a fair number of them Catholic missionaries. Some of these missionaries organized the Société Notre-Dame de Montréal and, in 1642, decided to establish an evangelizing mission near the deserted village of Hochelaga. Called Ville-Marie, it would eventually become Montréal.

While colonists cleared forests and cultivated the land, the thriving fur trade attracted a different kind of young explorer, one daring enough to go farther and farther in to the continent seeking bearskins, mink furs, and, above all, the popular and coveted beaver pelts. Called *coureurs des bois* (wood runners, or woodsmen), these adventurers are legendary figures in Québec, since they represent a life of freedom and a particular connection with nature that characterized the colonization of the continent. These *coureurs* also paved the way for the explorers and voyageurs to whom we owe the exploration of the regions of the Great Lakes and the Mississippi Valley, much of which they claimed for the French. These explorers left their mark on places all over the United States, including Detroit, St. Louis, and Baton Rouge.

The commercial relations brought on by the trade helped the French secure alliances with the Hurons, who in exchange for the pelts received copper and iron utensils, alcohol, and rifles. This alliance put the French colony in the middle of a bloody war when the English-backed Iroquois Five Nations launched an offensive campaign to wipe out the Hurons, their long-time enemies. The war lasted 25 years and seriously affected the young colony.

TOWARD DEFEAT

The conflicting commercial and political interests of the French and the English caused a succession of inter-colonial wars. In 1713, following a military defeat in Europe, the Treaty of Utrecht resulted in France relinquishing

Coming North: United Empire Loyalists

When things started looking really bad for the British during the American Revolution, a number of colonists who wanted to remain loyal to the British crown were offered free land and passage to other—non-rebelling—parts of the British colonies.

Called United Empire Loyalists because of their unyielding devotion to King George III, many chose to escape north, settling in the regions of southern Ontario and Québec. So many immigrated to the province, close to 50,000, that it sent the Québécois into a breeding frenzy and kicked off the

revanche des berceaux, the "revenge of the cradle."

By 1791 so many loyalists had arrived in the country that the government signed the Constitutional Act, dividing the province in two: Upper Canada, which would eventually become Ontario, and Lower Canada, the province of Québec.

Though many Loyalists and descendants of Loyalists eventually moved out of the province, their influence can still be seen in the Eastern Townships, where covered bridges, clapboard houses, and Victorian gingerbread moldings are the norm.

control of Newfoundland, Acadia, and the Hudson Bay, something that considerably hurt the fur trade and jeopardized the colony. This date marks the beginning of the end for New France, even if it took another 50 years for the British to secure power, a takeover that seemed inevitable considering the difference in population. Indeed, on the eve of the final battle, there were 60,000 French living in a huge territory, surrounded by two million British colonists living in the narrow strip of the 13 colonies.

The final showdown happened on September 13, 1759, on an open field by Cap-Diamant. After a two-month-long siege, the French Army, led by General Montcalm, was attacked by surprise early in the morning. General Wolfe and the British Army used a dried-up old creek to climb the cliff, something everyone thought was impossible. The Battle of the Plains of Abraham, which sealed the fate of French North America, was bloody, lasted barely 20 minutes, and cost the lives of both generals. One year after, Montréal capitulated and thus France lost all of its colonies in North America, leaving behind a small population of deeply rooted French Catholics in an ocean of British Protestants.

BRITISH REGIME

Though at first they tried to assimilate the French minority by imposing British Common Law and having them swear an oath to the British King, the victors decided that it was wiser to accommodate the French, wanting to secure their allegiance as social unrest and rebellion smoldered in the south. In order to cement the support of the French-Canadians, England wrote up the Act of Québec in 1774, recognizing both the French language and French civil law, and granting them freedom of religion. These concessions succeeded in preventing the

French-Canadians from joining the rebels in the south who started the American Revolution a year later.

At the end of that war, in 1783, 50,000 United Empire Loyalists (British Loyalists) had fled the United States for the province of Québec, many of them settling into the Eastern Townships region. To accommodate these Loyalists, who were an English minority in a French-speaking majority, a new Constitutional Act was signed in 1791, dividing the province in two: Upper Canada (which would eventually become Ontario) and Lower Canada (the province of Québec). The names Upper and Lower Canada were given according to their location on the St. Lawrence River.

The 19th century was marked by the power struggles between the Francophones and the Anglophones in Lower Canada. The elected French-Canadian representatives were constantly at odds with the colonial British executive and legislative powers. Over the years, the nationalist and re-formist Parti Canadien denounced the untenable situation, ending up in an armed insurrection. The Patriots War (Guerre des Patriotes) of 1837-1838 was immediately crushed and an emissary was sent from London to study the problems of this wayward colony. The solution proposed by Lord Durham was radical: make every effort to assimilate French-Canadians. This was the impetus behind the Union Act, laid down by the British government in 1840. Along with unifying Upper and Lower Canada and giving them an equal political power—despite the fact that Lower Canada was much more populated—it also made English the only official language, despite the fact that the vast majority were Francophone-speakers. These new laws and the constant arrival of English-speaking immigrants prompted a major exodus of Francophones, many of whom immigrated to the United States.

CONFEDERATION

The troubled politics of the subsequent years coupled with a dire economic situation prompted leaders of Upper and Lower Canada to unify. The British North America Act, signed in 1867, is the constitutional act that solidified Canada as an independent nation that would eventually stretch from the Atlantic to the Pacific.

It also created the two-level structure of government, in which power is split between the federal and provincial levels. Even though Québec's minority status was deepened by it, the new structure granted the province jurisdiction over certain aspects, like education, civil law, and culture. Québec maintained a central importance in the evolution of the country, and, before long, a French-Canadian, Wilfrid Laurier, became prime minister of Canada. Elected in 1896, he was the first of many Québécois, including Pierre Elliot Trudeau and Jean Chrétien, who would lead the country.

Faced with a prodigious period of economic growth at the beginning of the 20th century, Prime Minister Laurier declared it "Canada's century." The prediction fell short, though, when the Great Depression disrupted economic and social progress in Québec for many years. World War II finally put an end to the economic doldrums, and, in fact, Québec came out of the war economically stronger than ever before and ready for social change, as the anarchist manifest *Refus Global* (Total Refusal), signed by artists and writers, made clear.

Despite this exciting new energy and mind-set, the province would remain under the spell of Maurice Duplessis and his conservative party (Union Nationale) for another 15 years. In spite of its considerable economic growth, this period is often referred to as "La Grande Noirceur" (The Great Darkness), the last obstacle before real transformation.

A QUIET REVOLUTION AND CONTEMPORARY TIMES

After the death of Maurice Duplessis in 1959, Québec was ripe for change, and the Liberal Party government of Jean Lesage was elected the year after, kicking off what would be dubbed the Révolution Tranquille (Quiet Revolution), a wide range of bold economic and social reforms. The most important result of these reforms is the secularization of society, putting an end to the centuries-long overarching power of the church in every aspect of Québécois society. Education, health care, and social services were no longer under the control of the church as the state began to take over.

The most ambitious economic project of the time, the nationalization of the province's electric companies under Hydro Quebec is a powerful symbol of that new ambition. The Quiet Revolution also witnessed the rise of nationalism. Jean Lesage's Liberal government election slogan, *maîtres chez nous* (masters in our own home), meant to put a stop to the unbridled selling of the province's natural resources to foreign business interests.

Montréal hosted two major international events that still define its identity: the 1967 World's Fair (Exposition Universelle—Terre des Hommes) and the Summer Olympic Games in 1976. The sentiment of empowerment at the time exacerbated enthusiasm for the idea of a stronger autonomy within the Canadian federation, and more and more people became attracted by the idea of building a new country instead, some groups even falling into extremism. Thus, the Front de Liberation du Québec (FLQ), founded in 1963, used terrorist tactics against the Québec and national governments and businesses with the aim of establishing a socialist independent country.

In 1970, during the October crisis, when the FLQ kidnapped Québec Labour Minister Pierre Laporte and eventually killed him, Pierre Elliot Trudeau, then Canadian prime minister, launched the War Measures Act against Québec dissidents, putting the country under martial law to much public controversy. After that, the FLQ declined drastically and eventually disappeared.

Despite these radical actions and a certain support the FLQ gained with the public, the majority of pro-sovereigntists preferred moderate nationalism. In 1967, René Lévesque, a rising star of the Liberal government, quit the party and founded the Parti Québécois (PQ). Soon after, in 1976, a stunning and unexpected victory brought the PQ to power, putting the question of sovereignty at the forefront of political and social life of Québec society for decades. Bill 101 in 1977 made French the only official language of Québec. In 1980 Lévesque's government launched a referendum on the issue of independence, losing when the "no" side won with 60 percent of the vote. In time, the tensions with the federal government became aggravated, mostly over constitutional matters and Québec's refusal to ratify the repatriated Canadian constitution in 1982.

In 1995, a second referendum campaign was launched. This time the results were extremely close, and Canada held its breath: 49.4 percent of Québecers voted "yes" and 50.6 percent voted "no," underlining the deep division of the population over the issue.

However, the national question has faded in importance over the last 20 years, with public attention drifting toward other public matters like the environment and economy. In 2003, the PQ was ousted from power after 10 years, and the Québec Liberal Party, resolutely federalist, was elected. Led by Premier Jean Charest, they were voted in for a third term in 2009.

Thanks to political unrest related to the rising costs of tuition, the PQ regained political power with a minority government in the autumn 2012 election. Lead by Pauline Marois, the party is focused less on the question of sovereignty than during their previous term in power.

Government and Economy

POLITICS

Canada's political system is modeled after the British parliamentary system it historically inherited. Central in the government organization is the House of Commons, sitting in Ottawa, a democratically elected body consisting of 308 members known as Members of Parliament (MPs). Each MP in the House of Commons is elected by simple plurality in an electoral district, also known as a riding. Elections are called within four years of the previous election or when the government loses a confidence vote.

The leader of the party that won the most seats becomes the new prime minister and forms the new government. Canada being a federation, this political structure is reproduced for every province. Therefore, each of them has its own parliament. In Québec, it is called the Assemblée Nationale, and its 125 elected members sit in Québec City. The Canadian Constitution divides the power between federal and provincial governments. For example, defense, postal services, and international relations are under federal jurisdiction, while education, health, and natural resources are under provincial jurisdiction. Since the Constitution is not always clear about these divided powers, constitutional conflicts arise, a situation that has been particularly true between Québec and the federal government.

Canada is also a constitutional monarchy. People are often surprised to know that there is a queen in Canada: Queen Elizabeth II of England is the Canadian head of state. Actually, it is mostly a formal and symbolic title, although she does have a representative in Canada acting on her behalf: the governor general. She is represented by the lieutenant-governor in the provinces.

This type of governmental structure favors a two-party system, but in

Canada's case, four parties make up the federal government: the right- **207**
leaning Conservative Party, centrist Liberal Party, left-leaning NDP (New
Democratic Party), and the Bloc Québécois, the Québec sovereigntist party.
In major political battles, the Conservatives and Liberals are always the
front-runners, but the NDP and Bloc parties are instrumental to how government is run and what bills are passed in the House of Commons.

Since 2010, Prime Minister Stephen Harper of the Conservative party
has been the head of the federal government, but the government only rules
with a minority. The Conservatives have ruled with a minority government
since their re-election in 2011. The province of Québec is largely responsible
for the current political landscape, due to its overwhelming support for the
left-leaning National Democratic Party (NDP) during the 2011 election.
The province's support for the NDP and its leader, Jack Layton, single-
handedly shattered the Conservative's dream of a majority. Québec's political death knell was christened "Orange Crush."

On the provincial stage, two parties have been exchanging power for half
a century: the centrist, federalist Québec Liberal Party, and the sovereigntist Parti Québécois founded by René Lévesque. In the 1980s and '90s, the
Parti Québécois (PQ) became the center of international attention when it
organized two referendums on Québec sovereignty, the outcome of which
threatened to break up Canadian unity. The consecutive defeats of the PQ
in these referendums and in recent elections has laid the sovereigntist question aside for the time being.

ECONOMY

Since the beginning, Québec's natural resources have been the major asset
in the province's economy. Vast forests, mining resources, rich agricultural
land, and a huge potential for hydroelectricity—because of all the lakes—
make this province a gift from the gods. Historically everything began with
the fur trade, kicking off the European colonization of the territory and
sustaining it for over a century. In the 19th and most of the 20th centuries,
wood, pulp, and paper industries took the lead and are still, along with the
mining sector and hydroelectricity production, the most important sec-
tors of Québec's economy.

The government plays an important role in the economy and is the
largest employer in the province. Despite the trend toward more priva-
tization, this strong state involvement reaches a certain consensus in the
population and is considered essential due to the small size of its economy.
Government-owned Hydro Québec, the world's leader in hydroelectricity,
remains a national pride, and dams and development projects in the north
are thoroughly followed by the population. Another economic national
jewel is aerospace and railway maker Bombardier, a world-class company
started 70 years ago by Joseph Bombardier, the inventor of the snowmobile.

Québec City has discreetly developed into a very successful city, with
one of the lowest unemployment rates in Canada at 4.5 percent. Most jobs
in Québec City are found in public administration, services, and tourism,
with a large proportion of civil servants, because it is the seat of the entire
provincial political apparatus.

The past few years have seen a particularly sound growth rate and many urban development projects, probably prompted by the enthusiasm occasioned by the city's 400th anniversary. The result of this growth meant that Québec City virtually averted the economic crisis of 2008 and has continued to grow since then.

People and Culture

FIRST NATIONS

Québec's first inhabitants were the Amerindians. Eleven different First Nations tribes, including the Inuit, called the province home before the early days of colonization. Today, they represent a small part of the population, and three-quarters of them live on reserves throughout the province: The Mohawk reserves Kahnawake and Kanesatake in the Montréal region and the Wendat-Huron reserve Wendake north of Québec City are some of the bigger ones in the province. Though some Amerindians live in areas where they can hunt and fish, many of them have lost their traditional way of life and endure social hardships.

One of the most important political events of the past 20 years was the Oka Crisis: For two months in the summer of 1990 Mohawks barricaded one of the main bridges into Montréal, protesting land claims and issues of self-government. The incident forced native issues to the forefront, and in recent years many agreements have granted Amerindians more autonomy.

FRANCOPHONES

The vast majority of the Québécois people are descendants of the settlers who arrived between 1608 and 1759. From the 60,000 French-Canadians in 1759 there are now seven million living in Canada. Part of the reason Québec has such a strong cultural and social heritage is because of the population's demographics. In the late 18th century with the arrival of the United Empire Loyalists, the French-Canadians became nervous at the idea of being over-populated by the English-speaking contingent. One response to this immigration was something that would later be called the *revanche des berceaux* (revenge of the cradle), which saw the families of French-Canadians growing larger by the year. Of course, the province's Catholic background helped, and throughout the years Québécois families were typically large and women had an average of 8 children (Celine Dion is from a family of 14 kids). In the 1970s, however, the birthrate dropped considerably, and it remains one of the lowest in the world.

Though today the province is experiencing a baby boom, it is a mere blip compared to the numbers in the mid-20th century. Much of the growth to the province's Francophone population now comes from immigration.

ANGLOPHONES

The first Anglophone immigrants arrived after the British conquest in 1759. Most of them were well-to-do Protestant merchants, forever forging the stereotype of the rich Anglophone. However, this wasn't always the case; one of the most important groups of immigrants was the working-class Irish, who arrived in the province as early as the founding of New France. The biggest wave of Irish immigrants came 1815-1860, driven from Ireland by the potato famine. They came to the province by the boatload, disembarking at Grosse-Île, an island off the shores of Québec City that was set up as a reception center. During the summer of 1847, thousands died during a typhus epidemic, and the orphaned children were adopted by Québec families. It is estimated that a staggering 45 percent of Quebeckers have Irish ancestry, even if most of them don't know it. In Québec City many immigrant families were relegated to the slum-like dwellings in Petite Champlain.

The arrival of the United Empire Loyalists between 1783 and the beginning of the 19th century shaped not only the Eastern Townships, where most of them settled, but also the future of the country. They fled the United States in such great numbers as to facilitate the division of the province into Upper and Lower Canada. The 19th century also saw the largest number of immigrants from the British Isles, many of whom would put down roots in Montréal and, in the case of the Scots, found McGill University.

In the 1970s, after the rise to power of the PQ and the October Crisis in particular, many English-speakers left Québec, many settling in Ontario. Nowadays, they make up only 10 percent of the total population of the province and live mostly in Montréal.

QUEBECKERS OF OTHER ETHNIC ORIGINS

Immigration from countries other than Britain and France only started in the 20th century. This growing ethnic diversity is particularly obvious in Montréal, whose history has been defined by successive waves of immigrants. After World War II, the majority of immigrants arrived from Italy, Greece, and Portugal, communities that continue to have a stronghold in neighborhoods like the Mile End and Little Italy. For the most part, these immigrants aligned themselves with the Anglophone community, raising Québec's perennial concerns over French language subsistence. In 1977, the Parti Québécois passed Bill 101 as a solution to that perceived threat, forcing new arrivals into French schools. Immigration demographics began to change in the latter part of the century, and the 1970s and '80s saw exiles from Vietnam and Haiti join the ranks, followed more recently by North African, Chinese, and Central European immigrants.

Québec also has a large Jewish community, whose roots can be traced all the way back to the British conquest, while a large Hassidic community can be found in Outremont.

Jewish Québec

King Louis XIV of France might have banned Jews from entering the colony of Nouvelle France, but Québec's Jewish roots can still be traced for centuries.

The first Jewish people to settle in Québec were members of the British Army who arrived after the initial conquest. Several are thought to have been a part of General Jeffery Amherst's battalion, four of which were officers. Of those officers at least one, Aaron Hart, remained in Canada, settling in Trois-Rivières and eventually becoming a wealthy landowner. One of his sons, Ezekiel Hart, later became the first Jew to be elected to public office in the British Empire.

Though the Jewish community in Montréal numbered little more than 200, the Spanish and Portuguese Synagogue of Montréal opened its doors in 1768 and became the first non-Catholic house of worship in the province. In Québec City the first known Jewish inhabitant was Abraham Jacob Franks, who settled in the city in 1767, but it wasn't until 1892 that the Jewish population in Québec City had enough members to warrant a proper synagogue. In the interim, however, they had founded a number of institutions, including the Québec Hebrew Sick Benefit Association, the Québec Hebrew Relief Association for Immigrants, and the Québec Zionist Society. By 1905, Québec City's Jewish population numbered 350.

As anti-Semitism mounted in Europe, over 155,000 Jews resettled in Canada, many of them in Montréal, where they became storekeepers, tradespeople, and workers in the city's numerous garment factories. The history of one of the city's greatest streets, boulevard St-Laurent, can be traced back to the immigrant families who worked and lived along the Main or in the factories nearby. Jewish businesses left an indelible mark on the city, and many of Montéal's most recognizable symbols—the smoked-meat sandwich, the bagel—come from that strong Jewish lineage.

At the end of World War II approximately 40,000 Holocaust survivors came to Canada, and in 1947, the Workmen's Circle and Jewish Labour Committee started the Tailors Project, aimed at bringing Jewish refugees to Montréal in the needle trades. Jewish immigration continued to expand in Québec, especially in the 1950s when North African Jews fled the continent, settling in Québec City and Montréal where their French language would be an asset.

The community today is concentrated in Montréal, in areas such as Hamstead, Côte-St-Luc, and Outremont, with a large Hassidic community in the Mile End. Though Québec City still has a Jewish community, the majority of the province's Jewish population lives in Montréal, and in fact, many of the city's most recognizable citizens come from this community, including literary giants Irving Layton and Mordecai Richler, poet and musician Leonard Cohen, psychologist and linguist Steven Pinker, and even American Apparel founder Dov Charney.

LGBT COMMUNITY

The first recorded gay establishment in North America, Moise Tellier's apples and cake shop, opened in Montréal in 1869. You can't get a better picture of Québec's attitude toward the gay, lesbian, bi, and trans community than that. Like all LGBT communities, Montréal's has faced discrimination and hardships, one of the most crucial being a raid in October

1977, during which 144 men were arrested. Those arrests, however, led to a 2,000-person-strong protest the following day.

Today, there are queer establishments and events all over Montréal. There is also massive support both within the city and community for younger members of the LGBT community. The community is smaller and subtler in Québec City, but it's no less supported. Québec City hosts an annual pride celebration; decorations go up all over rue St-Jean, and Place d'Youville turns into a street party.

RELIGION

There is no denying the influence of the Catholic Church on the history of Québec, and almost every street corner features a three-story high cathedral, though today many of them have been converted into condos. Instrumental in the founding of the nation and throughout most of its history, the Catholic Church only really began to lose its prominence in the 1960s and '70s. For the most part, Francophones remain Catholic (though most are non-practicing) and Anglophones are Protestant, but there are also diverse religions encompassing Muslims, Jews, Hindus, and Sikhs.

LANGUAGE

The language issue is arguably the most important for Québécois Francophones since it's really what makes them both distinct and recognizable. They can be very touchy about how other people view their language, be it toward other Francophones who consider *joual* a mere dialect, or toward people who obstinately refuse to make any efforts to speak French. Don't be afraid, though; they're usually not hard to please, and using a mere *bonjour* (hello) or *merci* (thank you) is the safest way to gain their respect. They will often switch to English (even broken English) if they see you struggling.

In order to understand this somewhat intransigent stand on Québécois you have to understand the history. After the British conquest in 1759, even though language, religion, and other rights were granted to the French community, they were barred from political and economical power for a long time. This linguistic exclusionism, in which access to the upper levels of business and power was barred to the French-Canadians, lasted well into the 20th century. In fact, until the 1970s English-speakers were the minority that ran many of the businesses and held positions of power in the province.

The Quiet Revolution in the 1960s, however, helped to change all that as it fostered nationalist sentiment, which reached a peak when the Parti Québécois was elected in 1976. In 1977, Bill 101 was passed, asserting the primacy of French on public signs across the province, and apostrophes were removed from store fronts in the 1980s to comply with French usage. English is allowed on signage as long as it's half the size of the French lettering. Despite the debate that surrounded the bill when it was first implemented, many believe it has helped to preserve the language.

Anyone with a good ear will likely be able to tell that there's a big difference between the French spoken here and the French in France. The French here is said to be equivalent to the French spoken in the 17th and 18th centuries in France, preserved due to its geographical isolation. The language spoken in everyday life is very specific and somewhat entertaining, since it's full of funny expressions and syntax. Depending on where you are in the province, some accents are harder to understand than those in the cities.

Unlike in France where they've integrated English terms like "weekend" into regular usage, Québec is much more ardent about the preservation of the language. That's not to say English words aren't in common usage in Québec; there is simply a heightened awareness of them. The Office Québécoise de la Langue Française is an institution whose mandate is to translate new words, typically those related to IT or technology, into a French equivalent. For example, in Québec, email is *courriel,* the French contraction of electronic mail, and Québec's stop signs are also written in French, with the word *arrêt* at their center, though even in France the signs read "stop."

Festivals and Events

There's no helping Québec—it's simply a province that wants people to get together and have a good time. If you had to spend six months locked up indoors, you'd want to get out and celebrate too, which is why one of the biggest festivals of the year, Québec City's Carnaval de Québec, is held during the coldest months. Of course, when the warm weather finally arrives, Québec City throws it a big party too, in the form of the Festival d'Été de Québec.

WINTER
Carnaval de Québec

The most iconic of all the festivals in the province, **Carnaval de Québec** (various locations, 418/626-3716, www.carnaval.qc.ca) has its roots in the early days of New France, when everyone got together in the weeks leading up to Lent to drink and let loose. Following tradition, the festival is held between the end of January and early February. The first big Carnaval took place in 1894 as a way of combating the winter blahs, and it's in this spirit that the festival has taken place every winter since 1955. Lead by Bonhomme, a life-size snowman with a floppy red hat and a *ceinture fléchée* (a traditional Québécois belt), the festival is all about fun in the outdoors. From parades to dog-sled races, tobogganing to ice canoeing, ice-skating to outdoor dance parties and snow sculpture competitions, there's always something going on. It's also the only festival to give adults full rights to wander the town in snowsuits without shame while sipping on something to keep them warm. An added bonus? Most events are free.

Mois Multi

The international festival **Mois Multi** (various locations, 418/524-7553,

Clockwise from top left: one of the many churches that can be found throughout Québec City; typical architecture in St-Jean-Baptiste, Québec City; city hall, Québec City.

www.moismulti.org), founded in 2000, focuses on multidisciplinary and electronic arts. Artists from such diverse countries as Russia, Australia, and Mexico have exhibited here, bringing with them their various light and sound installations and multimedia performances that explore topics like synesthesia, sound-architecture, and light chaos. Throughout the month-long festival in February, visitors are invited to witness these manmade realms, making it more than just an event, it becomes an experience.

Red Bull Crashed Ice

If you think walking the icy streets of Québec City is tough, imagine skating down them. That's the challenge with the yearly **Red Bull Crashed Ice** (various locations, 877/643-8131, www.redbullcrashedice.ca), which takes place in March. Competitors from all over the world, kitted out in full hockey gear, take to the ice track laid out throughout the steep winding streets of Old Québec and attempt to skate their way to the bottom. Fans are free to line the 550-meter track and watch as both the men's and women's heats go by like a flash in this mash-up between downhill skiing, hockey, and boardercross.

SPRING
Carrefour International de Théâtre de Québec

The city's preeminent theater festival, **Carrefour International de Théâtre de Québec** (various locations, 418/692-3131, www.carrefourtheatre.qc.ca) presents innovative theater work from Canada and beyond. Though established playwrights often present here, there's an eye on emerging playwrights and artists as well. Held from the end of May to early June, all the productions presented are premieres in the province—they do not accept pieces that have already been mounted in Québec. Since it is an international festival, there are often a few English or bilingual selections.

Festival de la Gastronomiede Québec

For gourmands interested in seeing and tasting the latest in cuisine, the **Festival de la Gastronomiede Québec** (Gastronomy Festival, Expo Cité, 418/683-4150, www.crq.ca, $12 adult) brings out the best in new merchandise. Over three days in mid-April, 200 exhibitors invite the public to taste their wares, from wineries to microbreweries, pastries to cheese, with over 60 percent of the products coming from Québec. Visitors are welcome to browse the aisles, pick up some cooking tips, and indulge in all kinds of different food. Restaurants from around the city are also here, cooking up new or classic dishes. A word of warning: With fees for entering, parking, and the occasional bite, it can add up to be an expensive day.

Manif d'Art

Simply put, **Manif d'Art** (various locations, 418/524-1917, www.manifdart. org) is the Québec City biennial, held in May and June. Every even-numbered year, the city and the world's established and up-and-coming artists present their works at what is the biggest contemporary art festival in Québec City. Events outside of the exhibitions are held as well, including colloquiums and forums, and satellite activities with other disciplines such as live performances and shows. A nominal fee allows visitors to see all the exhibitions and gives them access to guided tours, theme-related events, and creative workshops.

SUMMER
Expo Québec

The largest agricultural fair in Eastern Canada, **Expo Québec** (Expo Cité, 250 blvd. Wilfrid-Hamel, 888/866-3976, www.expoquebec.com, $30 adult, $20 senior, $12 child) was founded in 1911 and has been celebrating with a public exhibition every August since. The 10-day event is aimed at families, with attractions like candy, inflatable castles, mini-rollercoasters, educational exhibits on science and organic food production, and concerts for kids and adults alike. The real draw here, however, is the animals; with close to 2,000 animals on view, kids and adults have a chance to learn more about horses, ponies, cattle, sheep, goats, alpacas, and a host of other, smaller animals.

Festibière

It isn't summer without a beer festival. **Festibière** (100 Quai St-André, 418/948-1166, www.festibieredequebec.com, $12 adult) takes place along the waterfront for three days in August and couldn't be better located. In order to expand the tastebuds of beer lovers everywhere, various tents are dedicated to various beers with locations dedicated to both local and international brews. There's also a conference dedicated to the art of brewing where you can test your knowledge of hops against that of the experts. Legal drinking age in Québec is 18, so don't be surprised to find yourself surrounded by a few amateur, yet eager beavers.

Festival des Journées d'Afrique, Danses et Rythmes du Monde

Celebrating African dance and music, this two-week **Festival des Journées d'Afrique, Danses et Rythmes du Monde** (various locations, 418/640-4213, www.festivaljourneedafrique.com), which occurs late July-early August, sees artists from all over the world performing a diverse range of African-roots music. Everything is represented here, from soukous from the Congo to Trinidadian calypso, South African Afro-beat, and roots reggae from Québec. Dance troupes, drumming, and dance workshops are also part of the fest. Prices vary depending on venue with some events free.

Festival d'Été de Québec

One of the biggest events in the entire calendar year, **Festival d'Été de Québec** (Québec Summer Festival, various locations, 888/992-5200, www.infofestival.com, $80 adult pass) is essentially one 11-day-long concert. With literally hundreds of shows—some of them for free—happening during the beginning of July, this event gives the city the attitude of a nonstop party. Started in 1968, the focus was mainly on Francophone and world artists, but since 2000 the festival has presented some of the most interesting international acts in the world, including Ethiopiques, Andrew Bird, Caribou, Black Eyed Peas, and a number of emerging talents. The biggest outdoor shows take place on the Plains of Abraham and in the past have featured musicians like Iron Maiden, Arcade Fire, and Paul McCartney.

Fête Arc-en-Ciel de Québec

Taking place in early September, usually over Labor Day weekend, **Fête Arc-en-Ciel de Québec** (Rainbow Celebration, various locations, 418/809-3383, www.glbtquebec.org, $12 adult) is Québec's gay pride celebration. Each year, the three-day event is based on a different theme, usually one that can be loosely interpreted and allow for some great street decorations. Though the center of the celebrations is the gay pride parade, they include a number of free performances, concerts, and conferences that look at important topics like homophobia in high schools.

Fête Nationale St-Jean Baptiste

Fête Nationale St-Jean Baptiste (Plains of Abraham, 418/640-0799, www.snqc.qc.ca, free) is Québec's national holiday, which takes place on June 24. "Nationale" refers to the nation of Québec; this holiday isn't celebrated elsewhere in Canada. Though Saint-Jean-Baptiste Day has been celebrated in Québec since the first European settlers, it took a patriotic turn in 1834 after Ludger Duvernay, who would later found the Saint-Jean-Baptiste Society, was inspired by St. Patrick's Day celebrations in Montréal. In celebration of the province's national holiday, the people of Québec usually spend the afternoon with an aperitif before heading out to the free concert on the Plains of Abraham in the evening, featuring famous Québécois performers and stars.

Les Fêtes de la Nouvelle-France

For four days in August, the public is invited to step back in time during **Les Fêtes de la Nouvelle France** (various locations, 866/391-3383, www.nouvellefrance.qc.ca, $12 adult, children under 12 free) to experience Québec as it was during the French regime. Bringing to life over a dozen sites in the Vieux-Québec's Lower Town, each year is centered around a theme in order to give viewers a fuller picture of what life was like in New France. Past events have included the baptism of an Amerindian and a public blessing of women's pregnant bellies. Visitors are encouraged to dress up in period costumes, which are available to buy or rent. This is good family fun.

Le Grand Rire

The Québec City equivalent of Just for Laughs, **Le Grand Rire** (The Big Laugh, various locations, 877/441-7473, www.grandrire.com, $20 and up, children under 12 free) caters to a Francophone audience. Occasionally, however, they have some big-name English acts like Bill Cosby on the bill. It runs throughout the month of June and into early July, and with over 70 shows on the schedule, there are often a few offered in English. Shows take place at indoor and outdoor venues all over the city.

Québec City International Festival of Military Bands

For five days at the end of August, military bands and a few dancers from all over the world take to the stage and streets for the **Québec City International Festival of Military Bands** (various locations, 888/693-5757, www.fimmq.com). Bands from all over Canada, Germany, France, Italy, and the United States regularly participate, including surprising acts like the New York City Police Department's Jazz Band. Locals line the Grande-Allée during the opening parade, then head to the main stage near the Manège Militaire to catch a free show. Most events are free, but some shows require tickets, including the grand finale Tattoo.

FALL

Envol et Macadam

The alternative music festival **Envol et Macadam** (various locations, 418/522-1611, www.envoletmacadam.com) was founded in 1996, with the aim of both nurturing up-and-coming talent and bringing established artists to the city who wouldn't necessarily play here otherwise. Taking place in September, the festival has three main outdoor stages in the downtown core and takes over a number of indoor venues during the fest. Though "alternative" isn't as defining a moniker as it was in the 1990s, bands here are still outside of the mainstream, and have included acts like Bloc Party and Metric as well as punk, hardcore, and metal bands like Mastadon, Pennywise, and Bad Religion.

Festival Antenne-A

Music, books, art, film, theater: It's all here at arts-focused **Festival Antenne-A** (various locations, www.antenne-a.com), which brings together emerging artists from all disciplines from late September to early October. Though the schedule is often heavy with bands and DJs from Québec, Canada, and the world, there is a focus on acts that go beyond just the musical aspects and delve into the realms of visual art and technology.

The festival also presents a number of group talks and conferences in both English and French around various themes, including emerging culture.

Festival de Jazz de Québec

The **Festival de Jazz de Québec** (various locations, www.jazzaquebec.ca) is for real jazz buffs only; you won't find any Top 40 artists here. The target audiences for this fest, running from the end of September to early October, are jazz aficionados. Here you'll find entire sets dedicated to greats like Charles Mingus and John Coltrane. Local jazz musicians also take to the stage, including younger avant-garde artists.

Festival des Musiques Sacréesde Québec

The **Festival des Musiques Sacréesde Québec** (Québec Festival of Sacred Music, Église Saint-Roch, 590 rue St-Jean, 866/525-9777, www.imsq.ca) is just that: a three-week-long, October festival filled with compositions inspired by spirituality. Taking place at the Église Saint-Roch, where they are the proud owners of a (partly) Casavantes organ, programs include standards like Brahms's and Verdi's requiems, as well as occasional dance performances, gospel concerts, and compositions from lesser-known sources like sacred songs from Anatolia.

Journées de la Culture

The province-wide **Journées de la Culture** (various locations, 866/734-4441, www.journeesdelaculture.qc.ca, free) opens a number of cultural and artistic hubs to the public by inviting visitors into architecture offices, design studios, and local theaters for a behind-the-scenes look. Also called "Days of Culture," this free, three-day event runs at the end of September, with cities offering complimentary shuttle services to various sites and events, so there's no excuse to miss out. Various workshops and kid-specific events make it an adventure for the whole family.

Parade des Jouets

Held annually at the end of November, the **Parade des Jouets** (Children's Parade, various locations, 418/780-3006, www.paradedesjouets.ca, free) has a long history. It was started at the end of World War II by fireman Marcel Bourassa. Firefighters of the city worked together to repair old toys and make new ones for the less-fortunate children in the city. The tradition continues today, and since 2004, 900 underprivileged children are the recipients of new and refurbished toys each year. This parade is run in celebration of that event and includes floats and marching bands.

The Arts

MUSIC

Without a doubt the province's best-known recording artist is Celine Dion. Born in the small town of Charlemagne 30 kilometers from Montréal, she was a mega-star in Québec and France when she was just a teenager and well before she started singing in English. Although she was criticized at first by her Francophone fan base for "selling out," her worldwide success is now a huge source of pride for the province, and fans now love (and buy) her English albums just as much as her French ones.

The province's second biggest export, music-wise, is Montréal's Arcade Fire, who took over the airwaves in 2004 with their infectious indie rock anthems and haven't looked back. Despite their rock star status—they've shared the stage with everyone from David Byrne to David Bowie—they remain active in the community, and many of the group's members play in other bands. Their success in the early 2000s was also part of a bigger indie rock explosion, with bands like The Dears, Wolfe Parade, and the Unicorns, among others. The scene has continued to grow since then and is constantly evolving. In recent years Francophone bands like

Malajube, Radio Radio, and Karkwa—who won the 2010 Polaris Music Prize, Canada's largest for an "indie" band—have been gaining fans across the language divide.

Poet and singer/songwriter Leonard Cohen is one of the city's most-loved inhabitants, and many of his melancholy and soulful compositions were inspired by the city, including the song *So Long Maryanne.* Grammy Award-winning artist Rufus Wainwright is also from Montréal, though he now resides in New York. Mixing symphonic sounds with a pop mentality, his sweeping compositions are utterly unique and catchy. His sister, Martha Wainwright, also a musician, is somewhat less experimental in her style, but continues to push the boundaries of pop. On one of her more recent albums *(Sans Fusils, Ni Souliers, à Paris)* she sings the songs of Edith Piaf. Of course, it helps when you have good genes, and the Wainwrights have them in spades: Their father is American folk singer Loudon Wainwright III, and their mother is Kate McGarrigle; Kate and her sister Anna are two of the biggest folk singers in the province. Since the 1960s, the McGarrigle sisters have sung and written in both French and English.

It wasn't until the 1960s that modern music really started to hit its stride in the province. Québec held a festival of experimental music in 1961, and by the mid-1960s, the symphony was starting to attract a larger audience. It was also the heyday of folk singers or *chansonniers* like Félix Leclerc and Gilles Vigneault. Leclerc in particular had been singing and writing for a long time, even finding success in Paris, before returning to find the same success at home. Singing about themes like nature and celebrations has made him one of the most revered musicians in the province.

CINEMA

After being under religious censorship during the first half of the 20th century, Québec cinema really kicked off in the 1960s, when a generation of directors formed the National Film Board (NFB). This film board gave them a platform, and they started to make movies mostly about the Québécois identity. Part of the enthusiastic social transformations that were happening in arts in this period, they shot documentaries and features that gained international recognition, despite their local flavor. Experiments in documentary film led to the Direct Cinema genre, which included Pierre Perreault's *Pour la Suite du Monde,* a vivid documentary about the ancestral beluga hunt in Isle-aux-Coudres, and Michel Brault's *Les Orders,* a rendition of the October crisis of 1971.

In the 1970s, a number of feature films gained wide critical acclaim and today are seen as part of a golden age in Québec cinema. Among these are *La Vraie Vie de Bernadette* by Gilles Carle (1972), *J.A. Martin Photographe* by Jean Beaudin (1977), and Frank Mankiewicz's *Les Bons Débarras* (1979). Most important of all is Claude Jutra's 1971 movie *Mon Oncle Antoine,* a coming-of-age story set in the rural Québec of the 1940s, which is considered to be the greatest Canadian film.

The Québec film industry is seen as the strongest in the country, and Québec films regularly win top accolades at the Genie Awards, which are the Canadian film industry awards. Québec's French cinema has a stronger character than its English counterpart, which often struggles to differentiate itself from American cinema.

With movies like *Le Déclin de l'Empire Américain* (1986) and *Jésus de Montréal* (1988), Denys Arcand is probably the best-known Québécois director. *Les Invasions Barbares* (2003), a poignant critique of the aging generation of the Quiet Revolution, won the Oscar for Best Foreign Film and was Best Screenplay at Cannes. Other stand-out directors have been scooped up by Hollywood including Jean-Marc Vallée, whose most recent film was *Dallas Buyers Club,* and Denis Villeneuve, who directed *Prisoners.* Newcomer Xavier Dolan has won big at the Cannes Film Festival for his films *J'ai Tué Ma Mère, Les Amours Imaginaries,* (*Heartbeats*) and *Lawrence, Anyways,* and has set the course for a new generation of filmmakers.

LITERATURE

Playwright and author Michel Tremblay wrote *Chroniques du Plateau,* which has made him one of the most prolific and well-recognized authors in the province. His stories about working-class French-Canadians in the 1960s, written almost entirely in *joual,* defined the writing of his generation. Other writers include Hubert Aquin, Dany Laferrière, Marie-Claire Blais, and Anne Hébert, whose *Kamouraska* looks at treachery and love in 19th-century Québec. Gabrielle Roy's *The Tin Flute* tells the tale of a young woman in working-class Verdun during the Depression.

The region's English-language literature has pretty much been defined, and reigned over, by the acerbic wit of Mordecai Richler, who continues to be one of the strongest voices in Anglophone literature, even after his death in 2001. His novels *The Apprenticeship of Duddy Kravitz, Son of a Smaller Hero,* and *St-Urbain's Horseman* defined not only the city's Jewish population but the city itself.

The witty and poignant novels and short stories of Mavis Gallant continue to weave their way through Montréal, despite the fact that she's long since emigrated to France.

New writers include Rawi Hage, who moved to Montréal in 2001 and whose 2006 novel *De Niro's Game* was nominated for the Scotiabank Giller Prize. His second novel, *Cockroach,* is an intimate look at an immigrant's experience in Montréal.

VISUAL ARTS

Early-Québec art can be divided into two subject matters: landscapes and religion. The province's first painters were Catholic missionaries who used paintings and engravings to convert the Amerindians. Since many of the works were by priests and nuns, they have a particularly naïve quality, a trend that continues in Québécois art. The first great Québécois painters emerged in the 19th century and included Théophile Hamel, known for portraits of explorers; Dutch-born Cornelius Krieghoff, who depicted settlers and images of the wilderness; and Ozias Leduc, whose portrait *Boy with Bread* is one of the defining images of Québécois art.

Work continued to be defined by snowy city-scapes and bucolic farm-land until the modern era of Canadian painting was ushered in by Paul-Émile Bourduas, John Lyman, and Alfred Pellan in the 1940s. Bourduas was the most prolific and outspoken of all three and developed a radical style of surrealism that came to be identified with a group called the Automatistes.

In 1948 Bourduas published the manifesto *Refus Global* (Global Refusal), rejecting traditional social, artistic, and psychological norms of Québécois society and the religious and bucolic art that defined it. The manifesto called instead for an untamed liberation of creativity and championed abstract art.

Canadian art and Québec's artistic community were never the same again. Automatiste artist Jean-Paul Riopelle would soon emerge as the movement's newest driving force, and his abstract works, called "grand mosaics," would become world-renowned.

The 1960s and '70s were defined by artists like Claude Tousignant and Guido Molinari, whose abstract works used hypnotic geometric shapes and unusual color combinations to almost psychedelic proportions.

Some of Québec's biggest contemporary artists include David Altmejd, known for mixed-media pieces that incorporate various materials—everything from a decapitated werewolf head to shards of broken mirrors—into something cohesive and anthropomorphic. Valérie Blass also plays with a mix of materials and human yet non-human forms. Adnad Hannah's film and photographic works play with traditional art history. Two of the province's biggest artists are collectives: The work of BGL plays with conventional objects or pop culture icons in unconventional ways—a melted Darth Vader, or a motorcycle covered with snow in the middle of a gallery floor. Cooke et Sasseville play with similar ideas, and one of their works involves a giant flamingo laying its head down on train tracks.

DANCE AND THEATER

The established Québécois culture and the province's bohemian disposition help nurture a particularly diverse arts scene in both languages.

French theater is some of the best in the world, while English theater struggles to keep the pace. The country's top performing arts educational institution, the National Theater School, is found in the Plateau, attracting Canada's most promising playwrights and stage actors in either language.

There is an innovative contemporary dance scene in the province that has fostered internationally recognized companies like La La La Human Steps, O Vertigo, and Fondation Jean-Pierre Perreault, as well as the careers of dancers and choreographers Margie Gillis, Marie Chouinard, and Benoît Lachambre. Québec also supports two classical ballet companies, Les Grands Ballets Canadiens and Le Ballet de Québec.

THE CIRCUS

Cirque du Soleil is undoubtedly the most famous Québécois circus, founded in Baie-Saint-Paul in the early 1980s by a group of street performers. These

Architecture in Québec

When settlers first arrived in Québec their main concern was with security; with that in mind all of the first towns started out as fortified enclosures. These were made of wood or stone and designed in the five-pointed Vauban style. By the end of the French regime, New France closely resembled provincial towns in the old country, with hospitals, convents, colleges, and churches whose steeples peeked out over the walls.

Early-1700s inhabitants had trouble adapting their homes to the cold weather, and many froze to death before the colony got it right. The design was altered and structures were made of rubble stone instead of wood, with small casement windows that were few and far between. The number of rooms in the house matched the number of chimneys. In 1721, wooden houses with mansard roofs were banned after a devastating fire, and stone firewalls and attic floors covered in terracotta tiles became the standard.

Although the British conquest took place in 1759, it wasn't until the 1780s that English influence could be seen in architecture around the province. A few high-ranking officials started building homes in the popular Palladian and Regency styles, with open-air porticoes and Italian columns. The Regency balconies and windows allowed for a perfect mix between inside and out, while also stopping the snow from blocking windows and doors in winter. Roofs became less slanted so the snow no longer fell directly on your head as you closed the door on your way out. All buildings during this period, commercial or residential, resembled country homes. You can still get a sense of this today on rue St-Jean in Québec City. Commercial buildings were set up to look like homes in part because the Catholic Church disapproved of the expansion of commerce.

stilt-walkers, jugglers, and fire-eaters banded together to create a performance platform, since the circus tradition didn't exist in the province at the time. In the years since then, they've become part of a rich circus culture they helped to create. There are now two schools dedicated to the circus arts: the National Circus School, established in 1981, and Tohu, established in 2004, are both located in Montréal.

Cirque d'Éloize, established in 1993, is another professional company situated in Montréal that is quickly following in the footsteps of Cirque du Soleil when it comes to pushing boundaries and innovation. They bring an edginess and dance sensibility to their shows, which can be seen throughout the world. This dedication to circus arts also means that the province has some of the best street performers in the world, who are especially visible during festival season.

Essentials

Getting There

BY AIR

A number of major airlines fly directly into Québec City's teeny-tiny **Aéroport International Jean-Lesage de Québec** (418/640-2600, www. aeroportdequebec.com). Most air traffic comes from Montréal, though there are a few direct flights from within Canada as well as some international flights, mostly from France and from a few major U.S. cities, including Detroit, Chicago, Newark, and Cleveland.

The airport is about 15 kilometers from downtown; there is no bus or shuttle service available, so the only way to get to downtown is by taxi, which will set you back about $35.

BY RAIL

Train passengers arrive at Québec City at the **Gare du Palais** (450 rue de la Gare-du-Palais, 418/525-3000) in Vieux-Québec's Lower Town. Depending on where you're staying and the amount of baggage you're carrying, it might be wise to take a taxi. City buses are also available just outside the terminal to Upper Town, including bus 800, which will take you through Saint-Jean-Baptiste and up to the Grande-Allée, Parliament, and the Plains area. A single ride costs $2.75.

BY BUS

Buses to Québec arrive at the same place as the trains at **Gare du Palais** (320 rue Abraham-Martin, 418/525-3000), near the Vieux-Port; most hotels will be a short cab ride or uphill walk away.

BY CAR

Québec City can be reached by Autoroute 20 in the south and Autoroute 40 in the north. The drive from Montréal will take approximately 2.5 hours, and though the drive along Route 40 is more scenic, it's also a little bit longer. From Toronto, Route 401 connects with Route 20, as do I-87 in New York and I-89 and I-91 in Vermont. Arriving on Route 20, follow the signs for Pont Pierre-Laporte, and once you've crossed the bridge, turn right onto boulevard Laurier, which becomes Grande-Allée. Route 40 turns into boulevard Charest as you approach the city.

TRAVELING TO MONTRÉAL
By Air

Short-haul 50-minute flights depart from Québec City 12 times a day on **Air Canada** (800/247-2262, www.aircanada.com), though by the time you go to the airport, check in, and collect your baggage afterwards, it might be just as fast to drive.

Previous: Jardin St-Roch; St-Jean-Baptiste neighborhood.

By Rail

The train is a fast and fairly efficient way to travel, though the costs can sometimes be prohibitive. **VIA Rail** (888/842-7245, www.viarail.ca) runs the only service between the two cities and offers four daily departures from both **Montréal's Gare Centrale** (895 rue de la Gauchetière W., 514/989-2626) and **Québec City's Gare du Palais** (450 rue de la Gare-du-Palais, 418/525-3000). Train times run anywhere from 3 to 3.5 hours, and a regular one-way ticket costs $102 before taxes, though seat sales can bring the price as low as $60.

By Bus

Both cities are served by the **Orléans Express** (888/999-3977, www.orleansexpress.com), with hourly departures from both **Montréal's Gare d'Autocars** (505 blvd. de Maisonneuve E., 514/842-2281, www.stationcentrale.com) and **Québec's Gare du Palais** (320 rue Abraham-Martin, 418/525-3000). A round-trip ticket costs approximately $80 and the ride can take anywhere from three to five hours.

By Car

Driving is often the quickest and easiest way to get to Montréal from Québec City. The drive can last anywhere from 2.5 to 4 hours depending on traffic. Take Autoroute 20 or Route 40 and head west. Heading into Montréal on Route 20, follow the signs for Pont Jacques-Cartier, which will take you straight into the heart of the Plateau. From Route 40, exit on any number of southbound streets, including Papineau, St-Denis, and St-Laurent.

Taking the 40 instead of the 20 will add approximately 20 minutes onto your trip, but it's more scenic and you have the option of stopping off at Trois Trois-Rivières at about the halfway point.

There are also a couple of ride-share companies that can help save costs for both drivers and passengers: **Allo Stop** (www.allostop.com) and **Amigo Express** (www.amigoexpress.com).

Getting Around

PUBLIC TRANSPORTATION

Québec City buses (www.rtcquebec.ca) are fast and efficient, with three major bus lines, called **MétroBus,** that run frequently and cover all the major areas of the city—some will even take you as far out as Chute Montmorency. A single bus ticket costs $3 and also acts as a transfer if you're transferring lines; if you don't have a ticket the bus accepts exact change.

The city also has a few buses aimed at tourists. The **Navette Desjardins** runs from June to mid-October and carries passengers from Beauport and Domain des Maizrets, north of the city, through the Vieux-Port and Lower Town and out to the Aquarium du Quebec and Promenade de Samuel de

amplain. A ticket costs $3 for all-day unlimited use, and a child under 5
es for free. Carrying approximately 20 passengers at a time, the **Ecobus**
ts $2 and takes you from Vieux-Québec Lower Town to Upper Town.

DRIVING

Driving in Québec City is not ideal, especially if you're heading into Vieux-Québec's Upper and Lower Towns. The small, winding streets make them difficult to navigate, especially if you're not used to that type of driving. In the summer, many of the streets are blocked off to accommodate pedestrians, mainly during the day and into the night. In the winter, it's these same streets that are covered in ice and snow. Though there is light traffic in general in Québec City, parking is still a problem, especially on streets with slopes of 45 degrees. The city has very few underground parking lots.

The speed limit on Canadian highways is 100 kilometers per hour (kph), and it's 50 kph on city streets unless otherwise noted. U.S. citizens don't need an international license and neither do drivers from England or France. If your driver's license is in a language other than English or French, you need an International Driver's Permit; see the Québec government website (www.saaq.gouv.qc.ca) for more information. Members of AAA (American Automobile Association, www.aaa.com) are covered under the Canadian equivalent CAA (www.caa.ca). Gasoline is more expensive than in the United States so fill up before crossing the border.

Rental Cars

Many of the large rental companies (Avis, Budget, Discount) are available in Québec City. The minimum age to rent a vehicle is 25, and rates run the gamut from $34 to $60 per day depending on time of year.

TAXIS

Québec City has a ton of different taxi companies. Try **Taxi Coop Québec** (418/525-5191). The initial charge is $3.30, each kilometer adds $1.60, and each minute of waiting is $0.60. Tip is usually 10-15 percent. Some drivers know the city well, others not so much, so make sure you have your destination with the cross street written down to show the driver, especially if it's a word you're unsure how to pronounce.

BICYCLING

Unless you're an experienced biker and brought your own ride, biking in Québec City is not recommended; there are some seriously steep hills that aren't fun going up or down. That being said, if you're planning on staying exclusively, or at least mostly, in Lower Town or Upper Town, then renting a bike is a great way to get around, and will allow you to ride along the river and the Vieux-Port.

Visas and Officialdom

PASSPORTS AND VISAS

All visitors must have a valid passport or other accepted secure documents to enter the country, even those entering from the United States by road or train. Citizens of the United States, Australia, New Zealand, Israel, Japan, and most western European countries don't need visas to enter Canada for stays up to 180 days. U.S. permanent residents are also exempt. Travelers who travel regularly between Canada and the United States should consider getting a Nexus membership; details are available online (www.cdp.gov).

Nationals from South Africa, China, and about 150 other countries must apply for a temporary resident visa (TRV) in their home country. Full details can be found at **Citizen and Immigration Canada** (888/242-2100, www.cic.gc.ca). Single-entry visitor visas are valid for six months and cost $75; multiple-entry visas last for two years, as long as a single stay doesn't last for longer than six months, and cost $150. A separate visa is required if you intend to work in Canada.

CUSTOMS

Depending on how long your stay in Canada is, you're allowed to take various amounts of goods back home without paying any duty or import tax. There is a limit on the amount of tobacco and liquor you can bring back duty-free, and some countries have a limit on perfumes. For exact amounts, check with the customs department in your home country. Also check the **Canadian Border Services Agency** (505/636-5064, www.cbsa-asfa.gc.ca) for details on bringing in and taking home goods.

There are very strict rules on bringing plants, flowers, food, and other vegetation into the country, so it's not advisable to bring them. If you're 18 years or older, you're allowed to bring into the country 50 cigars or 200 grams of tobacco, as well as 1.14 liters of liquor, 1.5 liters of wine, or 24 cans or bottles of beer. If you bring more, you'll face a hefty fine. Those traveling with their pets will need a health certificate and a rabies vaccination certificate. The vaccination must be carried out 30 days before your departure. Nonresidents can be refunded for the GST (government sales tax) paid on purchases made in Canada. If you want a refund, however, keep your receipts; to be eligible, your receipts must add up to $200. Call 800/668-4748 for details.

Blasphemy the Québécois Way

In Québec, swearing is its own language. Instead of being derived from naughty sexual innuendo, however, swear words come from Catholicism and its practices. Originating in the early 19th century, many of the swear words or *sacres* developed out of a frustration at the church that seemingly controlled everything. The church is much less influential since the Quiet Revolution of the 1960s, and though the swear words are still in use, they are no longer as powerful and have become part of common language. Even English-speakers get into the habit, especially when talking with Québécois friends.

Among the most popular *sacres* and the ones you'll likely hear the most are *crisse* (Christ), *tabarnak* (from tabernacle), *ostie* (from host), and *sacrement* (from sacrement). Like all good swear words, however, they work best when used together, as in *criss d'ostie de tabarnak,* which defies translation.

Another word you might hear is *fucké,* which, weirdly enough, has nothing to do with the English pejorative; instead it means strange or bizarre, as in *"ce film était vraiment fucké,"* or "that film was really weird."

Conduct and Customs

MOVING DAY

While the rest of the country celebrates Canada Day, the nation's national holiday, on July 1, Quebeckers move. It is the unofficial moving day for renters across the province—this is the day most leases change hands—and it is usually a hot, sweaty day with cars, vans, trucks, SUVs, and even bikes loaded to the hilt and headed for new digs. It's also not uncommon to see people simply schlepping their belongings by foot.

Don't even think about renting a car on this day, as there likely won't be any left. A thrifter's paradise, the aftermath of the move leaves sidewalks and alleyways littered with discarded belongings and unwanted junk, which may turn out to be your treasure.

ALCOHOL

As in most Canadian provinces, if you're looking for wine, beer, or spirits, you have to get it at the **SAQ** (Société des Alcools de Québec, www.saq.ca), the store run by the provincial liquor board. Found all over the city, they carry a wide selection of wine and spirits and a small selection of imported beer. Québec differs from most other provinces in that beer and wine can also be purchased in your local grocery and corner stores.

The selection of wine and beer varies from store to store; if you're in an upscale neighborhood, the selection of wine at both the *dépanneur* (corner store) and the grocery store will likely be of a higher caliber than what you'd find elsewhere. If you're looking for beer, a *dép* is your best bet. If you don't find the brand you're looking for, just step into the fridge yourself; it might look like just another display case but step through the camouflaged door and you're in beerville. Drinking age in Québec is 18, and stores stop selling alcohol at 11pm.

TIPPING

Tips and service charges aren't covered in the bill; instead a 15-percent tip should be added to the total bill at restaurants and bars at which you run a tab. When you order a drink at a bar, you're usually expected to pay when the drink is brought to you; a $1-2 tip for drinks is the standard. Tip the same for valet parking attendants, bellhops at the hotel, and coat-check attendants. Housekeeping staff should be tipped $3-5.

SMOKING

Smoking is illegal in bars, cafés, clubs, and restaurants and not permitted in enclosed public spaces. Outdoors on the sidewalk or on a restaurant's or bar's patio is fair game. Some hotels, however, still have smoking and non-smoking options, though it's becoming rarer. There are a few cigar bars, including Société Cigare in Québec City, where smoking indoors is allowed due to specialized ventilation systems. You must be 18 years or older to buy tobacco in Québec.

Tips for Travelers

TRAVELING WITH CHILDREN

There are a ton of kid-friendly activities in Québec City, most of which will tucker any kid out by the end of the day. Top choices include ice-skating and tobogganing in winter, wading pools and bike rides along the canal in summer. Public parks with playgrounds can be found throughout the city and are perfect for blowing off some steam. However, some of the sleeker, cooler boutique hotels might not be the most fun for the kids. Children are also given half-price or free entry to most museums and attractions; some venues offer family rates. Hotels will recommend babysitting services if none are available in-house.

WOMEN TRAVELERS

Québec is a relatively safe city and women should feel at ease traveling alone. Still, the usual rules apply: Women should avoid walking alone on quiet streets and dimly lit areas late at night. Violence is far less prevalent here than in the States, but if you are attacked or sexually assaulted call 911 or the **Sexual Assault Center** (418/522-2120).

LGBT TRAVELERS

Québec is one of the top destinations for gay travelers. In 1977 Québec became the second political entity (after Holland) to include a non-discrimination clause on the basis of sexual orientation in its charter of rights. Gay marriage is legal in Québec, and attitudes toward homosexuality in the province are open and tolerant.

Though there are a number of LGBT publications, monthly magazine *Fugues* (www.fugues.com) is the most comprehensive and has information on everything from hotels to saunas and upcoming gay events.

TRAVELERS WITH DISABILITIES

Most public buildings, including tourist offices, museums, and sights, are wheelchair accessible.

Access to Travel (www.accesstotravel.gc.ca) is a guide to accessible transportation across the country.

Kéroul (514/252-3104, www.keroul.qc.ca) is an association that specializes in tourism for people with disabilities. It publishes *Québec Accessible,* which lists 1,000-plus hotels, restaurants, museums, and theaters that are accessible. For English speakers, there is *The Accessible Road,* which offers information on everything from the most accessible top sights to how to get a disabled parking sticker. It can be downloaded for free from the website.

Health and Safety

HOSPITALS AND CLINICS

Canadians have free health care, but it's not free for visitors, so get travel insurance before you leave your home country. Emergency room waits can be lengthy, and if you're not a Canadian citizen, the treatment could be pricey (though not compared to U.S. hospitals).

For emergency treatment in Québec City, head to the **Hôpital Laval** (2725 chemin Ste-Foy, 418/656-8711).

For minor maladies in Québec City, the closest clinic can be found by calling 418/529-4777 or checking online at www.csssvc.qc.ca. Though the clinics will be glad to help you, you will have to pay cash to see a doctor; they don't take debit or credit.

If you're feeling unwell and just want some advice, call the health hotline (811) from any land line to speak with a nurse 24 hours a day.

PHARMACIES

In Québec City, the largest pharmacy is **Jean Coutu** (110 blvd. René-Lévesque, 418/522-1235, Mon.-Sat. 9am-9pm, Sun. 10am-9pm), near avenue Cartier.

EMERGENCY SERVICES

The fire department, police, and ambulance can all be reached by dialing **911.** When in doubt, you can reach the operator by dialing **0.** There's also the **Poison Center** (800/463-5060) if you're worried about something you've ingested.

CRIME AND HARASSMENT

Québec City is relatively safe and violent crime is rare. Tourists are more likely to be the targets of thieves, like pickpockets at crowded bars, markets,

Winter Essentials

If you want to fit in among the locals during winter's deep freeze you need two things: a parka and a pair of Sorel boots.

- **Parka:** When it comes to parkas, there are two schools: The younger generation goes for a selection from Canada Goose, while many mature Quebeckers opt for the Kanuk. Both are made in Canada and offer that important balance of warmth without the puffiness. When buying a parka the goal is to avoid the "Michelin Man" look; don't buy white and stay away from anything that has a ringed effect. Make sure it's got a fur-trimmed hood and covers your bum—good coverage is essential, especially when you want to take a crazy carpet down Mont-Royal.

- **Boots:** Made with a heavy insulated rubber sole and sturdy leather, Sorel winter boots have been a Canadian staple since 1959. Introduced to the market by Kaufman Footwear of Kitchener,

Ontario, the boots were an instant hit. Originally they were made in Canada, but the company was bought by Columbia Sports in 2000. Though the boots are no longer Canadian owned and made, there is still a strong connection to their Canadian heritage. The ingenious construction of a thermal, waterproof sole paired with a more stylish upper is ideal for city life when 99.9 percent of the time you're walking through freezing gray slush.

- **Fur:** Another popular winter material in Québec is fur, and it's not unusual to see both men and women covered in fur from head to toe. If you find fur offensive, try to suppress your inner activist and instead take a deep breath—see that? Your nose is now completely frozen. Fur in Québec is less about style and more about survival and heritage, and many of the furs have been passed down through family members.

and bus stations. Cars with out-of-province license plates are also targets, so make sure not to leave anything of value in the car and remove your car registration and identification papers.

Information and Services

MONEY

Prices quoted in this guide are in Canadian dollars. Canadian coins come in 5-cent (nickel), 10-cent (dime), 25-cent (quarter), $1 (loonie), and $2 (toonie) pieces. Paper money comes in $5 (blue), $10 (purple), $20 (green), $50 (red), and $100 (brown). In 2013, the government phased out the penny, so most companies round up their prices to the closest 5-cents. Though the Canadian dollar's value was once much lower than the American dollar, it now trades at a few cents off par; www.xe.com has the most current rates.

ATMs

ATMs are all round the city, not just in banks. Though if you're getting money out from a foreign account, the safest way is to get it from a proper bank machine, to avoid fraud. Most banks charge you an additional fee when you withdraw a currency different from that of your home country as well as the original transaction fee. Check your daily withdrawal limit, so you don't get caught short.

Changing Money

Counters dedicated solely to exchanging money are becoming rarer. It's much simpler just to head to the bank. Foreign-exchange desks can also be found at the main tourist office and at the airport. Try **Transchange International** (43 rue de Baude, 418/694-6906).

Credit Cards

Major international credit cards are accepted at most stores, hotels, and restaurants. Carrying a credit card means you don't have the worry of carrying cash and it also gives you excellent exchange rates. Visa and MasterCard are the most widely accepted, though certain places also accept American Express and Diners Club.

MAPS AND TOURIST INFORMATION

Airports have information offices open year-round. For Québec province info about Montréal, Québec City, and environs, visit **Bonjour Québec** (www.bonjourquebec.com).

In Vieux-Québec's Upper Town there's **Centre Infotouriste** (12 rue Ste-Anne, 800/363-7777, late June-early Oct. daily 9am-7pm, early Oct.-late June daily 9am-5pm), and backing on to the Plains of Abraham is another **Centre Infotouriste** (835 ave. Wilfrid-Laurier, 800/266-5687, late June-late Aug. daily 9am-7pm, late Aug.-mid-June daily 9am-5pm).

COMMUNICATIONS AND MEDIA
Phones

Thanks to the massive popularity of cell phones, public pay phones are becoming almost impossible to find, but if you do manage to fine one, a single local call will set you back $0.50. Though many are coin operated, some also accept phone cards and credit cards. Québec City's area code is **418.** When dialing local numbers, you must include the area code.

Toll-free numbers begin with **800, 866,** or **888** and must be preceded by a 1. Most of these numbers work in both Canada and the United States, but some may only work in a specified province. Dialing **0** for the operator or **911** for emergency services is free of charge from land lines and public phones, but calling **411** for directory assistance will cost you.

Cell Phones

Tribrand model cell phones working on GSM 1900 and other frequencies are the only foreign cell phones that will work in Canada. If your phone doesn't work, it might be worth picking up an inexpensive phone at an electronics store and getting a pay-as-you-go plan. Travelers from the United States will likely have service, though roaming charges will probably apply; check with your provider for details.

Mobile Apps

Québec City's tourism board has created apps for both Android and iPhone, and their website is also mobile-friendly. Head to www.quebecregion.com to check them out before downloading from the appropriate app store.

Internet Services

A number of cafés offer free Wi-Fi; you can register for free at **Île Sans Fil** (www.ilesansfil.org) and find out where the 150-plus places are where you can get online with your laptop. Visit www.zapquebec.org for free Wi-Fi in Québec. If you left your computer at home and can't check your email at your hotel, your best bets are the local libraries.

In Québec City, a couple of libraries offer free Internet access to visitors. **Bibliothèque Saint-Jean-Baptiste** (755 rue St-Jean, 418/641-6798, Mon.-Tues. and Thurs. noon-5pm, Wed. noon-8pm, Fri. 10am-5:30pm, Sat. 1pm-5pm), in the Faubourg Saint-Jean-Baptiste, offers an hour of free access, and **Bibliothèque Gabrielle-Roy** (350 rue St-Joseph E., 418/641-6789, Mon.-Fri. 8:30am-9pm, Sat.-Sun. 10am-5pm) in Saint-Roch offers two hours of free access.

Many hotels, though not all, offer free Wi-Fi access, and the majority also have public computers.

Mail Services

Québec City's main post office is at 5 rue du Fort in Upper Town and offers a number of services. Stamps can also be purchased at newsstands, convenience stores, and tourist shops. Standard first-class airmail postage for letters and postcards costs $0.65 to Canadian destinations and $1.10 to the United States. Other destinations cost $1.85.

Newspapers and Periodicals

The Globe & Mail (www.globeandmail.com) and the *National Post* (www.nationalpost.com) are the country's two national papers, and while both cover national and international events as well as the arts, the *Globe* leans more to the center-left and the *Post* to the right.

For French readers there's the federalist *La Presse* and separatist-leaning *Le Devoir,* both of which cover the news and art of the entire province, not just the Francophone community (though that's a large part of it). In Québec there's *Le Soleil,* a great little paper with a focus on events in the capital. There's also the Francophone alternative weekly *Voir* (www.voir.ca), great for getting the latest scoop on what's going on in town or for scoping out their restaurant reviews.

L'actualité is the Québec monthly news magazine, and *Maclean's* is Canada's only weekly news magazine.

Television

The main public-radio and television stations are run by the Canadian Broadcasting Corporation. The CBC is the English-language component and Radio-Canada is the French-language component; both are revered for their long broadcast history. The other major English-language network is the Canadian Television Network (CTV), which broadcasts both Canadian and U.S. programs as well as nightly newscasts.

For Francophone audiences there's Télé-Québec (TVA) and Télévision Quatre-Saison (TQS), both of which broadcast news programs, movies, and shows from France, as well as dubbed American sitcoms and dramas.

Radio

Radio stations in Québec are mostly Francophone, with the exception of the English-language artists they play. Anglophones can tune into CBC Québec 1 (104.7 FM streaming), the city's only English-language radio station for all their cultural, news, and educational programs. Tune into CHYZ (94.3 FM) to hear what the students at Université Laval are listening to. CHIK (98.9 FM) gives you top pop and Francophone hits, and Radio-Canada (106.3 FM) keeps you informed in French about news and culture.

WEIGHTS AND MEASURES
Electricity

Like the United States and Japan, Canada uses 110-volt, 60-cycle electrical power. Canadian electrical goods have a plug with two flat, vertical prongs and sometimes a third rounded prong. Travelers from outside North America should bring a plug adapter for small appliances.

Measurements

Canada uses the metric system of measurement. Distances are measured in kilometers, liquids in liters and milliliters, but height, strangely enough, is measured in feet.

Time

Québec City is on eastern standard time (EST/EDT), the same as New York and Toronto. Canada switches to daylight saving time (one hour later than standard time) from the second Sunday in March to the first Sunday in November. "Spring forward, fall back," is a simple way to remember how to set your clocks properly. In Québec the 24-hour clock is used for most schedules, including movies and trains.

Resources

Glossary

l'Abitation: the first settlement (habitation)

allongé: a long espresso coffee, the French name for an Italian *lungo*

Anglophone: a native English speaker

Bill 101: a Québec law that deals with French and English language issues

boîte à chansons: a place where you can hear singer/songwriters *(chansonniers)* play

boréal: the type of forest that is found in the province of Québec

branchée: plugged in, which translates to hip, or cool, in the French vernacular

brasserie: a brewery or pub

brioche: a type of sweet French bread

cabane à sucre: a sugar shack; this is where you go to see maple syrup tapped from trees and eat maple-drenched treats

café: where you buy coffee as well as the drink itself; usually refers to an espresso

calèche: a horse-drawn carriage

chansonnier: a folk singer/songwriter

côte: hill; if a street has *"côte"* in its name, it's on a hill

coureurs de bois: early fur hunters and adventurers who helped explore North America

dépanneur: meaning "to help out"; it's the name for convenience stores in Québec, which are commonly referred to as *"dép."*

First Nations: the name for Canada's Amerindian population

frites: French fries

joual: a popular form of slang

loonie: Canadian one-dollar coin

Nouvelle France: the name given to Québec by the French; it also means New France

pâté chinois: a meat, potato, and vegetable pie similar to shepherd's pie

patriotes: the name given to patriots who led an uprising against the government in 1837; it's used today to denote those who are against federal rule

pont: a bridge

poudreuse: blowing snow

quai: quay that juts out into the water

Quebecker: English name for all native citizens of the province of Québec

Québécois: the name for the Francophone population in the province as well as the language they speak

Refus Global (Total Refusal): a manifesto of a group of Québec artists that radically changed the face of modern Québec art

sacres: the name for Québécois swear words
sandwicherie: a place that makes sandwiches
sloche: slush made from melted snow
sovereigntists: those who want Québec to separate from the rest of Canada
stimés: hot dog with a steamed bun
Sulpicians: society of Catholic priests founded in Paris in 1641 who were part
   of the founding of Québec
table d'hôte: a fixed-price meal
terrasse: an outdoor patio
terroir: food products that come from the area, as in "terroir" cooking
tire sur la neige: maple syrup that has been frozen on snow, a popular treat
   during the sugaring-off season
toastés: hot dog with a toasted bun
toonie: a Canadian two-dollar coin
tourtière: a meat pie made with everything from pork and beef to game
viennoiseries: pastries and sweet breads usually eaten at breakfast

French Phrasebook

If you're uncomfortable about breaking out your rusty 10th-grade French, relax. In Québec City locals' English isn't as fluid as in Montréal, but those who work in tourism and hospitality speak it flawlessly. Even if you do feel confident with your French, the Québécois accent will take some getting used to, and the language you hear on the street won't have much to do with the words you read in this phrasebook. The Québécois also have a tendency to speak very fast, so don't be afraid to ask them to slow down if you're having trouble understanding.

As has been explained throughout the guide, language is a central issue in Québec, so a good rule of thumb is to be polite; the Québécois are especially receptive to people who are at least trying to speak a little French, and they're always encouraging. Throw in a few easy French words here and there like *bonjour* or *merci* and you'll soon earn a friend for life, or at least gain their respect.

PRONUNCIATION

French is known for being difficult to pronounce—and as payback for creating such a difficult language, French-speakers are unable to properly pronounce any other language. When it comes to phonetic pronunciation, French is as bad as English. Most of the spellings and the pronunciations don't have much in common, which can make learning French difficult. Here are a few guidelines to get you started.

Vowels

Vowels in French can be confusing for an English speaker: the "a" is **e,** the "e" is **i,** and the "u" is from outer space. Here is the secret:

a   pronounced a, as in "cat"
i   pronounced ee, as in "free"

y pronounced the same way as **i**

o pronounced ah, as in "dog," or oh, as in "bone"

u This vowel has always been a tough one for English-speakers. The closest you can get would be to put your lips and tongue in position to say "oh" and try to say "ee" instead. Something like the ew in "stew" is not that far off.

e pronounced uh, as in "about." Before two or more consonants, it is pronounced eh as in "set." At the end of a word, such as *chaise* (chair), **e** is silent, except in words of one syllable like *je* (I), where it is pronounced "uh."

Vowel Groups

To make things harder, French assembles certain letters to produce new sounds.

ai pronounced eh, as in "set," as well as **ei**

au pronounced oh, as in "bone," as well as **eau**

eu pronounced uh, as in "about." It is sometimes spelled **œu**, as in *œuf* or *sœur*

oi pronounced wa, as in "wagon"

ou pronounced oo, as in "foot"

Nasal Vowels

A typical aspect of French speech is nasal vowels, vowels pronounced through both the mouth and nose. They are as difficult for English-speakers to reproduce as the **u** and will require quite a bit of phonetic gymnastics before you get it right.

an, am pronounced ahn, as in "aunt"

en, em pronounced pretty close to ahn, combined with the on of "honk"

in where the a of "bag" is nasalized as in "anchor." You'll find more or less the same sound in many different spellings, such as **im, un, um, yn, ym, ain, aim, ein,** and **eim**

on, om pronounced on, as in "long"; a nasalized **o**

Accents

French has five different accents that stick to vowels and make French as exotic to read as it is to hear: In French they are called *accent aigu* (´), *accent grave* (`), *accent circonflexe* (^), *accent tréma* (¨), and the *cédille* (ç), which is only used with the letter **c**.

The circumflex and grave accents appear as **è, à, ù, ê, â, û, î,** and **ô**. Except for **ê** and **è**, which are pronounced eh as in "set," and **ô,** which always sounds like oh as in "bone," the accents don't change the pronunciation of the letters; they are mere decoration.

The acute accent, as in **é**, is pronounced ay as in "day," but shorter. The cedilla makes **c** sound like **s**.

Last but not least, the dieresis (*tréma*) separates two vowel sounds, such as **ï** in *naïve*, which is not pronounced nev, but as two separate syllables, na-ive.

Consonants

Most French consonants are similar to their English equivalents, even if there are a few differences. For example, *some* final consonants are silent; rather than pronouncing *vous* as "vooz," you'd say "voo." In general the following consonants are usually silent: **b, d, g, m, n, p, t, x,** and **z. S** is always silent in plurals but often pronounced otherwise. Others are generally pronounced: **c, f,** and **l. R** is usually pronounced, except in the endings **er** and **ier.**

c pronounced k as in "kick" before **a, o,** or **u,** and s as in "set" before **e, i,** or **y.** Combine **c** and **h,** as in *chance* (luck), and it is pronounced like sh as in "ship"

g pronounced g as in "god," except when placed before **e, i,** or **y,** when it is pronounced zh as in "measure." Combine it with **n,** as in *vigne* (vine), and it is pronounced like ny in "canyon"

h always silent

j pronounced zh as in "measure"

ll pronounced y as in "yes," in words like *famille*

r emphasized more strongly than in English and comes from the far back of the throat

BASIC EXPRESSIONS

Hello Bonjour

Hi Salut

Good-bye Au revoir/Salut

Good morning/afternoon Bonjour

Good evening Bonsoir

Good night Bonne nuit

How are you? (courteous) Allez-vous?

How are you doing? (colloquial) Ça va?/Vas-tu?

Fine, thank you. Ça va bien, merci.

And you? Et vous?

See you later. À plus tard/À bientôt.

Nice to meet you. Enchanté.

Yes Oui

No Non

Please S'il vous plaît

Thank you Merci

You're welcome Bienvenu/de rien

Excuse me Excusez-moi

Sorry Pardon/désolé

What's your name? Comment vous appelez-vous?

My name is . . . Je m'appelle...

Where are you from? D'où venez-vous?

I'm from . . . Je viens de...

Do you speak English? Parlez-vous anglais?

I don't speak French. Je ne parle pas français.

I don't understand. Je ne comprends pas.

I don't know. Je ne sais pas.

Can you please repeat? Pourriez-vous répéter?

What's it called? Ça s'appelle?
Would you like ...? Voulez-vous ...?

TERMS OF ADDRESS

I je
you tu
he il
she elle
we nous
you (plural) vous
they ils/elles
Mr./Sir monsieur
Mrs./Madame madame
Miss mademoiselle
young man jeune homme
young woman jeune fille
child enfant
brother/sister frère/sœur
father/mother père/mère
son/daughter fils/fille
husband/wife mari/femme
friend ami/amie
boyfriend/girlfriend copain/copine
married marié/mariée
single célibataire
divorced divorcé/divorcée

QUESTIONS

When? Quand?
What? Quoi?
What is it? Qu'est-ce que c'est?
Who? Qui?
Why? Pourquoi?
How? Comment?
Where is ...? Où est ...?
What's it called? Ça s'appelle?
Would you like ...? Voulez-vous ...?

GETTING AROUND

Where is ...? Où est ...?
How far away is ...? À quelle distance est ...?
How can I get to ...? Puis-je aller à ...?
bus bus
car voiture
train train
bus station la station d'autobus
train station la gare de trains
airport l'aéroport

What time do we leave? À quelle heure est le départ?

What time do we arrive? À quelle heure arrive-t-on?

a one-way ticket un aller simple

a round-trip ticket? un aller retour

Can you take me to this address? Pourriez-vous m'emmener à cette adresse?

north nord

south sud

east est

west ouest

left/right gauche/droite

straight ahead tout droit

entrance entrée

exit sortie

first premier

last dernier

next prochain

ACCOMMODATIONS

Are there any rooms available? Avez-vous des chambres disponibles?

I'd like to make a reservation. J'aimerais faire une reservation.

I want a single room. J'aimerais une chambre simple.

Is there a double room? Y a-t-il une chambre double?

private bathroom salle de bains privée

key clé

one night une nuit

Can you change the sheets/towels? Pourriez-vous changer les draps/ les serviettes?

Could you please wake me up? Pourriez-vous me réveiller?

Is breakfast included? Est-ce que le petit déjeuner est inclus?

FOOD

to eat manger

to drink boire

breakfast déjeuner

lunch dîner

dinner souper

Can I see the menu? Puis-je voir le menu?

We're ready to order. Nous sommes prêts à commander.

Can I have some more wine? Puis-je avoir un peu plus de vin?

Can you bring me the bill please? Pourriez-vous apporter l'addition?

Is the service/the tip included? Est-ce que le service est compris?

I'm a vegetarian. Je suis végétarien.

It was delicious. C'était délicieux.

hot chaud

cold froid

sweet sucré

salty salé

bread pain
rice riz
Enjoy! Bon appétit!

Meat and Fish

meat viande
beef bœuf
pork porc
lamb agneau
chicken poulet
ham jambon
fish poisson
salmon saumon
mussels moules
oysters huîtres
shrimp crevette
tuna thon
rare saignant
medium à point
well done bien cuit
roasted rôti
boiled bouilli
grilled grillé
fried frit

Eggs and Dairy

milk lait
cream crème
butter beurre
cheese fromage
ice cream crème glacée
egg œuf
hard-boiled egg œuf dur
scrambled eggs œufs brouillés
poached egg œuf poché

Vegetables and Fruits

vegetables légumes
carrot carotte
tomato tomate
potato patate/pomme de terre
cucumber concombre
pepper poivron
mushrooms champignons
eggplant aubergine
peas petits pois
cabbage chou
apple pomme

RESOURCES
FRENCH PHRASEBOOK

pear poire
banana banane
orange orange
lemon citron
grape raisin
strawberry fraise
blueberry bleuet
raspberry framboise

Seasoning and Spices

sugar sucre
salt sel
black pepper poivre
onion oignon
garlic ail
olive oil huile d'olive
vinegar vinaigre
cinnamon cannelle
basil basilic
parsley persil
mint menthe
ginger gingembre

Drinks

drinks boissons
beer bière
wine vin
wine list la carte des vins
cheers! à votre santé!
water eau
ice glace
juice jus
filtered coffee café filtre
coffee with milk café au lait
black coffee café noir

SHOPPING

money argent
ATM guichet automatique
credit card carte de crédit
to buy acheter
to shop magasiner
I don't have change. Je n'ai pas de monnaie.
more plus
less moins
a good price un bon prix
sales soldes
How much does it cost? Combien ça coûte?

discount rabais
Can I try it on? Est-ce que je peux l'essayer?
It's too tight. C'est trop serré.
It's too big. C'est trop grand.
Can I exchange it? Est-ce que je peux l'échanger?

HEALTH AND SAFETY

Can you help me? Pouvez-vous m'aider?
I don't feel well. Je ne me sens pas bien.
I'm sick. Je suis malade.
Is there a pharmacy close by? Y a-t-il une pharmacie pas loin?
Can you call a doctor? Pouvez-vous appeler un docteur?
I need to go to the hospital. Je dois aller à l'hôpital.
medicine médicament
condom condom, préservatif
Is this neighborhood safe? Est-ce que ce quartier est sécuritaire?
Help! À l'aide!, Au secours!
Call the police! Appeler la police.
thief voleur

COMMUNICATIONS

to talk, to speak parler
to hear, to listen écouter, entendre
to make a phone call faire un appel téléphonique
cell phone cellulaire
What's your phone number? Quel est ton numéro de téléphone?
What's your email address? Quelle est ton adresse électronique?
collect call appel à frais virés
Do you have Internet? Avez-vous Internet ici?
post office bureau de poste
letter lettre
stamp timbre
postcard carte postale

NUMBERS

0 zéro
1 un
2 deux
3 trois
4 quatre
5 cinq
6 six
7 sept
8 huit
9 neuf
10 dix
11 onze

12 douze
13 treize
14 quatorze
15 quinze
16 seize
17 dix-sept
18 dix-huit
19 dix-neuf
20 vingt
21 vingt-et-un
30 trente
40 quarante
50 cinquante
60 soixante
70 soixante-dix
80 quatre-vingt
90 quatre-vingt dix
100 cent
101 cent un
200 deux cent
500 cinq cent
1000 mille
2000 deux mille

TIME

What time is it? Quelle heure est-il?
It's 2 o'clock. Il est deux heures.
It's 2:15. Il est deux heures et quart.
It's 2:30. Il est deux heures et demie.
It's 2:45. Il est deux heures quarante-cinq.
in two hours dans deux heures
now maintenant
before avant
after après
late/early tard/tôt
When? Quand?

DAYS AND MONTHS

day jour
night nuit
morning matin
afternoon après-midi
yesterday hier
tomorrow demain
today aujourd'hui
week semaine
month mois
year année

Monday lundi
Tuesday mardi
Wednesday mercredi
Thursday jeudi
Friday vendredi
Saturday samedi
Sunday dimanche
January janvier
February février
March mars
April avril
May mai
June juin
July juillet
August août
September septembre
October octobre
November novembre
December décembre

SEASONS AND WEATHER

season saison
spring printemps
summer été
autumn automne
winter hiver
weather temps/météo
sun soleil
It's sunny. Il fait soleil.
rain pluie
It's raining. Il pleut.
snow neige
It's snowing. Il neige.
snowstorm tempête de neige
ice glace/verglas
It's hot. Il fait chaud.
It's cold. Il fait froid.

Suggested Reading

HISTORY AND GENERAL INFORMATION

Dickinson, John A., and Brian Young. *A Short History of Québec*. Montréal: McGill-Queen's University Press, 1993, revised 2008. Originally written in 1992, this book is now into its fourth edition and offers a comprehensive overview of the province's social and economic development from pre-European to modern times. This latest edition includes reflections on the Bouchard-Taylor Commission on Accommodation and Cultural Differences, which examined attitudes toward immigration and immigrants in the province.

Grescoe, Taras. *Sacré Blues: An Unsentimental Journey through Quebec*. Toronto: Macfarlane Walter & Ross, 2001. Montréal author Taras Grescoe's modern account of Québec explores the stranger side of the province's pop culture, takes readers to a Francophone country-and-western festival, meets up with UFO-obsessed followers of Raël, and, of course, deconstructs a Montréal Canadiens hockey game. The book won the Québec Writers' Federation First Book Award and the Mavis Gallant Prize for Nonfiction in 2001.

Jenish, D'Arcy. *The Montreal Canadiens: 100 Years of Glory*. Toronto: Doubleday Canada, 2008. Published to coincide with the hockey team's 100th anniversary, this is the definitive history of the team—from the days of their first Stanley Cup win to the return of former player Bob Gainey as general manager. Even if you're not a fan, this book provides an insider's look at one of the NHL's most storied teams.

Lacoursière, Jacques, and Robin Philpot. *A People's History of Québec*. Montréal: Baraka Books, 2009. First published in French, this concise book looks at the history of the province through the people that discovered, explored, and inhabited it. The focus is on day-to-day life and offers little-known details, like the despicable "mixed dancing" at times of celebration and early settlers' love of *charivari,* a loud, rambunctious party through the streets.

FICTION AND MEMOIRS

Carrier, Roch. *The Hockey Sweater*. Montréal: Tundra Books, 1979. This semi-autobiographical children's picture book is one of the most memorable Canadian stories. It tells the tale of a boy in small-town Québec who orders a Canadiens hockey sweater from the Eaton's catalogue only to receive a Toronto Maple-Leaf jersey. Full of subtle comments on Québec and the rest of Canada, it's a touching story that has been immortalized by an NFB film.

Doucet, Julie. *365 Days: A Diary.* Montréal: Drawn & Quarterly, 2008. Born and raised in Montréal, comic artist Julie Doucet first gained recognition as an artist for her zine *Dirty Plotte,* a funny, demented take on her own life experiences. *365 Days* offers an intimate look at the artistic community Doucet surrounded herself with in her early days and the experience of an artist in Montréal.

Hage, Rawi. *Cockroach.* Toronto: House of Anansi Press, 2009. IMPAC-Dublin award-winner Rawi Hage's second effort, *Cockroach* tells the tale of a struggling immigrant living in Montréal's underbelly. Hage, who is originally from Lebanon, brings a unique perspective and an adept eye to the Montréal experience.

MacLennan, Hugh. *Two Solitudes.* Toronto: McClelland & Stewart, 1945. The title of this book has become emblematic of the country's French/English cultural and linguistic divide. Set between World War I and 1939, the book takes place in Saint-Marc-des-Érables, a small Québec town, and the booming, predominantly English city of Montréal. Centered on Paul Tallard, a Québécois at home with both languages, the book follows him on a quest to find his own identity and a way of defining the Canadian experience.

O'Neill, Heather. *Lullabies for Little Criminals.* Toronto: Harper Perennial, 2006. Heather O'Neill was born and (mostly) raised in Montréal, and her debut novel tells the story of Baby, a 12-year-old girl growing up in the seedy area of lower St-Laurent with her young, well-meaning junkie father. There is a touching humanity to O'Neill's writing, and her depiction of Montréal in all its real, gritty glory is fascinating.

Proulx, Monique. *Les Aurores Montréales.* Toronto: Douglas & McIntyre, 1997. Twenty-seven short stories make up this collection that takes place in pre- and post-referendum Québec. Weaving in and out of Montréal, the stories look at the lives of Quebeckers and how they are affected by the changing times.

Tremblay, Michel. *Les Belles Sœurs.* Vancouver: Talonbooks, revised ed., 1992. Arguably the most important Québécois writer of his generation, Tremblay was only 23 years old when he wrote this play in 1965. First presented in 1968 at Théâtre du Rideau Vert, it ushered in a new era of Québécois theater. Written in *joual* (working-class slang), the play is set in the triplexes of Montréal's Plateau and follows the exploits of an extended family.

Internet Resources

Bonjour Québec
www.bonjourquebec.com
The province's official tourism website has comprehensive information on anything and everything to do with the province, from national parks to kid-friendly fun.

Foodie in Québec City
www.foodiequebec.com
This English language blog covers all aspects of the food and restaurant scene in Québec City and beyond.

Québec T'aime
www.quebectaime.com
This Québec City-based blog run by the hippest writers in the city offers information on everything from the 10 Best Ice Cream Shops to the latest art openings.

Said the Gramophone
www.saidthegramophone.com
This music blog offers an interesting insider take on the Québec and Montréal music scenes.

Voir
www.voir.ca
The online component to the Francophone alternative weekly, Voir has event listings, restaurant reviews, and a weekly webcast that takes you behind the scenes of the weekly photo shoot and gives you a rundown of the week's biggest events.

Index

Restaurants Index

Nightlife Index

Shops Index

Hotels Index

Photo Credits

Title page: © Songquan Deng/123rf.com; page 2 (top) © Songquan Deng | Dreamstime.com, (bottom) © Sacha Jackson; page 14 (all) © Sacha Jackson; page 15 © Sacha Jackson; page 16 © Sacha Jackson; page 17 © Sacha Jackson; page 19 © Wangkun Jia/123rf.com; page 20 (left) © Musée de la Civilization, (right) © Sacha Jackson; page 22 © Sacha Jackson; page 23 © Susan Peterson/123rf.com; page 24 © Songquan Deng/123rf.com; page 25 © Sacha Jackson; page 26 (all) © Sacha Jackson; page 35 (all) © Sacha Jackson; page 43 © Sacha Jackson; page 46 (all) © Sacha Jackson; page 55 (top) © Sacha Jackson, (bottom) Chez Boulay; page 56 © Sacha Jackson; page 61 (all) © Sacha Jackson; page 71 (top left) © Sacha Jackson, (top right) © Clocher Penché, (bottom) © Sacha Jackson; page 85 (top) © Songquan Deng/123rf.com, (bottom) © Ivan Mikhaylov/123rf.com; page 91 (top left) © Sacha Jackson, (top right) © Sacha Jackson, (bottom) © Le Drague; page 99 © oksix/123rf.com; page 103 (top) © Sacha Jackson, (bottom) © Ferenz | Dreamstime.com; page 110 (top) © Sacha Jackson, (bottom) © Edward Fielding | Dreamstime.com; Page 116 (top) © Songquan Deng | Dreamstime.com, (bottom) © Sacha Jackson; page 118 © Commission des Champs de Bataille Nationaux; page 128 (all) © Sacha Jackson; page 136(top left) © Dubuc, (top right) © Sacha Jackson, (bottom) © Benjo; page 144 (top left) © Jupon Pressé, (top right) © Sacha Jackson, (bottom) © Wangkun Jia | Dreamstime.com; page 153 (top) © Sacha Jackson, (bottom) © Alex Strohl; page 160 (top) © Fairmont Hotels & Resorts, (bottom) © Sacha Jackson; page 162 © Fairmont Hotels & Resorts; page 170 (top) © Sacha Jackson, (bottom) © Renaud Philippe; page 174 (top) © Justek16 | Dreamstime.com, (bottom) © Misscanon | Dreamstime.com; page 182 © (top left) © Sacha Jackson, (top right) Ritu Jethani | Dreamstime.com, (bottom) © Sacha Jackson; page 187 © Sacha Jackson; page 190 (top) © Fairmont Hotels & Resorts, (bottom) © Sacha Jackson; page 198 (all) © Sacha Jackson; page 213 (all) © Sacha Jackson; page 223 (all) © Sacha Jackson

MAP SYMBOLS

▦ Expressway	★ Highlight	✗ Airfield	⚑ Golf Course
▦ Primary Road	○ City/Town	✈ Airport	🅿 Parking Area
▦ Secondary Road	◉ State Capital	▲ Mountain	◢ Archaeological Site
▦ Unpaved Road	◉ National Capital	✛ Unique Natural Feature	♟ Church
▦ Trail	★ Point of Interest		🚰 Gas Station
▦ Ferry	● Accommodation	🌊 Waterfall	Glacier
▦ Railroad	▼ Restaurant/Bar	▲ Park	Mangrove
▦ Pedestrian Walkway	■ Other Location	⊡ Trailhead	Reef
▦ Stairs	△ Campground	⛷ Skiing Area	Swamp

CONVERSION TABLES

°C = (°F - 32) / 1.8
°F = (°C x 1.8) + 32
1 inch = 2.54 centimeters (cm)
1 foot = 0.304 meters (m)
1 yard = 0.914 meters
1 mile = 1.6093 kilometers (km)
1 km = 0.6214 miles
1 fathom = 1.8288 m
1 chain = 20.1168 m
1 furlong = 201.168 m
1 acre = 0.4047 hectares
1 sq km = 100 hectares
1 sq mile = 2.59 square km
1 ounce = 28.35 grams
1 pound = 0.4536 kilograms
1 short ton = 0.90718 metric ton
1 short ton = 2,000 pounds
1 long ton = 1.016 metric tons
1 long ton = 2,240 pounds
1 metric ton = 1,000 kilograms
1 quart = 0.94635 liters
1 US gallon = 3.7854 liters
1 Imperial gallon = 4.5459 liters
1 nautical mile = 1.852 km

MOON QUÉBEC CITY
Avalon Travel
a member of the Perseus Books Group
1700 Fourth Street
Berkeley, CA 94710, USA
www.moon.com

Editor: Leah Gordon
Series Manager: Erin Raber
Copy Editor: Naomi Adler-Dancis
Graphics Coordinator: Darren Alessi
Production Coordinator: Darren Alessi
Cover Design: Faceout Studios, Charles Brock
Moon Logo: Tim McGrath
Map Editor: Albert Angulo
Cartographers: Albert Angulo, Stephanie Poulain

ISBN-13: 978-1-63121-145-4
ISSN: 2376-7707

Printing History
1st Edition — May 2015
5 4 3 2 1